19.35.

WILLIAM IRVINE

The Life of a Prairie Radical

ANTHONY MARDIROS

James Lorimer & Company, Publishers
Toronto 1979

ISBN   0-88862-237-6   paper
ISBN   0-88862-238-4   cloth

Cover design: Don Fernley

6 5 4 3 2 1   79 80 81 82 83 84 85

Canadian Cataloguing in Publication Data

Mardiros, Anthony, 1912-
  William Irvine

Bibliography.
Includes index.

ISBN   0-88862-238-4   bd.   ISBN   0-88862-237-6   pa.

1. Irvine, William, 1885-   2. Politicians —
Canada — Biography.

FC581.I78M37   971.06'32'0924   C79-094230-5
F1034.I78M37

James Lorimer & Company, Publishers
Egerton Ryerson Memorial Building
35 Britain Street
Toronto M5A 1R7, Ontario

Printed and bound in Canada

CONTENTS

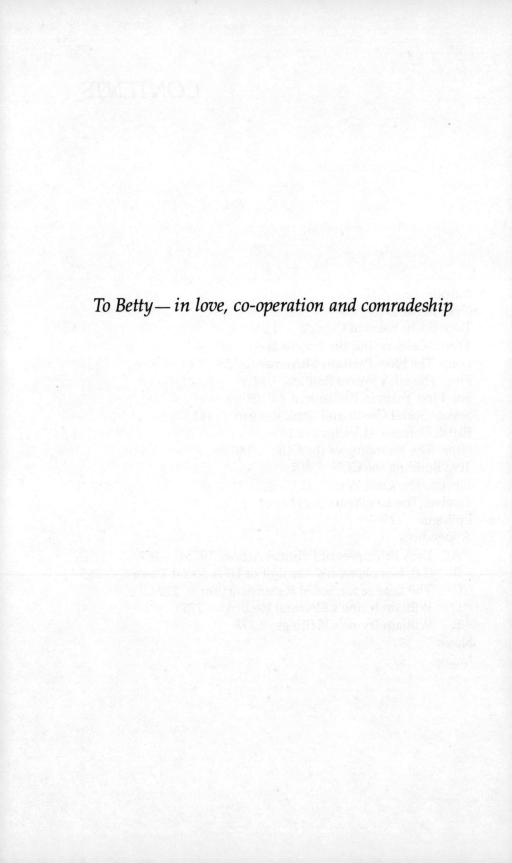

To Betty— in love, co-operation and comradeship

ACKNOWLEDGMENTS

Many people and institutions have helped me to write this book. My special thanks are due to the Alberta Woodsworth House Association for its generous financial aid in support of publication, and to the University of Alberta for granting me a sabbatical leave during which part of my research was accomplished.

The following institutions allowed me to use their materials and facilities: the Glenbow-Alberta Institute, Calgary; the Archives of Alberta, Edmonton; the Public Archives of Canada, Ottawa; and the microfilm library of the University of Alberta. I am grateful to the staffs of these institutions for their valuable help and unfailing courtesy.

My thanks are due to the Irvine family, particularly Mrs. Delia Irvine, for their help and encouragement.

Many friends of William Irvine have helped me in numerous ways, but special thanks are due to Ernie Cook, the late Floyd Johnson and to Nellie and Roy Peterson.

This book would not have been written without the constant advice, criticism and encouragement of my wife, who also typed the many versions of the manuscript.

A.M.

AUTHOR'S NOTE

In addition to the research material to be found in archives at Edmonton, Calgary and Ottawa, which I have indicated in the chapter notes, I have had in my possession William Irvine's papers, which include correspondence, a fragment of autobiography, unpublished manuscripts and documents relating to the Alberta CCF. These will later be placed in the appropriate archives.

INTRODUCTION

For nearly fifty years, William Irvine played a significant role in Canadian political movements, and for seventeen of those years he was a Member of Parliament. Sixty years ago in Alberta, he organized farmers and labour to enter the political arena. He hoped that jointly these groups would bring an end to the political monopoly of the old-line parties and gain political power for the farmers and urban workers, who coproduce the real wealth of any country. He and his supporters also aimed at destroying the economic power and monopolies of the large corporations and financial institutions, seeking to replace them by a form of socialism they frequently referred to as the Co-operative Commonwealth. Although many people worked in this movement, none did so more devotedly and in so many diverse ways than William Irvine, who might rightly be called the founding father of the radical democratic socialist movement in Alberta.

However, during his triple career as parliamentarian, journalist and political organizer, his activities and influence went far beyond Alberta, for he organized and campaigned in nearly every province in Canada. His earlier activity laid the groundwork for the birth of the CCF, of which he was a founding member, and of its successor, the New Democratic Party. Strangely enough, although he is frequently mentioned in historical accounts, he has never been given extended treatment and his importance has never received due recognition. This may be because he did not attain either high political office or national party leadership, but it may also be due in part to the fact that he almost entirely lacked personal ambition and was prepared to work in another's shadow if that seemed to further their common cause. The purpose of this book is to rectify this relative neglect of an important figure, and by so doing to throw light on certain aspects of our recent history.

Irvine was an impressive speaker in the House of Commons with his gift for oratory, his sharp and ready wit, and his passion for social justice and a more rational economic order. His talents were so remarkable that he often earned the respect of his bitterest political opponents. An objective observer, the late John A. Irving, wrote of him:

> I consider that William Irvine was one of the great Canadians of the twentieth century. He left an indelible impression on the House of Commons, and Mackenzie King admired the contribution he made there during the Twenties, Thirties and Forties, whether as a UFA or CCF Member of Parliament. I always found it a sheer delight to discuss Albertan, Canadian and world politics with Bill, and the world does not seem the same without his robust and dynamic mind and personality.[1]

From a somewhat closer standpoint, Grant Notley, MLA and leader of the Alberta New Democratic Party, wrote of Irvine, in 1962:

> He loved controversy, and fought with people vigorously, inside and outside the House of Commons. Political success was no incentive to sacrifice his political beliefs, nor was failure a rationalization to weather the struggle for a better society.... You always knew that Bill would stand and be counted whether the public acclaimed him as a hero, or condemned him as a menace to society. In an age when so many refused to take a stand.... a man like Bill Irvine stands as an inspiration to us all. One of his most endearing qualities was his warmth as a human being. Too often social reformers shield themselves from public antipathy by retreating behind the shell of self-righteousness. This was not the case with Mr. Irvine.... Perhaps it was because he refused to be-

come a martyr in his own mind that he became an inspiration to the rest of us.[2]

Of course, not everybody responded favourably to Irvine's ideas and personality. Some people found him infuriating and, among other things, accused him of being inconsistent, vacillating and even opportunistic. Irvine's reply to such criticisms is illustrated in a story told by his old friend, J.E. Cook, when he introduced Irvine as the main speaker at an NDP rally at Sedalia in 1962:[3]

> I remember a lady at a meeting we attended in about 1936 or '37 who was quite irritated with Mr. Irvine. She was sensitive about any criticism of Mr. Aberhart, and Bill was quite free with some criticism of him. This lady.... suddenly jumped up and said: "I wish you'd stay put, sir. The first time I remember hearing of you, you were a Unitarian minister in Calgary. Next you were a labour man. Next you were in the UFA, and after that you are now CCF. Why don't you find one place and stay there?" "Well," Bill said, "It's like this, madam. If some time early in the spring, you went out and looked in the water in the ditch, you would see some little nodules. You go back in a day or two and these things are moving around; you go back in another day or two and you'll have pollywoggles, darting here and there, and if you wait another few days and go back, you'll have a frog. Would you say to that frog: 'You there, jumping around like that. When I first saw you you were just a speck in the water, then next you were a pollywoggle, and now you're a frog. Why don't you stay put?'" Then Bill said: "This is where we fit.[3]

Irvine always thought things out for himself, disdaining secondhand opinions. He could be persuaded to change his mind, and often did, but only if he thought there were good reasons to do so. As a result, he was often in conflict with the conventional wisdom of his time; throughout his life he was repeatedly branded a heretic of one sort or another. As a pastor, he rejected the traditional dogmas of religion — and was indeed subjected to

trial for heresy. During wartime, he demanded that there be conscription of wealth as well as of men. As a parliamentarian, he
trenchantly criticized the system for being undemocratic and co-
ercive of individual judgement. In times of economic depression,
he proclaimed unorthodox monetary theories and held them to
be compatible with his socialism, and in the climate of the Cold
War that prevailed in the Forties and Fifties, he worked for world
peace and urged the necessity for coexistence among the world
powers despite the conflict of ideologies.

A biographer-historian has a double task. The first is to establish what happened; i.e., what was said and done. The second is
to use this material to reconstruct what it meant in the minds of
the men and women who participated in these events. Since I
knew Irvine as a close friend and fellow socialist during the last
five years of his life, this biography has a certain personal dimension, but in order to perform the first task, I have striven to attain
objectivity by going back to what was said and written in the past
by Irvine and his contemporaries, both his friends and his critics.
In performing the second task I am on my own.

ONE

Beginnings

William Irvine was born at Gletness, Shetland, 19 April 1885. Gletness lies on the coast in the parish of Nesting, some fifteen miles north of the capital, Lerwick, on the main island of Shetland. Most of the islands lie close together stretching for seventy miles north of latitude 60°. No place in Shetland is more than two and a half miles from the sea.

"Man makes himself but not the whole cloth," said Karl Marx, and William Irvine forcibly demonstrates the truth of this aphorism. More than most men, Irvine shaped his own life and made his own choices in thought and action; but the material he worked on was as surely created by the geographical and social environment of the Shetland Islands as are the famous products of Shetland sheep and Shetland skill in weaving and knitting. The stone cottage where Irvine was born stands a few yards from the rugged shore in a wild and somewhat desolate landscape. Two rocky islets — Iplin and Berrier — lie just off shore, uninhabited except by sea birds.

William Irvine senior was a seaman who had, in his younger days, sailed as far as China, but who later acquired a fishing sloop, *The Wild Duck*, and this brought a measure of very modest prosperity to his family and to the small village of Gletness. For centuries Shetlanders have been crofters with small holdings, the produce of which was insufficient to pay the landlord's rent and also provide a subsistence. So most crofters had additional employment, usually fishing or some other job connected with the sea.

In the year of Irvine's birth, the Crofter's Commission came to Shetland, and in the following year, the Crofter's Act was passed, which established rent control for the crofts and some security of tenure for their occupants. Nevertheless, life for the Irvines, as for most Shetlanders, was still hard, the more so since William was the eldest son and third child in a family of nine girls and three boys. Crofting and fishing had been the occupations of his forebears for generations. However, his mother's father, James Pottinger, after being a fisherman for many years, began preaching in local meeting places and eventually was ordained and became Congregational minister for the parishes of Nesting and Tingwall. For some years, young Irvine wavered between choosing a life at sea or one in the church. His mother was resolutely opposed to his becoming a seaman and eventually her influence prevailed.

In 1872, the Scottish Education Act made education compulsory for all children between the ages of seven and fourteen, unless they resided more than three miles from the nearest school. Young Will walked barefoot the two miles to school. He had no shoes, but in any case they would have been useless, since there were no roads and the water from the sodden peat bog oozed up over his feet. In winter each child carried a couple of dry peats as his contribution to the school fireplace. The two-room stone school and the teacher's residence still stand. There was only one teacher, Mr. Spence, although he often picked an older pupil frequently one of his own daughters — to take charge of the lower grades. The curriculum consisted largely of the "three Rs" and in addition Mr. Spence taught the principles of navigation to those pupils, among them Irvine, who had ambitions of becoming ship's officers. However, Irvine's ambitions were not fulfilled. The only secondary school in Shetland was at the capital, Lerwick, and the Irvines could not afford the cost of board and tuition for any of their children. Instead, Irvine went to work at fourteen and subsequently served his apprenticeship as a carpenter and boatbuilder, a craft he practised at frequent intervals throughout his life. At the same age he began preaching in the little Methodist church at Nesting as a lay preacher, presumably substituting in the absence of the regular minister. His religious views were then completely orthodox and were doubtless a repetition of the kind of sermons he had himself heard, but he was an able speaker.

Shetlanders are frugal and hardworking people, but neighbours met in occasional social gatherings or "soirees" as they were called and provided their own entertainment. Irvine acquired some reputation as a mimic:

> I could mimic the peculiar people around the countryside. Maybe they thought I was peculiar too, but there wasn't anybody who could mimic me, and my mimicry seemed to be acceptable to the families I visited.[1]

Shetland also has a long tradition of professional or semi-professional fiddlers, going back to at least the seventeenth century. Their services were mainly though not exclusively in demand for providing the musical accompaniment for dancing. Irvine, in addition to his skill at mimicry, became a reliable performer on the fiddle. He also early acquired a pleasant singing voice and a wide repertoire of songs.

The urge to seek higher education and wider opportunities has encouraged young people to emigrate from Shetland since the 1860s, so that the population declined from a peak of 31,670, recorded in 1861, to 17,809 in 1961.[2] Irvine's first move towards achieving his educational ambitions came early in 1902 when he was no more than sixteen. The City of St. Louis, Missouri, in the United States, decided in 1903 to celebrate the 100th Anniversary of the Louisiana Purchase by holding a centennial exposition. It was a lavish trade fair which drew exhibitors from every state and from about sixty foreign countries, at a cost of approximately $44.5 million. It was not actually held until 1904, but Irvine and two companions from Gletness went some two years in advance to take advantage of the demand for labour. To raise his fare, Irvine sold for nine pounds a purebred Shetland pony he had raised himself. The steerage fare across the Atlantic cost him three pounds ten shillings: during the seventeen-day passage on the *S.S. Phoenician,* he lived on deck in some very rough weather and this probably cured him of any lingering seafaring ambitions. When the ship arrived at New York, Irvine's remaining five-pound note was put to multiple use. Each new immigrant had to show the Immigration authorities that he had some minimum means of support. Irvine showed his five-pound note and then passed it behind his back to his companion. The journey to St. Louis used up what was left of his savings and he arrived penniless. A motherly landlady of Scots origin gave him board and lodging until he found a carpentry job and was able to repay her. Work continued to be plentiful until the close of the World's Fair. After that Irvine walked the streets for weeks without finding a job. As luck would have it, however, he had been speaking at meetings of the Epworth League,[3] which met after the church service every Sunday night. Many of the congregation stayed for the young people's meetings, and at the conclusion of one, a middle-aged man approached Irvine and asked him questions about his background and his ambitions. Irvine told him that his greatest ambition was to get an education. About a week later he received a letter from Dr. Morris, principal of Science Hall, Fayette, Missouri, informing him that an anonymous friend had deposited sufficient money with him to pay all the expenses for Irvine's university program, as far as he wanted to go. Irvine had misgivings about accepting charity and suspected that his family would disapprove if they knew of it. However, necessity was more pressing than pride, and he accepted the offer. At that time, practically every home in Fayette burned tamarack or hickory, both for cooking and heating, and Irvine was able to earn sufficient extra money by contracting to split firewood.

After a year in college he went back to St. Louis, where he immediately became ill with tonsillitis.

> I went to a doctor. The upshot of it was that he told me I had only a few months to live and that it would be best for me to go home and die. This was a smashing blow to me. I do not think I was afraid to die, but I did not feel like doing so. However, I thought if I was that near to the end, I might as well end it. The doctor told me not to climb stairs, not to work, etc. So I asked a young strong friend of mine to come with me to climb a mountain. I thought if I got to the top of it and compared my condition with his, I would find out that the doctor was mistaken. We climbed the mountain, it was

really just a big steep hill about a thousand feet up. At the top I took my pulse and his and found that his heart was beating faster than mine! I felt no bad effects, and while this encouraged me somewhat, influenced by my faith in doctors and my homesickness, I could not disregard the medical diagnosis. So I returned to Shetland, although I hated to do this since I had only been away about two and a half years and I felt that I had accomplished nothing. When I arrived in Shetland I had only two pounds left. The first thing I did was to see our family doctor. He gave me a very careful examination and said that there was nothing the matter with my heart. I still found this hard to believe and replied that I had been told that it beat faster than it should. He answered "It is not doing so now, just let it beat." He went on to say that my tonsils should come out, for an attack of tonsillitis made the heart beat faster because of high fever. (This I found to be true in future years and eventually I had my tonsils taken out.)

It was surprising how quickly homesickness left me. I was not home a month before I was bored and wanted to get away. I was never homesick again.[4]

Very soon, following in his grandfather's footsteps, he took a Methodist lay preacher's position, which he held for the next two years, in a remote district in the northern part of the main island. He had charge of three churches situated in a straight line running north to south and covering a distance of twenty miles. Every Sunday he had to preach in each one and in order to do so he walked the entire twenty miles. In addition he had to study the Bible and Methodist theology and take examinations in these subjects. For this he was paid twenty-five shillings a week. Nevertheless, in two years he had saved the money for his passage back across the Atlantic.

At this time, in 1907, the Reverend Dr. James Woodsworth (father of J.S. Woodsworth) arrived in Britain seeking to recruit a hundred young men to train for the Methodist ministry in Canada. Woodsworth accepted Irvine's application with alacrity because of his previous experience in the U.S., and so, at the age of twenty-two, William Irvine came to Canada. But before his departure he was already committed to socialism. His father was a socialist, although apparently not a very active or articulate one. However, three of his cousins, some ten years or more older than himself, were leading socialists in Shetland.

Frank and James Pottinger were the sons of his mother's brother, while James Robertson was the son of his mother's sister. All were compositors on the *Shetland Times* in Lerwick, and had spent a period in Edinburgh to gain further experience in their trade. James Pottinger and his cousin, James Robertson, went to Edinburgh in 1893. They had already been influenced by an older generation of Shetland socialists and they promptly joined the Edinburgh branch of the Social Democratic Federation. James Pottinger corresponded with his brother Frank, who remained in Lerwick, and, after a lively debate, converted him to socialism. In 1896, Frank joined his brother and cousin in Edinburgh and together they regularly attended socialist meetings and heard such famous speakers as R.B. Cunninghame Graham and John Connolly. After their return to Shetland they took an active part in the Lerwick Literary and Debating Society, founded in 1902. James Robertson read a paper on "Socialism: The Workers' Only Hope" at one of the first meetings. He was also the first socialist in Shetland to be elected to a public body, by becoming a member of the school board in 1897. Frank Pottinger was also elected to the school board in 1903. Several of the young men in the society spoke and wrote against the Boer War, including Frank, who wrote letters to the *Shetland Times* on this and other topics.

In 1905 they formed the Lerwick Working Men's Association, the first socialist organization in Shetland, which attracted to its meetings many of the more thoughtful young men of Lerwick. At the early meetings of the LWMA, a difference arose in principles and program. Frank, and probably his brother and his cousin, spoke for affiliation to the Marxist Social Democratic Federation, while others opposed this, advocating instead affiliation to the Independent Labour Party. After full discussion, the SDF faction were victorious, though most of the ILP supporters agreed to remain in the Association.

The LWMA was active in many ways. Its members helped to

form trade union branches and exposed the scandalous housing and sanitary conditions and the long working hours at low wages that workers endured. The association popularized cheap reprints of political, philosophical and scientific pamphlets and promoted the sale of such radical papers as *Justice*, the *Clarion*, *Forward* and the *Christian Socialist*, not only in Lerwick but throughout Shetland. They held frequent meetings and from 1905 on socialist speakers visited Lerwick, attracting large crowds to the Esplanade and town hall. When the speakers left by the mail steamer, the younger members of the association would follow them to the pier and sing *The Red Flag* as the ropes were cast off. Many visiting fishermen and other workers first heard of socialism at these meetings. The association ran candidates for the school board, town council and county council. In 1905, the Association's municipal candidates, William Sinclair and Alexander Ratter, were successful. They were the first workingmen returned to the town council on a straight socialist program, much to the disgust of the local merchants and landlords.

Irvine learned a great deal about socialism from his cousins and they lent him books on the subject, in particular two works by a leading popular socialist writer of the time, Robert Blatchford, whose *Merrie England* now ranks as an early socialist classic. In it Blatchford argued, among other things, that trade unionism, though necessary and important, was not enough. Workers must send their own individual representatives to Parliament. *Guilty Men* was a critique of the social role of religion and the church. Irvine said that it made a tremendous impression upon him, and for the first time shook his belief in, and respect for, the doctrines of Christianity. Nevertheless, at this time, he associated socialism with Christianity, and identified Christian with socialist ethics. Keir Hardie became one of his heroes; he admired him for his rugged stalwart honesty, his sterling character, his scorn for pomp and his fidelity to the workers who had elected him. Hardie too identified Christian ethics and socialism and had struggled hard to build trade unionism and labour representation in Parliament. He was also a resolute opponent of war. Although at that time Irvine had no thought of a political career, he remembered consciously deciding that Keir Hardie and Abraham Lincoln were the models he would like to follow throughout his life.

One must conjecture that although Irvine's cousins undoubtedly influenced him by their actions and by the literature they supplied him, his contacts with them were neither close nor frequent. They were members and supporters of the Social Democratic Federation, which claimed to be more Marxist and more revolutionary than either the Fabians or the Independent Labour Party. All we know of Irvine at this time, and of his subsequent development in Canada, strongly suggests that he was closer to the socialism of the ILP than to that of his cousins.

However, not only was there roughly a ten-year age gap, but there was also a geographical gap. His cousins did not become politically active in Lerwick until 1902, and in the following five years before he left for Canada, he spent two and a half years in the United States and much of the other two and a half preaching in the northern part of Shetland. Therefore, although Irvine's socialist convictions were already formed and were firmly based before he left Shetland, they were the result of diverse influences and were flexible and undogmatic.

In spite of the fact that his prime aim in coming to Canada was to seek an education, there is a very real sense in which it could be said that he already had formed the fundamental concepts upon which his future activities would be based. He had learned to speak eloquently in public; he knew intimately the lives of working people, crofters, fishermen and artisans; and he had himself acquired the skill of carpentry. In addition, he could sing and fiddle. Most important of all, already he had acquired the basic political convictions that remained with him throughout his life.

TWO

Early Years in Canada

Irvine arrived in Canada after a ten-day crossing and proceeded to Winnipeg, where he was enrolled in Wesley and Manitoba Colleges, the Methodist and Presbyterian theological colleges respectively. The two colleges had anticipated the much discussed and debated union of the two churches, which was not actually consummated until 1925, and had set up a common theological training program leading not to a university degree but to ordination as a minister in either church. Irvine discovered that he was first of all required to complete matriculation at the colleges and then to proceed to a special theological course rather than to the university degree program. This was a considerable disappointment to him, for although he had not yet seriously questioned the church creeds he had not even then much taste for theology; but he decided that even a theological education was better than no education. The churches proved to be none too generous. Students were expected to preach in small out-of-town centres during the weekends and to spend their summers out in the field, making a circuit of small rural churches and doing what often amounted to missionary work in isolated communities. Even then, the student often had to find other work in order to raise the money to support himself through the fall and winter semesters.

Irvine's college career was extended over more than six years because of the need to take long periods, ranging from a summer to a whole year, to find money to study. Aside from ministerial and missionary work in remote townships, Irvine spent most of this time on farm work. The hardest farm work he undertook was stooking wheat, following in the path of a binder. For this he got a dollar a day and food. His first winter in Canada was not spent in college in Winnipeg but working as a preacher in the lumber camps around Prince Albert, Saskatchewan.

The church and the superintendent of missions seemed to think that there was a great need for a man to preach to the lumberjacks in northwest Saskatchewan. Since this was thought to be a very difficult assignment, they called for volunteers from about one hundred students. Very few wanted to go into the bush to rough it with the hard-drinking lumberjacks, but Irvine was one of the volunteers.

> "I had been accustomed to rough and ready sailors in the fo'castles of boats and ships and I liked them despite their rough exteriors. I didn't expect that lumberjacks would be very much different. My first night in the lumber camp I shall never forget. I arrived at the camp about 2 a.m. It was about −35°F. I put away my horses and made for the bunkhouse. I was assigned by the night watchman to a bed. It was the kind called a "muzzle-loader." The beds were in three tiers, one above the other. One had to crawl in through the "muzzle." I must have wakened one of the men in the bed next to me. He spoke and said, "Hullo pard, are you lousy?" "No!" I emphatically replied. "Well, you goddam soon will be."
>
> The preacher who had been in these camps prior to my coming arrived next day to introduce me to my parishioners. He was one of the narrowest-minded men I have ever met, and I soon found out that he was hated by every man in the camp. If he heard a man swear he would walk right up to him and give him a lecture on the wrath of God — not unnaturally he would often get some pretty irreligious answers in return. He took me into the bunkhouse after supper, stood up and introduced me to the men. They were silent at first, but very soon they organized a testimony meeting, which was as rough as it was possible to make it. The proceedings were opened by a large unshaven rough-looking monster of a man rising and saying, "Brothers, the time has come for us to tell what the good Lord has done for us. True!

He freezes us here all winter, feeds us slops, and gives us lice for company. That was what the children of Israel got. Here are the words of the sacred inspired book: 'They were tried with frogs and bloody water. None of these proved so nice; so then Moses said to Aaron, "Brother give these fellows lice."'" Then the crowd shouted, "Hallelujah! Praise the Lord!" Another shouted: "We have a lot to be thankful for. What would we do nights if we did not have lice here indeed as a pastime both elevating and beneficial? I say, gentlemen and brothers, let us raise our voices now and thank the good God for lice." "Hallelujah!" again came from the crowd. Then a fellow got up and said, "By the rip-roaring, bald-headed Jesus Christ Almighty, I do feel happy tonight." "Praise the Lord" came from everywhere. "I should like to say that I've not got one sin left, they have been washed away in the Blood of the Lamb. But what I want to know is: who the hell got the Blood of the Lamb? All we have is sour belly and stinking salt beef. Who got the roasted Lamb?"

Another got up and said, "I want to praise the Good Lord for what He did for me. He guided me to Nancy after the drive last spring." And he went on to describe all the mano-euvres of love-making and at every pause "Praise the Lord" came from every throat.

Long before this finale, my mentor had vanished. He urged me to leave too, but I stayed, trying to keep a solemn face. When they saw that they could not move me by that tactic, one got a fiddle and shouted: "Let's praise the Lord with music and dancing as the Scriptures saith," whereupon he began to saw away across the strings an awful tune on an awful fiddle by an awful player. This pretty nearly did make me give up, but I managed to stick it out. By and by I went to the fiddler and said "Don't you want to have a dance?" "Yes," he said, "but who will play?" "I will." And so it was that I played until they were exhausted.

Irvine greatly enjoyed his stay at the lumber camp. The men would do anything for him and often embarrassed him with their kindness. On one occasion, he found himself on a long train journey with very little money:

Fortunately I got a chance to take a railcar load of pigs to Winnipeg, which saved me my return fare. At Dauphin, Manitoba, we stopped to feed and water the swine. When finished I went to the restaurant to get some lunch. When I came to pay I found that I had eaten five cents' worth more than I had in cash. You can imagine how one feels in such a predicament. But I had a watch and I offered to leave it with the man at the counter until I got to Winnipeg and sent the nickel back. While we were discussing this, I saw one of my lumberjacks going into the bar, so I said "Just wait a minute." I went into the bar and met this man and with him were about fifty of the lumberjacks from the camp where I had been. I asked him if he could lend me a nickel until we got to Winnipeg. He said, "A nickel?" And with a great flourish he swiped his hat off his head and shouted to all in the bar: "Brothers, here is our sky pilot. He wants a nickel. Can we spare it?" He passed the hat around and I came out of the bar with $100. There was no stopping them, they simply wouldn't listen. They got on the same train to Winnipeg as I did, with a fiddle, and I fiddled them all the way to Winnipeg and we had a real uproarious time.[1]

Irvine never actually preached in the camps, preferring instead to organize debates, discussions, singsongs and concerts, and to distribute books and magazines he had collected and begged from church communities in the towns. These discussions were never about religious questions but about the problems of society with socialism as a basic theme. For these assignments Irvine received as stipend $800 a year. The collections taken in the camps often greatly exceeded this amount, but everything over $800 went to the church.

During his student years, Irvine went back to the lumber camps a number of times. Sometimes he lived in a small rural centre and preached twice on Sunday at two different churches to farming communities, while during the week he travelled about sixty miles to visit the lumber camps. On such occasions he often had to accept the warm hospitality of farm folk, albeit sometimes in rather cramped circumstances. Irvine relates how on one occasion he was given a temporary shakedown bed in the farmhouse kitchen while the farmer and his wife retired to the only bedroom. In the morning, much to Irvine's embarrassment, the farmer's wife set about her household chores in the kitchen before he was able to get up and get dressed. While he pondered on how to get dressed while preserving the modesty and decency demanded of a student minister, the woman opened a trapdoor in the kitchen floor and descended into a cellar, where the household stores were kept. Irvine seized the opportunity, jumped out of bed and desperately attempted to get into his trousers before she reappeared. He succeeded in getting one leg in and was hopping about trying quickly to get the other in also, when he inadvertently hopped, half-clad, down the cellar opening, just as the lady of the house was ascending. The rough life of the lumber camp had not hardened him to the point where he could face such a situation with equanimity.

It was at the small town of Shellbrook, not far from Prince Albert, that Irvine met Adelia Maple Little. Her parents had lived at High Bluff, near Portage la Prairie in Manitoba, but had recently moved to Shellbrook. Adelia played the organ in the Methodist Church and Irvine stayed with the Littles. Once he brought home a derelict from the lumber camp; after Mrs. Little deloused him, he stayed for the remainder of the winter and his fine singing voice was much appreciated. Bill Irvine and Adelia became engaged, but the Methodists did not approve of students entering matrimony before ordination. The Presbyterian church was more liberal in this regard, so Irvine changed his allegiance from the Methodists to the Presbyterians. This was easy to do since they had a common educational program for student ministers and there were no serious doctrinal differences between the two churches, which were in any case already engaged in the negotiations which would eventually bring the United Church into existence.

Adelia and Bill were married on 29 December 1910, in the small town of Swan River, Manitoba, just across the border from Saskatchewan. Probably Irvine was a supply minister in the area at the time. Soon after they moved to Togo, about fifty miles south in Saskatchewan, and here Irvine built a four-room cottage for them to live in, a few yards from the church. Irvine said about his marriage: "I found out that two people could live as cheaply as one, provided one of them had foresight and prudence. When I first got married I tried to hide from my wife the fact that money was short; I simply had no thought about more until I did not have any. Eventually I decided to give her every cent earned and to let her manage the home without any advice from me. This worked admirably."

The tribute is well deserved and to it might be added the fact that not only was Delia Irvine the economist and financial manager of the household, but also, because of Irvine's preoccupation with first community and later political affairs, she ultimately carried the major burden of bringing up the four sons and one daughter who blessed their marriage. But he exaggerated the ease with which marriage solved their financial problems. At Togo, as well as serving a number of churches, he found it necessary to hire himself out as a farmhand at harvesting time, and to work every evening in the local drugstore. Thus, despite the birth of their first child, Ronald, in January 1912, Irvine had earned and saved enough to take him back to college in Winnipeg in the fall of that year. In 1913, at the end of the college year, he was back in the ministerial field, this time at Minitonas, Manitoba, and in the fall he returned to college. Finally, in the spring of 1914, he completed his theological training and was ordained.

Irvine was in some ways disappointed with his college experience:

> College was not inspiring to me. Reading the New Testament in Greek, studying Church history, which always seemed to me much ado about nothing, or following the peregrinations of systematic theology highly flavoured with medieval concepts, were anything but inspiring.

Even so, he recalled several of his teachers as having made a genuine contribution to his education:

> Even systematic theology under Dr. Eliot of Manitoba College had its compensations. He somehow or other persuaded us to challenge every religious view and to think our way

through, not as parrots but as students.... but very few really wanted to do that. They wanted to be instructed and assured of the truth of the old doctrines and were apt to be critical of anyone who suggested that there might be something wrong with these doctrines. At his classes, all the doubts which had been growing in my mind about religious doctrine brought me at last to question everything and to realize that the test of truth was to be found in fact and natural law.

Irvine's college education was not as unproductive as his first reaction to it suggests; six years of theological training produced in him a critical mind that eventually rejected practically all of the traditional Christian beliefs. He also pursued an informal education under the guidance of two men. The first was Dr. Salem Bland, who taught New Testament Greek at Wesley College. Dr. Bland's central concern was the removal of social injustice and irrationality in society, and its rebuilding on socialist lines. Throughout his ninety years, by preaching, teaching and writing, he supported the claims of working people, both urban labour and farmers, to a just economic reward and a fair share in political power. He taught that this could only be achieved in a socialist society in which co-operation replaced competition and concern for human beings and human values replaced the profit motive. All this seemed to him to be linked with the Christian ethic as he saw it portrayed in the New Testament. In his book, *The New Christianity* (1920) he saw Christianity as undergoing changes and being moulded by the different forms of society through which it had passed, but finally emerging in a purified form with the development of a socialist commonwealth. Thus Bland was a leading exponent of the Social Gospel, which developed in Canada chiefly, though not exclusively, within the ranks of the Methodist clergy, and which was espoused by a small band of critically minded and intelligent men who had strong social consciences and a disdain for religious dogma.

Irvine always claimed that he had been greatly influenced by Bland:

Dr. Salem Bland had a tremendous influence on his students.

Many of them rejected his humanistic concepts of Christianity, but it drove them to question some of the old basic creeds. Religion to Dr. Bland was not a compartment into which one entered to get away from the world. It was like the golden thread which runs through a necklace. There is no part of human life which can escape from the humanistic test of morality. This strengthened our views on socialism and helped to give an intelligent purpose for living.

Irvine's other influential teacher was from outside the college. J.S. Woodsworth was the son of the man who had recruited him for the ministry in Canada. Eleven years older than Irvine, Woodsworth, following in his father's footsteps, had become an ordained Methodist minister, but subsequently ceased to believe in much of the Christian creed. He offered his resignation to the Methodist Conference but was persuaded to withdraw it and was appointed to the post of Superintendent of All Peoples' Mission in Winnipeg in 1907. This enabled him to work with the poor and oppressed and gave expression to and reinforced his adherence to the Social Gospel.

Woodsworth became more and more convinced that the church was out of touch with the needs of the people. He approached Irvine and asked him to try to organize a group in the college where he could come and discuss social questions with the theological students. Irvine organized a study group in sociology and persuaded a few students to attend.

Woodsworth used to take us out at least once a week to some part of the city to study what was happening there. For instance, we would one night visit the Labour Council meeting and hear them discuss their problems, and another time we would visit the slums or we would visit a large industry. We would talk with the men about their hours of labour and what wages they were getting. We visited the provincial legislature and we visited every institution that we possibly could just to see how the affairs of people worked, and from that we learned a great deal more perhaps than we did by taking theology.

In the fall of 1910, Woodsworth also organized a People's Forum which met on Sunday afternoons and Sunday evenings in the Grand Theatre. The afternoon programs consisted of a lecture on some topic of social importance followed by general discussion. In the evening there were concerts, often provided by one or more of the ethnic groups that made up the population of Winnipeg. Irvine also attended meetings of the Socialist party and the Social Democratic party, and once he spent a Sunday afternoon debating with Joseph Barretts, a member of the Socialist party of Canada. There was a large crowd present and a lively debate took place, but as a result Irvine was on the carpet before the college authorities and threatened with expulsion for debating socialism on the sabbath with a radical.

All in all, despite Irvine's expressed dissatisfaction, the formal and informal education he received between 1907 and 1914 could hardly have been better. The socialism of his youth had been deepened and broadened, while the religious doctrines he had been brought up with were subjected to critical scrutiny and replaced by the Social Gospel. Finally, he had travelled extensively through two of Canada's western provinces and met with all sorts and conditions of people.

When the time came for Irvine's ordination, he told his professors at the college that he could not conscientiously sign the Articles of Faith in which he no longer believed, but that he did believe in the social and humane ideas of Jesus, whose preachings were the basis of Christianity as he saw it. He was allowed to receive ordination without signing the Articles, possibly because a number of his instructors shared his views and also because the movement towards the union of churches must have led to the development of a more relaxed, tolerant and broadminded attitude towards sectarian beliefs. After discussion with such teachers as Bland, Irwin and Fleming, Irvine hoped that he could have a career in the church preaching the Social Gospel.

Even before graduation, he was called to a church in Emo, in the Rainy River district of southwestern Ontario, close to the Manitoba and U.S. borders. The church had been Presbyterian,

but it had joined with the Methodists to form a Union Church.
Before receiving the appointment, Irvine had to go to Emo to de-
liver a trial sermon, and later when he wrote a letter of acceptance
he informed the church board that he was going to preach the
Social Gospel and received in return the assurance that this was
what they wanted. So he moved to Emo with his family and took
up his first fulltime pastorate.

> I was preaching sheer humanism. The supernatural had
> vanished. There were no miracles, no virgin birth, no atone-
> ment and no resurrection. Of course I did not put it to my
> congregation in that way. I used everything in the Bible
> which could in any way support the Social Gospel. I did not
> mention nor criticize church doctrine except by inference to
> those who could follow logic. It took nearly two years for it
> to dawn on the people of Emo that I was not preaching to get
> people into heaven but that I was much more interested in
> getting heaven into people.

In the summer the religious communities of Emo, Rainy River
and Fort Frances, under the guidance of their three pastors, held a
summer school for several weeks in a holiday setting. One such
was held on an island in Rainy Lake. The participants — close to
one hundred people — were a cross section of the three communities, professional men, business people, farmers. They, together
with camping equipment and supplies, went down Rainy River
by barge to Rainy Lake and were set ashore on an island with no
means of communication with the shore except one canoe. Each
of the ministers gave a series of lectures followed by discussion.
Irvine dealt with two subjects. One was what was then called the
"Higher Criticism," that is, the attempt to apply to the Bible the
same rational standards and methods of criticism that historians
would apply to any secular historical document. It was of course
disruptive of literal, traditional and orthodox interpretations of
the scriptures. His other topic was the social implications of the
teaching of Jesus. At the time, he regarded both higher criticism
and the Social Gospel as putting new life into the worn shibbo-
leths of the Christian religion. Irvine's lectures gave rise to lively

and no doubt interesting discussion, but he found that most of his audience was firmly wedded to the oldtime religion in which they had been brought up.

The summer camp was dramatically enlivened by one incident which Irvine has described. The minister from Fort Frances suggested to Irvine that they take a canoe out on the lake. Irvine agreed although he urged the man to put on a bathing suit and to take off his heavy boots. This Irvine's companion refused to do, asserting that there was no danger.

> We paddled off for a distance of about a mile into the middle of the lake. It was a nice day, calm and beautiful, but suddenly he made a shift in the canoe from one end to the other and over she went. He went down like a rock and stayed under. I guess I haven't got the stuff that heroes are made of, I was more scared than of anything in my whole life. I feared that I couldn't go home without him, I couldn't bear to face his wife and child, both of whom would be on the beach waiting for us, but I wasn't going to commit suicide if I could help it. He didn't come up and the water was about one hundred feet deep there and as black as night. I knew very well that if I dived for him I wouldn't be able to see him and I'd have to take a chance just to find him, and if he happened to grab me by the arms or throat or something, we might both stay down. So I thought: "Well, I'll give him just half a minute to cool off down there. There is no use trying to save a man who is struggling and doesn't know what he is doing". I could see a sort of whirlpool in the water just above where he was struggling, so I knew just about where he was. It occurred to me that I might try to catch him on the end of the canoe. So I upended the thing and shoved it down and by good luck he grabbed the keel and I managed to lever him up. He was unconscious but still holding on like grim death to the keel. I had to keep the canoe upside down because he was on the keel and I was certainly not going to risk letting him fall off. Then I swam to the front end of the canoe and got the painter and made a bowline of it and put it around my neck and under my arms and started to swim. Though it

was only a mile, it seemed more like two or three before I made it.

There was an anxious crowd awaiting them on the beach but Irvine's friend soon regained consciousness and was none the worse although perhaps the wiser for his experience.

No doubt the summer school helped to spread knowledge of and emphasize the unorthodox nature of Irvine's religious convictions, but perhaps it was his more positive and social commitments that some of his congregation found disturbing. He was also an open advocate of votes for women at a time when this was a controversial issue and he put on a small play called *The Spinsters' Convention*, which, whatever its entertainment value, was a piece of propaganda for women's suffrage.

When World War I broke out, Irvine's younger brother, James, who had come to Canada and was working in a hardware store in the nearby town of Fort Francis, went to the recruiting office and joined the army. Irvine considered that James did not really know what he was getting himself into, so he went to Fort Francis and obtained his brother's release, probably on the grounds that he was not yet eighteen. James, however, promptly rejoined and was a member of the First Canadian Expeditionary Force. He died in the second battle of Ypres in April 1915, after fighting bravely, but his body was never traced. Irvine's attempt to prevent his brother's enlistment gave rise to the rumour that he was pro-German, and shortly thereafter he was subjected to surveillance by the authorities. One Sunday evening after church, a secret service officer came to the manse and told Irvine that he had been in Emo for a couple of weeks, had heard him preach four times and had heard him discussing matters in the street, and that his investigation was now concluded. He added: "You've got some enemies in this town and I just wanted you to know that I'd been here and that I am giving you a clean sheet".

Many of the small farmers in the area were living on the edge of poverty. In some cases they were in the process of clearing the land, felling heavy timber and taking out the undergrowth, and meanwhile keeping a cow and a few chickens and growing a little grain for sustenance. Around Christmas Irvine happened to be in a store when a farmer drove up with a frozen carcass of beef on a sleigh, which he tried to sell to the merchant. The merchant said, "Well, really I have more of this than I can handle, I'm afraid I can't take it from you." The farmer replied, "I've simply got to have something. This is Christmas time, my children have no boots or shoes and I would like to have a little extra for them at Christmas. I've just got to sell this thing." "Well," said the merchant, "if you like to leave it, I'll let you have five dollars for it."

Irvine later commented: "I thought that was terrible. Five dollars for a steer that, when it was alive, would weigh a thousand pounds at least! Here was a man who had been working hard to try to feed his family and here was another, comparatively rich, who offered him five dollars with the prospect of making a handsome profit on the deal."

Irvine immediately set about organizing a farmers' co-operative for the buying and selling of their produce. Irvine had no official position in the co-operative; it was run by the farmers themselves. The co-operative had no store but it brought in supplies, flour, fencing wire, fruit, etc., on order from its members and it shipped out carloads of baled hay and frozen meat. In the first month it did $60,000 worth of business, which of course was lost to the merchants who had previously been taking advantage of the farmers. Several of the merchants concerned were on the church board. They summoned Irvine to a meeting at which they told him: "We did not hire you to preach socialism but Jesus Christ and Him crucified." Irvine replied: "You will crucify Him without any help from me," and he reminded them that when he first accepted his position he had warned them that he proposed to preach the Social Gospel and that they had agreed.

The structure of the church polity was such that the board could not dismiss him except on a majority vote of the whole congregation, which they could not get. So Irvine remained in his pastorate, but from then on he refused to take his salary even though the congregation contributed to it. Again he went out during the week and earned his living at any jobs he could get in the community. He built a hall for the fair grounds, blew out tree stumps with dynamite for farmers who were clearing their lands, dug ditches and tended his own vegetable garden. Sometimes he was paid in cash, but more often in kind with food. Although by 1914 his second son, Harry, had been born, Irvine managed to provide his family with all essentials.

Finally, he received a dinner invitation from a church elder:

> Well, I went to supper. There was another man there whom I had not met before. After supper the elder led the discussion into the ancient bogs of superstitious doctrine. I was careful to counter every step with another toward a fuller and more ethical life for man. Eventually, he suggested that I was evading the issue. I agreed and told him I was doing so because his mind had been frozen in the cold icy environment of superstition and that it was impossible to penetrate his mind with a new idea, no matter how meritorious. I further said that if these doctrines he had been repeating were the only things he had to cling to, I did not want to try to remove them, just as I would not kick a crutch from the armpit of a physical cripple, neither would I kick away his mental crutches he had used for so long that he could not function without them.

However, Irvine proceeded to do just that. He told his host that the Bible was not the Word of God, nor was it to be taken as literal truth, but rather as a heterogeneous collection of writings derived from ancient peoples, interesting and valuable if read critically in this context, but not infallible. He argued that man did not suffer a fall; on the contrary, he had evolved and risen. The fall described in the mythology of the Bible really stood for the time when man developed an awakened consciousness of right and wrong. Irvine also contended that the doctrine of atonement was immoral, for no person can rightfully take upon himself the burden of another's wrongdoing, and the notion of vicarious punishment is morally repulsive. Finally he argued that the doctrines of the virgin birth and the resurrection of Christ were incredible both from the point of view of science and commonsense.

That night the elder walked seven miles to the nearest railway station and wired to the church assembly, which was meeting in Winnipeg, and laid a charge of heresy against Irvine. The case was referred to the presbytery (consisting of the ministers and elders of the church) which held its hearing at Fort Frances. The Reverend Reid, as moderator, was in the chair. There was only one witness, Mr. Leveridge, whom the elder had asked to supper at the same time that Irvine was invited. Leveridge was asked if, on that occasion, he had heard Irvine say anything which as a minister of the church he should not have said. Leveridge replied, "No, on the contrary, I should say that if he hadn't said what he did he'd be entirely unfitted for any ministry."

The majority of the presbytery were young men, recently out of college, like Irvine himself, and may, to varying degrees, have shared his unorthodoxy. When the vote was taken a substantial majority voted for acquittal. The following day, however, Irvine resigned. He felt that the disparity between his own views on religion and that of many of his congregation was too wide and that they would be paying him for something he could not give them.

A few days later he received a wire from the Unitarian church headquarters in Boston saying that they had read an account of the trial and, judging from the charges laid against him and his replies, he was the kind of man they wanted to go to Calgary. The First Unitarian Church of Calgary had been in existence for some time, but had only a small congregation and for several years had lacked a pastor. Irvine accepted for it seemed to offer him the opportunity of supporting himself and his family in the profession for which he had been trained, without imposing upon him a set of dogmatic beliefs and, perhaps most important of all, it gave him an opportunity to pursue his social concerns.

Irvine's experience at Emo was to be typical of that of other adherents of the Social Gospel. J.S. Woodsworth, Irvine's lifelong friend and companion-in-arms in the fight for social justice, suffered a similar series of struggles and frustrations, which culminated in his resignation from the Methodist church in 1918. William Ivens, who had been a fellow student at Wesley College and had also studied with Salem Bland, under pressure from the board of the McDougall Methodist Church in Winnipeg, in 1918 gave up his charge there and proceeded to found the first of the Labour churches, sometimes called People's churches. In June 1919, A.E. Smith under similar pressure from the Brandon Methodist church resigned and formed a People's church.

Salem Bland himself stayed to the end with the Methodist church although in the course of his struggles to bring the church into the forefront of the fight for social justice and social reconstruction, he was dismissed from Wesley College in 1917, and in 1919 he successfully resisted an attempt to oust him from the pulpit of the Broadway Methodist Tabernacle in Toronto. Bland, although sympathetic to the People's church movement tenaciously held to his position in the Methodist church until his retirement at the age of sixty-eight.

It is clear that all these men, and others of less eminence, were politically radical and dedicated to changing the structure of society in a socialist direction. It is also clear that they thought their socialism was compatible with, and indeed an expression of, the Christian ethic which could be discovered in the scriptures, in the life of Jesus, and in the early Christian church under the Roman Empire. What is not clear is what their religious beliefs amounted to beyond this.

In 1920, when the Reverend A.E. Smith came to Calgary to assist in the formation of a People's church there, although the need for social change was central to Smith's concern, nevertheless he went to some pains to remould traditional religious conceptions. Thus, he declared that although external authority in religion was to be rejected, nevertheless Jesus Christ was the first of all spiritual teachers and none higher had ever appeared on this earth. The Last Supper was not a sacrament but a communistic rite, while the Lord's Prayer was a revolutionary prayer that was meaningless in a church that served as a buttress for the capitalist system.

Irvine, who was at this time active in the formation of the People's church and who chaired one of Smith's meetings, never wrote or spoke in such terms. His fundamental concerns were human, social and ethical and he regarded the Christian church as an influential social institution that *might* be used as an instrument of social change although it had been sadly lacking in this regard. What made it a potential force for good were the ethics, more preached than practised, that in the western world had become associated with the Christian religion.

A month after A.E. Smith's visit to Calgary, Irvine published an article on "The Labour Church in Canada" in the *Nation*. The general tone of this article is remarkably secular and anti-clerical:

> In this period of general readjustment, it is, of course, natural and inevitable that the church, or institutionalized religion, should be called upon to square itself with the need for human service, or go out of existence.
>
> In Canada, and presumably in most other countries, the church is among the most backward of all institutions.... The failing power of churchianity is due to the growing conviction that the church is a class institution, depending for its existence not on truth, but on preaching the gospel of those with financial power. In gaining the purse-strings of the rich, it lost the confidence of the masses, and in Canada today it can be reckoned with only as a reactionary force.
>
> The Great War had its effect upon the church as definitely as upon trade or national debt. Up to the moment that war was declared the clergy had been the professed champions of peace.... This was profitable doctrine during an industrial struggle between the workers and the masters, but presto! the Gospel changed over night when Germany declared war. Forthwith every sanctuary became a recruiting office and the convener of the Presbyterian Assembly appeared with his sword at his belt....
>
> But why does the church go back to the old Gospel as soon as the war is over? This is the action which has completely destroyed public confidence. No sooner was peace declared than the wage earners, the many returned soldiers, decided to take "direct action" in securing industrial amelioration; the One Big Union was born and became portentous. At that moment the church abandons its war philosophy, quickly strips the armour from the fighting Saviour, and presents him once more as the meek and lowly carpenter who said: "Render unto Caesar the things that are Caesar's."

New churches are springing up everywhere under the leadership of men like the Reverend J.S. Woodsworth, the Reverend S.G. Bland, the Reverend A.E. Smith, and the Reverend W. Ivens....

The basis of membership in this new church does not rest upon a belief in a theological syllogism. "Anyone," it is declared, "shall be eligible for membership who believes in the need for and possibility of a better day for human society, and who is willing to make some systematic, consistent, and constructive contribution of thought, time, influence and means towards that end."[2]

Seven months later Irvine wrote:

The religion here referred to is that which is inseparable from the interpretation which people give to life, not the narrow concept which centring around creeds and churches often passes for religion.... My purpose in referring to religion does not involve a discussion of the relative merits of creeds, sects, or churches, nor does it admit any consideration of the question in its theological aspect. I am concerned only with the new social appeal which indicates a reinterpretation of that deeper spiritual truth for which religion stands. The trend of religious thought as expressed by church conferences and from the pulpits, is away from the old individualistic outlook, and more and more towards making a social application of Christian principles.... It is now recognized to be impossible to save the world one individual at a time as long as the conditions from which people need to be saved are allowed to go unchallenged.... This kind of religion cannot be kept out of politics. Being inseparable from life it permeates its every department, and extends the domain of the sacred to what have been called material things. The line between the sacred and the secular is being rubbed out. This does not mean that everything is becoming secular, on the contrary, everything is becoming sacred. In the past the sacred things of life have been extremely limited. We had but one sacred day in seven, one sacred

building in a community, one sacred calling in all the voca-
tions of men, and one sacred book in all literature. . . . The day
is coming when the land by which we live will be considered
as sacred as the little plot in which we bury our beloved
dead. When that time fully arrives, there will be no more
speculation in land, for the privileged few who now hold out
of use land which should be utilized in growing bread will
no longer be able to do so. When that time comes the privileged few will have disappeared. We are approaching the
time when every employment will have service for its aim
and will be looked upon as being as sacred as that of a
clergyman. And just think what a day it will be when our
factories become sacred — so sacred that there will be no
sweating, no exploitation, no unsanitary conditions — and
when the man who would not perform a bad deed on Sunday will find that all other days have also become sacred.[3]

The book in which this passage appears, *The Farmers in Politics*,
has a short introduction by Salem Bland, but the section which
discusses religion occupies only six of the total of 253 pages. By
this time, Irvine had resigned from his ministry in the Unitarian
Church and was devoting himself to political organization and
political journalism. However, during his period as an MP in Ottawa, from 1922-35, Irvine renewed association with the Unitarian church there, often speaking from the pulpit and sometimes
acting as a substitute minister. In 1935 he published a thirty-page
pamphlet entitled *Can a Christian Vote for Capitalism?*, again with
a foreword by Dr. Salem Bland. He answers No to his question on
the grounds that: "Ethics cannot be separated from Christianity
in its social implications. A person may be ethical without being a
Christian, of course, but he cannot be truly Christian without being ethical."

In his 1945 booklet, *Is Socialism the Answer?*, Irvine devotes
three out of ninety-three pages to the same theme and concludes:

Socialists would remind the church that even the preaching
of what is called "the Social Gospel" is not, in itself, enough.
The church must find ways and means of inspiring the com-

mon people to take whatever action is necessary for translating the great ideals of Christianity into a living reality. It must strive to recover its lost position as a "people's church" — a role it fulfilled in the beginning.[4]

These fading hopes were doomed to disappointment, and although the Christian churches generated a small and active group of crusaders for social justice, they never managed to carry with them the significant support of their congregations. The role of the Social Gospel proponents is an honoured one in the history of Canada's struggle to achieve social justice, but it was mainly their work in secular organizations that bore fruit.

In Irvine's case, by the time of the Emo trial, and probably before, his religion on all essential points had been replaced by humanism. As a student he had read Marx, Darwin and Huxley's defence of Darwin, Herbert Spencer, and James Frazer's *Golden Bough* which treated Christian beliefs in the context of pre-Christian mythology. Under the impact of this reading and reflection, he soon came to reject all the supernatural elements of religion and to place his reliance upon the natural and the social sciences for explanations of the origin and constitution of both the natural world and the peoples and societies who inhabit it.

His activities in the churches in Canada were always entirely directed towards the enlightenment of people's minds and the betterment of their conditions of life. In doing this he appealed to what he considered to be a valuable core of Christian ethics, although he recognized that these ethics were not unique to Christianity. However, he was well aware that the supernatural and mythical elements in Christianity had a disturbing effect upon its ethical theory and practice. Adherence to the myths of *Genesis* led Christians to oppose well-established scientific theories and facts, the most notable being the theory of biological evolution. Irvine noted that churches and Sunday schools continued to teach children fables about the world as if they were fact, thus producing confusion in their minds and inhibiting the development of a rational outlook. Christian teaching about original sin and the virgin birth of Jesus had led to an unhealthy attitude towards sex, to the extent that people were led to believe that uncontrolled sex was the major form of immorality. Irvine did not condone loose sexual behaviour, but he thought that the evils of our economic and political systems were far more immoral. He complained that economic injustice was not recognized as immoral and that exploitation of labour was in fact encouraged by both church and state.

Irvine also rejected the other-worldliness of Christianity, with its claim that through suffering, deprivation and pain here on this earth, we are buying happiness in the hereafter. This resignation to the evils of this world was utterly unacceptable to Irvine, with the consequence that he abandoned the Social Gospel for socialist humanism. He ceased all association with churches of whatever kind and joined the International Humanist and Ethical Union, a worldwide association dedicated to rational and scientific thinking and to an ethic based upon the need for improving human conditions and human relationships.

In an unpublished manuscript written in the last year of his life, Irvine wrote:

> The watchword of humanism is service to humanity in this existence, as contrasted with the salvation of individual souls for a future existence, and the glorification of a supernatural supreme being. Humanism urges men to accept freely and joyously the great gift of life and to realize that life in its own right and for its own sake can be as beautiful and splendid as any dreams of immortality.... Humanism adheres to the highest ethical ideas, fosters the so-called goods of the spirit, while at the same time it insists that all values are grounded in the world of human experience and natural forms.... As a humanist I find the greatest of all pleasures in devoting myself to furthering the humanist civilization. The first essential of that sort of civilization is to attain the widest, most universal application of the democratic principle to every aspect of human life. The participation of all the people on earth in the good things of life should be an acceptable definition of democracy. This, as a goal to be sought, is worthy of everyone's devotion. In this world which is the common home of man, we must learn to share

together on the basis of equality and co-operative effort, the vital work to be done. At present the life of man on this planet earth is threatened by the possibility of nuclear war. The choice for us is universal democracy in all things vital for human happiness or to continue with an individualistic striving for gain, which spells annihilation.[5]

THREE
Calgary and the *Nutcracker*

The Irvines left for Calgary in January 1916. It was the middle of a particularly hard winter. Drifting snow frequently held up the train as it crossed the prairies and it became so cold in the carriages that the guard lined his van with blankets and gathered mothers with young children, including Mrs. Irvine and the two boys, into the van to give them some protection against the biting cold.

On arrival in Calgary, they received a warm welcome from the Unitarian congregation and Irvine was installed as pastor of the First Unitarian Church of Calgary on Sunday, 9 January, at Unity Hall. In his installation address the Reverend Horace Westwood of All Souls Church, Winnipeg, spoke of the courage and independence shown by the new pastor in leaving his former church and in joining the Unitarians. He went on to make a plea for the open mind and declared that the majority of evils were those of human hands and human hearts and therefore the remedy lay not in asking for divine intercession but in ourselves. The Reverend Charles Potter of Edmonton also spoke and said that the congregation must share its minister with the community. The Unitarian tradition was that one-tenth of the pastor's time was spent on the needs of his congregation and nine-tenths upon work in the community at large. The minister should not be required to give more than one sermon a week but he should maintain the Unitarian ideal of public service.

It seemed clear that Irvine was entering into a situation congenial to his ideals and which gave him freedom to pursue his concern for social justice and his role as social critic. He became the centre of what some termed "progressive" and others "radical" thought and action in the Calgary community. Within a few weeks he was reported as saying in a public address: "All political parties are corrupt; all newspapers, or nearly all, are cowardly, and the churches are either venal or woefully lacking in courage."[1] Soon thereafter he was addressing a public meeting on "The Franchise for Women," a cause which he strongly supported.

During the next four years, the Unitarian church served Irvine as a base from which he carried on numerous activities in the fields of journalism, public speaking, political organization, and sociology, all designed to arouse the awareness of people and make them critical of the society in which they lived, and encourage them to take active steps to change it. He was aided and abetted by a loyal following from his congregation, among whom were William Davidson and his wife. Davidson was the founder and publisher of the *Morning Albertan*, a relatively progressive Calgary newspaper and rival of the *Calgary Herald*, which took a more conservative stance on most issues. Davidson was a Liberal and later became an MLA, but he appreciated Irvine as an intellectual catalyst in the community and gave him a good deal of coverage in his paper. Soon Irvine was contributing both signed and unsigned editorials.

R.J. Deachman was another member of the Unitarian congregation who was closely associated with Irvine in most of the projects he undertook in Calgary. Deachman frequently wrote letters to the press, in many of which he set forth his opposition to the imposition of tariffs and his advocacy of the nationalization of Canada's railways. He was associated with Irvine in his journalistic ventures, in the People's Forum, and in the development of labour political parties in Calgary.

Among the most active members of Irvine's congregation were Miss Rachael Coutts and her sister, Marion Carson. They shared a passionate sympathy for the disadvantaged — victims of ill-health, economic injustice, or racial prejudice — and they were prepared to join with others to eradicate the causes of these conditions. Rachael Coutts was a public school teacher and a charter member of the Alberta Teachers' Alliance and several times a member of its provincial executive. She attended, at her own expense, the first World Conference of Educationalists, held in Holland, and wrote accounts of this gathering for the ATA magazine. In 1934, she was awarded the OBE in recognition of her contribution to education and her qualities as a citizen. Her sister was a force in the local Council of Women from its inception, and to her and other like-minded women was due such legislation as the introduction of mothers' allowances. She was an organizer and for many years an active president of the Tuberculosis Association in Calgary; it was in part through her efforts that care for TB patients was eventually provided free in the province of Alberta.

The two sisters joined the Unitarian Church in 1913 and, from the time of his arrival in Calgary, they supported Irvine's activities in the cause of social justice. When J.S. Woodsworth lost his position as a social service worker in Winnipeg and eventually left the Methodist church because of his opposition to the war, they were glad to welcome him to their home when he visited Calgary. Resolute in her opposition to the war, Mrs. Carson wrote a letter of encouragement to a young man who had resisted conscription and who was in consequence brought before the courts. On hearing the news of the death of her son in action in France, Mrs. Carson said, when it was regarded as almost treason to speak thus: "I would be glad to clasp the hand of any German mother who sorrows as we do tonight."

Mr. and Mrs. Carson and Miss Coutts were founding members of the Labour Representation League in Calgary, which held its first meeting in their house at which Irvine and Alex Ross described the objectives of labour as a political force. Mrs. Carson was the first president (an office she held for many years) of the Women's Labour League (later to become the CCF Women's Club). She made sure that reports of meetings were submitted to the daily papers, for she believed that every opportunity should be seized to influence public opinion. Mrs. Carson was elected and re-elected to the Calgary school board with large majorities, and was largely instrumental in getting legislation such as the provision of free milk for needy school children passed.

Other members of Irvine's Unitarian group were A.G. Broatch, a machinist by trade, a labour man elected and re-elected city alderman and a well-known supporter of the One Big Union movement; A.J. Samis, alderman and later Calgary city commissioner; Alex Calhoun, city librarian; and finally there was Miss Amelia Turner, who lived with the Irvine family for some time and became Irvine's secretary. She was also active in the labour political movement (and later the CCF), serving for twelve years as a labour representative on the Calgary school board.

Thus, from his first arrival in Calgary, Irvine found himself surrounded by a group of men and women, who, though covering a fairly wide spectrum of opinion, nevertheless shared an interest in social issues, were prepared to engage in public debate and were not afraid to adopt unorthodox views which they were prepared to translate into political or social action.

In February 1916, Irvine embarked upon his first venture in Calgary outside of the church; recalling the People's Forum that Woodsworth had started in Winnipeg a few years previously, he decided to set up a similar organization. Details of the first meeting on Sunday, 20 February, are not on record, except for the fact that it was not well attended. Consequently Irvine and another of his congregation with whom he was to have a long association, Jack Ford, arranged to hold a noon-hour meeting with the men at the Ogden Workshops of the CPR, with the purpose of explaining to them the goals of the People's Forum to enlist their co-operation and support. Irvine emphasized the pressing need for education, particularly about industrial questions. He spoke of the proposed extension of the franchise to include women (they received the provincial franchise in April of that year), and urged the men not only to come to the Forum but to bring their wives. He pointed out that the value of the Forum to the working class would entirely depend on the extent to which they actively participated in it.

The second meeting of the People's Forum on 27 February 1916 was well attended. Irvine was in the chair and Harry Pryde, the president of the Calgary Trades and Labour Council, spoke on the origin and vicissitudes of the trade union movement in England. The meeting established the pattern for subsequent ones. The speaker's address was followed by questions and then by three-minute speeches from the floor. A month later the *Morning Albertan* was reporting that:

The People's Forum has been a success beyond the expectations of its most optimistic supporters. It was needed and it is somewhat surprising that many of Calgary's better-known citizens do not attend and take part in the discussion. It is becoming a principal asset.[2]

The *Albertan* does not tell us which "better-known citizens" it had in mind, but certainly in the ensuing two or three years, a great variety of people spoke on a great variety of topics. A little more than two years after its founding a report at its annual meeting showed that thirty-five meetings had been held during the season, divided into topics under the following classifications: nine, provincial and local interest; seven, purely Canadian in scope; seven, democracy and cognate subjects; six, origin and conduct of the war; four, religion and morals; two, public health. To this analysis, the comment was added that "although the range of subjects chosen by the various platform speakers is capable of classification as above, it is far otherwise with questions and discussion from the floor, in respect to which it would be difficult to mention any subject in the heavens above, the earth beneath, or the waters under the earth, which has not been incidentally debated upon."

From the beginning, the Forum attracted members of the Socialist Party of Canada, which appears to have been a sectarian group dedicated to a somewhat narrow interpretation of Marxism. They were aware that the Forum was one of the few places available to them to voice their views to an audience of any size, but at the same time, they seemed resentful of the fact that the Forum offered its platform to a broad spectrum of opinion. In response to their demands, a session of the People's Forum (8 October 1916) was given over to the presentation of "The Case for Socialism " by one of their members, W.J. Reid, with J.H. Ford, the newly elected president, in the chair. Reid told a sympathetic, and indeed an enthusiastic, audience that "when the working class knows what it wants it will get it, possibly by force." He went on to say that the questions discussed by the Forum were of no use in solving the problems of the working class. He scornfully described women's suffrage, proportional representation, the single tax and prohibition, as "nostrums" which would not help the situation or touch the cause of present conditions.

On another occasion, Alderman R.J. Tallon spoke to a well-attended but contentious Forum meeting on the eight-hour day, during which he spent some time defending the International Workers of the World. R.H. Parkyn, a member of the Carpenters' Union, later active in the formation of the Dominion Labour party, served as president of the Forum for a season and was referred to in the press as "an extremist, albeit a very gentle, mild-mannered one." On Sunday, 21 May 1917, the Reverend J. Austin Huntley of the First Baptist Church spoke to the Forum on "The Church and Social Service." He was very clearly a supporter of the Social Gospel, for in the course of his address he declared that "our industrial and economic life is un-Christian"; "A man is guilty of treason who makes great profits in war-time"; "Exploitation is the curse of this country"; "When the Church is told to keep out of politics, politics must be rank."

However, the members of his congregation present at the Forum, perhaps alarmed by their pastor's outspokenness, insisted that the meeting conclude by singing the national anthem. This caused some dissension and, as a consequence, a certain amount of adverse comment from outsiders and the newspapers, particularly the *Calgary Herald*. The Forum decided that in the future it would sing the national anthem set to new words and would retitle it *God Save the People*. The committee of the Forum, through its president, J.H. Ford, announced that there was no particular prejudice against singing *God Save the King* except that certain newspapers and individuals had tried to dictate to the Forum what song should be sung at the close of meetings. Ford intimated that the feeling of the Forum leaders was "that the King is getting along very nicely and that a national anthem that expresses more concern with the great mass of men is more in keeping with the purpose of the organization than the extolling of Kings and Queens." It was probably as a result of this incident that the proprietor of the Empress Theatre refused to rent to the Forum "for business reasons." The Forum moved without ado to the Grand Theatre and proceeded on its controversial career.

Despite the controversy it aroused, the Forum had its staunch defenders. The following editorial appeared in the *Morning Albertan*:

> A few months ago, during political excitement, a candidate for the provincial legislature condemned the People's Forum as a dangerous institution and caused the Forum Committee some embarrassment. The politician was not sure of its morals and loyalty.... The meeting yesterday (a debate, pro and con conscription) indicates the plan and purpose of the People's Forum. The Forum is not a place for party organization or propaganda. It is just a forum of the people, free to all, open to all to express their views.... For a democracy open discussion is essential. To provide a place for such discussion is the work of the Forum. The discussion in the Forum has become an important factor in the life of the city and a good influence upon public affairs.[3]

If Irvine had done nothing else during his stay in Calgary, his initiation, support and participation in the People's Forum would have been a notable achievement and a justification of the terms under which he entered upon his Unitarian ministry.

Some nine months after establishing the People's Forum, Irvine embarked upon a journalistic venture that was to continue for the next four years. Within a few days of coming to Calgary he had roundly criticized the newspapers, and although he had established friendly relations with the *Morning Albertan* through its editor and had begun writing the occasional column, he felt the need to seek a wider audience and a better medium for educating the people. In collaboration with J.H. Ford he set up a paper to be published twice monthly, called the *Nutcracker*. After nearly a year it became the *Alberta Non-Partisan* and later still the *Western Independent*, but throughout these changes it remained essentially the same paper with the same format, featuring cartoons, political comment, correspondence, articles and book reviews.

Its editor and principal contributor was Irvine, while Ford was the business manager. Other people were at various times associated with the venture, including R.J. Deachman and Alex Ross.

It is not clear what role they played, although at one stage Ross was one of the three proprietors, and perhaps Deachman also supplied some capital. It is certain, however, that the paper was largely the product of Irvine's writing and editorial abilities and Ford's business acumen. It was not intended to be a moneymaker, but it soon paid its expenses and provided a bank balance of several hundred dollars.

The first issue was dated 17 November 1916,[4] and the following day it received a generous welcome from the *Morning Albertan*:

> The Nutcracker: have you seen the new Calgary paper?...The latest addition to the Calgary newspaper family arrived on the scene yesterday afternoon in the form of a very bright, merry, happy, progressive little paper...It declares that "We are friends of everybody, the enemy of nobody, the hope of Calgary and the Saviour of the Empire. Modesty forbids our saying more about ourselves. A lady voter who saw our advance pages said 'It's perfectly lovely.' We were humiliated. We took the same female voter to the circus the last time it was in Calgary and she made the same remark about the hippopotamus."

The new paper prospered. At the end of the first year, the circulation, which was not restricted to Calgary but spread throughout the province, was 8,000 and it exceeded 10,000 before its ultimate demise in 1920.

Irvine's contributions to every issue were considerable, some of them acknowledged as coming from the editor and others written under various pseudonymns, so that it is a major piece of detective work to discover what Irvine did or did not write, and the mystery is not always solvable. There were many other regular contributors and a lively correspondence column. Now and again there were contributions in light verse, one obviously from Irvine himself giving the lie to his earlier contention that he had solved his financial problems by marriage:

> When in school I learned addition
> And I learned subtraction too;

And I learned a lot of other stuff
That's helped me out, 'tis true.
But experience and learning
Fail to mitigate the pain
Of that phone call from the banker:
"Bill, you're overdrawn again."[5]

A number of the regular contributors to the *Nutcracker* were women. Mrs. Louise McKinney, MLA, wrote regular reports of the proceedings in the provincial legislature and her speeches at public meetings were often reproduced. And then there was "Contrary Mary," who often wrote under the headline "Letters of an Unfashionable Woman." She was a rural school teacher, and one of her contributions takes a satirical poke at a pamphlet published by Irvine:[6]

Civics in a Rural School

Mr. Irvine, in his pamphlet *Public Ownership of the Government* regrets the lack of education in citizenship in our public schools. By a coincidence I had happened to give a lesson on government in the rural school which owns me on the very day on which I read the pamphlet; and it would surprise Mr. Irvine to know the shoals which a well-meaning teacher may land herself into when she attacks this subject.

In the intervals between telling the five-year-olds not to thump so loudly on their plasticene, and waiting for the school door to be opened with an axe whenever anyone wanted to go out, and telling the children in the back seats to stop eating snow (we only have a water supply at our school when it rains), I was endeavouring to explain the Government of Canada.

In rural log schools where the door has to be opened with an axe and so on, we don't have these lovely model lessons where the children sit as though they were in church and the teacher delivers an address. There are frequent interruptions and detours and even contradiction from the audience. The first detour was with reference to our noble King, whose portrait surrounded by all the little kinglets and queenlets, adorns our walls (by order).

"Didn't he make the laws?" "Why didn't he?" "What was he for?" "What would happen if he objected to a law and said it wasn't to be?"

"Well," I explained, "our King was just for show, to take part in processions where he looked quite grand in that crown."

"Gold?"

"Yes, all gold with diamonds in it, and a cloak lined with ermine."

"What's that?"

"Same as the weasels you get here when they turn white."

(Here a closure had to be put on an animated discussion in the back desk on trapping weasels.) I couldn't think of anything else the King was used for at the moment and I wasn't quite sure what "wages" the country gave him beyond a vague "millions."

Ambling along we came to provincial government and I explained that the provincial parliament was where laws were made about such things as roads (a burning topic in a new district), schools, homesteads, and so on. We got into difficulties when we reached the subject of our Member. Who was our Member?

"Mr. Price," said one boy.

"Aw, you're nuts," said his neighbour. "It ain't — it's Mr. Matheson."

"'Tis so Mr. Price. He gave dad $5 to vote."

"Listen," I said, "Mr. Price isn't the Member. He was paid to get people to vote for the member — Mr. Matheson."

"Matheson ain't no good, father says so. He's a Conservative and they're no good," hissed a girl across the aisle.

"Liberals ain't no good. . . ."

Closure again.

"Teacher, what's the difference between Liberals and Conservatives?" inquired one of the older girls.

"There isn't much difference. Once upon a time the Liberals were more go-ahead than the Conservatives, but now they're much the same. It is like baseball at our church here; there have to be two sides — one in and one out — or there wouldn't be any fun. When one side has been in so long that they get quite bold about stealing the country's money, the people put them out and let the other side in."

Here, before I could explain (in simple language) that we should vote for measures not party, there was another detour while a girl propounded the knotty question: "Why does the Government have to borrow money for the war when they could print as many dollar bills as they like, and it wouldn't cost them anything but the paper and printing?"

Irvine was an excellent editor, for in addition to his own steady stream of contributions, he drew upon the talents of a wide circle of independently minded men and women who were not afraid to challenge orthodox opinion. The *Nutcracker* had very definite editorial policies on the issues of the day. When it first appeared late in 1916, Sir Robert Borden was Prime Minister, leading a Conservative government which, under pressure of wartime conditions, was moving towards the imposition of compulsory allocation of labour and compulsory military service for men between the ages of twenty and forty-five. There was considerable opposition in Quebec to military service and recruiting was proceeding slowly in other parts of the country. For example, in Calgary in 1916, it was estimated that there were 10,000 able-bodied men between the ages of eighteen and forty-five, only half of whom had enlisted, despite a barrage of propaganda in the press and elsewhere.

Although Irvine regarded war as a great evil, and although he abhorred violence, he was not a pacifist. Indeed, when in October 1916, the Premier of Austria, Count Karl Stürgkh was assassinated, Irvine wrote a column in the *Morning Albertan* virtually approving the action of the assassin:

> Fredrick Adler was a clever thinker and writer devoted to the cause of the people and out of his love for his country he killed one of its chief oppressors.... It was the deliberate act of one who had tried every other conceivable method to stem oppression and who took his own life in his hand and committed a murder on a murderer for the sake of his suffering people.[8]

Thus Irvine's opposition to the conscription of men for military service and of labour for national service rested upon his conviction that these measures could only be justified if all classes in society bore their fair share of the sacrifice. He demanded that there should also be conscription of wealth and an end to war-profiteering. Concerning conscription he wrote in the *Nutcracker*:

> The reinforcement of Canada's forces at the front is one of the vital problems of today. Recruiting has almost ceased, enlistments are gradually decreasing, in spite of the fact that we have high-salaried recruiting agents parading the country trying to persuade people to enlist, while they themselves are holding down a sinecure. The cry for conscription is again heard throughout the Dominion, mostly from military officials and those people who cannot be conscripted; while the eligibles for conscription are awaiting their fate, some glad, some apathetic, others rebellious.
>
> Both political parties agree that Canada ought to have conscription, but both are afraid of the consequences. They may well be, if they attempt to force unconditional compulsory military service in this country. This is not the first demand for compulsion of some sort since the bogus National Service scheme was launched. The Canadian National Service scheme is now admitted by all to be an absolute failure....
>
> Let us look at some of the reasons why recruiting has fallen off.... We all know that Canadian officers have been selected because of political influence rather than by merit. Thousands of competent officers are in civilian clothes. These are men who have qualified but who have not the necessary pull to get commissions.
>
> Next comes the most important of all — profiteering in army supplies. No other country in the world has permitted capitalists to pile up fortunes at the expense of the soldiers in the trenches — 200 million dollars is the profit extracted by our army contractors since the war began. The man in the street believes that army officials and politicians have continued to exploit and bleed the masses. This belief is strengthened by the fact that eastern capitalists are living in the lap of luxury, and flaunting their ill-gotten gains in the face of that

class which must inevitably pay for it at the conclusion of
the war.

Another trouble lies in the fact that the authorities have
made no effort to control the price of foodstuffs in the country. The price of flour in western Canada is a striking example of the manipulation of food prices, and so far not a
single protest has emanated from Ottawa.

Inadequate pensions for soldiers and their dependents and
negligence in regard to the needs of returned soldiers add to
the annoyance of the people.[9]

In a later issue Irvine again argued:

Conscription must not be limited to men. ... Wealth is just as
necessary as men in this fight. Munitions, transportation and
food are absolutely essential, and if either fails, defeat is certain, no matter if we had a hundred million troops. If the
government be sincere in its expressed desire to win the
war, then all the resources of the Dominion must be utilized
to this end.

Had wealth been conscripted at the beginning of the war,
or should it be taken over at this late hour, we believe that
our army could be speedily raised without conscripting a
man.[10]

Borden's government moved steadily on towards conscription.
In September 1917, it passed a Wartime Election Act. This gave,
for the first time, the franchise to women in a federal election. (In
1916, Alberta women had already received the provincial franchise, but only those who had husbands or brothers in the armed
forces.) R.J. Deachman tersely remarked that many young Canadian women were being disenfranchised because their brothers
had flat feet. The Act also disenfranchised for the duration of the
war not only conscientious objectors, but all German- and Aus-
trian-born Canadians, even those who were naturalized. This Act
was opposed by Irvine in the *Nutcracker* and elsewhere.

If there is going to be any disenfranchisement we would
recommend ... to begin with the individuals who have exploited the patriotism and the resources of our country in its

time of grave danger, and to allow every alien, so-called, who holds the right of citizenship in Canada to retain it until it can be proved that this sacred trust has been violated.[11]

Parliament proceeded late in September 1917 to pass the Compulsory Military Service Act, conscripting men between the ages of twenty and forty-five. Early in October, Parliament dissolved and a coalition was formed of Conservatives and Liberals. The Liberal party was split, with Sir Wilfrid Laurier and his supporters opposing conscription, because of widespread opposition to it among French Canadians. The election that followed in December (anticipated by the War Elections Act) resulted in a sweeping victory for the Union Government, which remained in power until 1920, and steadfastly refused to conscript wealth or to restrict or tax wartime profits.

The *Nutcracker's* heretical opposition to the wartime government frequently led it into conflict with other journals in Calgary. Even the *Morning Albertan*, with its generally sympathetic attitude to Irvine's activities, sometimes found the *Nutcracker* too unorthodox. The *Calgary Herald* regarded Irvine as a dangerous radical. The most interesting journalistic conflict, however, was with a paper more in its own class and size. This was the *Calgary Eye Opener*, a weekly, published single-handedly by its editor, Bob Edwards. It appeared intermittently over a period of twenty years, from 1902 to 1922. Partly due to its longevity and partly to the flamboyant and eccentric personality of Edwards, it acquired a fame which has survived to the present.

Unlike the *Nutcracker*, the *Eye Opener* did not draw upon a circle of talented contributors, but was entirely written by its editor. It consisted of three- or four-line paragraphs separated by asterisks, a format not conducive to sustained, logical argument. There were cartoons and, as in the *Nutcracker*, considerable advertising. Edwards' role in Calgary became that of the licensed jester who occasionally delivers a few home truths. He showed the rough, coarse, hard-living side of western Canadian society, which was masked behind a puritanical facade.

A matter upon which the *Nutcracker* had strong views was the practice of patronage by both the Liberals and the Conservatives. Both parties, on achieving power, appointed their faithful supporters to lucrative public positions. On this issue the *Nutcracker* crossed swords with the *Eye Opener*:

> That worthy publication [*Eye Opener*] has been on every side of every question since the days of Vol.1. No.1. . . . It also has the distinction of being the only paper published in the Anglo-Saxon world which advocates the patronage system as we have it today. Other publications may tolerate. Some may defend it by the rather vacuous assertion that "one party must have it as long as the other one does." But Robert Edwards confesses to an open admiration for the Beast in the following paragraph: "Since the great Conservative victory of 1911, at least two-thirds of the choicest appointments have been bestowed on Grits. R.B. [Bennett] exultantly cried aloud at the rink on election night 'To the victors belong the spoils!' But we have not noticed the victors being overloaded with spoils. Not to any alarming extent. Have you?"
>
> He then proceeds to find fault with the Tories for not applying the Bennettian doctrine with all its full force. Even Bennett could scarcely follow that, but Mr. Edwards glories in the most vicious of political doctrines "to the victors belong the spoils." . . . It is regrettable that a man of so many excellent virtues and tastes as Mr. Edwards should be on the wrong side of every question. . . .[12]

Some six months later, the *Eye Opener* was attacking Sir Wilfrid Laurier, the Liberal leader, for his opposition to the imposition of conscription. In reply, the *Nutcracker* produced a fictitious letter from Laurier to Edwards in which the former defends and justifies his stand on conscription. In the course of the letter, Laurier (standing in for Irvine) addresses Edwards as follows:

> I love you, Robert, for your erratic ways and your unique powers of expression, but frankly you are the most reactionary political writer in Canada. I can recall no single occasion in which you have stood up for principle or advocated advanced legislation, and when a man at your age has held that course so long, the future is little likely to witness a change.[13]

When Sir Robert Borden, after imposing conscription and forming a Union Government with a portion of the Liberal party, dissolved Parliament and called an election for December 1917, Edwards renewed his attack on Laurier and others who opposed the Union government. Irvine himself ran in this election as a Labour candidate for East Calgary in opposition to the Union candidate and thus became a prime target for abuse in the *Eye Opener*. However, after the war, some four years later, when Irvine was again a Labour candidate for East Calgary, the *Eye Opener* published a photograph of Irvine with an announcement of his nomination as a Labour candidate. Edwards commented:

> William Irvine has been nominated to contest one of the Calgary ridings, probably East Calgary. He will make a strong candidate, though too far advanced in his views to suit most people. Bill is a capable upright man who enjoys the respect of all who know him. Also a fearfully eloquent chap. The man opposed to him will know he has been to the races.[14]

A few weeks later Irvine, addressing a large and enthusiastic campaign meeting, expressed appreciation of the support he was getting from the *Eye Opener* and *Morning Albertan*, thus bringing to an end a five-year verbal feud.

What might be called the progressive movement in Alberta, including the farmers' movement, much of the organized labour movement, the women's rights movements and the churches (whether progressive or not), were in favour of the prohibition of alcoholic beverages. Prohibition became law in Alberta in 1916 and nationally on 1 April 1918. Like most people, Irvine was a "social" drinker, and his feelings about prohibition seem ambivalent. The *Nutcracker*, unlike the *Eye Opener*, never advertised alcoholic beverages and sometimes expressed itself in favour of prohibition; certainly it was never against it. The following unsigned analysis of the issue may or may not have been written by Irvine:

> Through the deficiencies of the Alberta Liquor Act of 1916, the question of prohibition has again begun to prick the conscience of the moral reformer who endeavours to assume the responsibility for the well-being of the community. The issue is not one of economics or expediency, but one of moral and ethical responsibility. The "personal liberty" cry is bound to fail ... for despite hindrances human society is rap-

idly becoming socialistic, however reluctant it is to accept the pet program of socialists. Society does not hesitate to make its own collective welfare paramount to the individual right when convinced that social welfare demands this or that curtailment of the individual's right "to live his own life in his own way."

The evil of intemperance is beyond all question.... It is involved in all issues of poverty, social disease, crime and vice, of defrauded childhood, of corrupted politics. Beyond the personal right of the free man "to decide for himself what he shall eat and drink" stands the collective right and responsibility of decent men and women to live in a community unsmirched by the flagrant defilements of a corrupting evil.

The problem is in the end essentially altruistic and religious. For thousands of intelligent people the use of intoxicating liquors is innocent and harmless, and in an ideal society the law of personal restraint and self-control is more worthy than the method of enforced prohibition.

The temperance issue can be worked out in the truly temperance way — which is not prohibition. But experience makes plain the futility of waiting for this method. All Canada can rid itself of a costly evil when once it finds courage to take resolute methods instead of playing and bickering with the question. Its courage is growing. Will the man of progress or timid conservatism, the man of genuine goodwill or the man of dominant selfishness, hunt for arguments to stay the decisive step?[15]

Subsequently in 1921, when Irvine was running as a Labour candidate in Calgary East, and his friend and running mate, Joseph Shaw, was candidate for West Calgary, they were both asked their views on prohibition. Shaw waxed eloquent on the evils of drink, and Irvine contented himself with the laconic reply that he was "against the liquor interests."

A surprising feature of the progressive and radical movements of the period is the almost complete lack of concern for Canada's native population, whose plight was rarely mentioned. For the most part the *Nutcracker* reflects this apparent lack of concern, but in the *Western Independent* in 1920, Irvine raised the matter with some force. He wrote about the proposed celebration in Calgary of the 250th Anniversary of the Hudson's Bay Company:

> The Company was endowed with an exclusive and perpetual monopoly of trade and commerce of all the seas, straits, bays, rivers, lakes, creeks, and sounds, in whatever latitude they shall be that lay within the entrance of Hudson's Straits, together with all the land, countries and territories adjacent to those waters. . . .

> In return for all this, the Company was asked to pay two elks and two black beavers whenever His Majesty or his successors should enter the Company's territory. Here we have the most stupendous bargain in history. How could that Company help becoming wealthy? It had but to gather the riches from the forests, the fisheries, and the plains. It is no wonder that the Company still feels like celebrating the anniversary of that "bargain."

> What the Company gained in this "bargain" the people lost. The Native Indians were the first to suffer, the immigrant population has suffered from that bargain ever since, and are still paying part of the price. The fur trade was the most lucrative field for the Company at the beginning. It yielded large profits, and was comparatively easy in operation. The Indians in a sense became the subjects of the Company, and were plundered, exploited and debauched for the sake of profits.

> I understand that there are to be Indians in the procession on the anniversary day. These Indians will not know the price their forefathers paid to enrich the Company which they blindly honour. If they did they would not likely grace the procession. . . . There are thousands of Indian braves who would, if they could, lift up their voices in protest from the silent dust. . . .

> How can we celebrate by gorgeous pageant that Company which debauched and made slaves of the poor aborigines, that made a desert of the country and by its wealth and power brought the people of Canada into a long regime of exploitation? A day of mourning would be more fitting.[16]

FOUR

The Non-Partisan Movement

Although it did not make its owners rich, the *Nutcracker* (and its successors) was, by any other standard, an outstanding success. It succeeded in entertaining, educating and raising the political consciousness of thousands of people, but its chief task was the role it played in developing a farmer-labour political movement in Alberta. When Irvine first arrived in Calgary in 1916, the Alberta farmers were already a numerically strong and well-organized group. Seven years before, the United Farmers of Alberta had been formed by the amalgamation of two earlier farmers' organizations, the Society of Equity and the Alberta Farmers Association. The membership, beginning at approximately 6,000, had now surpassed 11,000. Farmers in Alberta and elsewhere in Canada and the U.S. were organizing to confront their problems. They were not getting their fair share of the national income, despite rising wheat prices, for these were offset by the increasing cost of production. Land, machinery, and marketing were all costing more. The farmers rightly blamed the rising cost of land upon the existence of land monopolies and speculators. In western Canada the chief culprits were the Hudson's Bay Company and the CPR, who along with foreign land speculators held vast acreages.

The railroads charged exorbitant rates for transporting farm produce and often failed to provide sufficient railroad cars for efficient delivery to markets. The cost of farm implements in the Prairie provinces was raised by discriminatory freight rates and by the existence of tariffs on imported and manufactured goods, which benefited eastern manufacturers. There was much criticism of the privately owned grain elevators, which were often inadequate in size, inefficient in management, and prone to dishonest practices. The Winnipeg Grain Exchange was dominated by five grain companies who through speculation manipulated the wheat prices to the disadvantage of both farmer and consumer. And last, but not least, was the farmers' dissatisfaction with the banking system. Farmers needed credit in order to buy machinery, land, livestock, and for other capital needs. Many farmers were unable to get sufficient credit and many were heavily in debt to the banks because of high interest charges.

All these grievances led the farmers of Alberta (and elsewhere) to organize in order to set up their own co-operatives for buying, marketing and storing grain and other farm products. The power of their collective opinion was used in lobbying provincial and federal governments. However, it was south of the border, in North Dakota, where farmers set an example of political action. In 1915, under the leadership of A.C. Townley, a Socialist party organizer, they set up the Non-Partisan League. As its name suggests, it was directed against the political domination of the two traditional parties, the Republicans and the Democrats. It held that both stood for the maintenance of privilege and exploitation and that neither represented the interests of the producers; i.e., the farmers and the industrial workers. They suspected that the political system, although it presented a democratic facade, really excluded farmers and workers, and that the apparent struggle for political power between these two parties, composed largely of lawyers, bankers, big businessmen and the members of highly paid professions, masked the real interests they both served.

The Non-Partisan League led a head-on attack on this system and aimed at getting farmers and workers elected to legislatures and to public office. Although primarily a farmers' movement, it sought and gained allies in the labour movement and was in effect a farmer-labour party. In 1916, the Non-Partisan League was successful in electing a majority of the state legislature of North Dakota, and at the same time they elected Lynn J. Frazier to the governorship by an overwhelming majority of 64,000 votes. After about two years spent in reforming the constitution, they proceeded to establish the state-owned North Dakota Mill and Elevator and the Bank of North Dakota. They also introduced state housing plans, farm loan organizations and state meat-packing plants. Non-Partisan influence began to spread to neighbouring states.

Upon U.S. entry into the war in April 1917, the Non-Partisan League opposed conscription of men without conscription of wealth and resources. The rising tide of jingoism and war hysteria was used to bring about the destruction of the Non-Partisan government and the movement. In 1918, Frazier's majority was reduced to 17,784, in 1920 it dwindled to 4,630, and by October 1921, the governor and the Non-Partisan administration in North Dakota had lost office.

Previously, the president of the Non-Partisan League, A.C. Townley, had been arrested while on a speaking tour in Minnesota, and charged with sedition. His crime was reported to be that he demanded that wealth as well as men should be conscripted, and denounced "the hypocrisy of those so-called patriots who wrapped the American flag about them the better to conceal the fact that they had their hands in the pockets of the American people." His remarks were interpreted as "tending to hamper enlistment during the war." At Jackson County Court in Minnesota, he was found guilty and sentenced to ninety days in prison.

In addition to its other troubles, the postwar economic depression drained away a good deal of Non-Partisan financial support so that the Non-Partisan League went out of existence in 1924. Much of its work and program was taken over by the Farmer-Labour Party, which sprang up in Minnesota and continued for another twenty years. In 1916, however, the Non-Partisan League in North Dakota was a growing movement spreading into the neighbouring states, and to Canada.

Mr. S.E. Haight, who farmed near Swift Current, Saskatchewan, visited North Dakota, where he worked with the Non-Partisan League. On his return in July 1916, he organized a Non-Partisan League in Saskatchewan, which grew to 1,200 members within two months and to 5,000 a year later. Harry Johnson, an Alberta farmer on a business trip to Regina in the same year, met some of the Saskatchewan Non-Partisans and enthusiastically brought the idea back to Alberta where, at Calgary on 16 December 1916, he met with four other people including Irvine. They agreed to form a provisional committee and Irvine became secretary of the group and agreed to lecture for the League wherever meetings could be held. Irvine became an able and enthusiastic proponent of the Non-Partisan League, and together with Johnson bore the lion's share in establishing the movement and setting its course of action. From the first, the organization was entirely distinct and separate from the Non-Partisan Leagues of either Saskatchewan or North Dakota, although it shared the same objectives and adopted similar methods for organizing support. Harry Johnson as head organizer set up a team of organizers to travel through Alberta, getting farmers to join the League for the then rather substantial fee of $15. A year after its inception, the League had a budget of more than $50,000 with a credit balance of over $12,000 and a membership exceeding 3,000.

The *Nutcracker* became the mouthpiece of the Alberta Non-Partisan League. The day before its foundation meeting, the non-partisan movement was first mentioned in the newspaper:

> From the Non-Partisan League of Canada, organized in Saskatchewan, we hear the first echoes of the fray. They have copied the whirlwind methods by which the farmers of North Dakota captured their state at the last election. The chief object of this movement is to destroy partyism, to obtain a government more representative of an agricultural country, and to secure for the farmer a fairer share of what he produces. Every farmer that joins the Non-Partisan League puts off his Grit and Tory garb and stands out as a man, capable of thinking for himself, of governing himself, and doing his own business. . . .
>
> The Non-Partisan League will not necessarily conflict with the farmers' organizations already in existence. The Grain Growers of Saskatchewan and the United Farmers of Alberta alike refuse to take political actions, believing that indirect influence is of greater value than direct action. The Non-Partisan League believes that nothing permanent in the way of reform can be secured without political action. . . .[1]

Irvine also discussed the relationship between Non-Partisan politics and socialism. After defining socialism as "the collective ownership and control of the means of production, distribution and exchange," he goes on to say that:

> The Non-Partisan movement is the first logical step for the socialist, but it is only the first step. We are not a socialistic organization, because we are an organization of the people and the people have not given us any mandate to adopt pure unadulterated socialism. We are just as socialistic as our members make us.... We are however a working-class movement. Not one capitalist so far as we know has espoused our cause.... We can take as big a chunk of socialism as we can digest and if we develop an appetite we can go the limit.[2]

The Alberta Non-Partisan League finally incorporated the following points into its program:

1. To overcome partisanship by the election of a truly people's government and the establishment of a business administration instead of a party administration;
(a) By educating our people to a higher sense of citizenship.
(b) By organizing them to co-operate in political action.
(c) By leaving the program of legislation to be enacted, and financing of all elections in the hands of the constituents.

2. The securing of government ownership and control of all natural resources and fundamental industries feasible to government control.
(a) Transportation and communication;
(b) Banks;
(c) Flour mills, Packing Houses and Farm Machinery Manufacturing and Insurance;
(d) Retaining of all lands now held by the Crown, and securing by the most equitable means those already alienated.[3]

The first set of objectives was directed against the domination of the party system and aimed at a government more democratic and more participatory. The second set clearly aimed at transferring the means of production, distribution and exchange from private to public ownership with special regard to those that affected the lives of farmers. Together they amounted to a fairly radical program of democratic socialism.

The Alberta Non-Partisan League, early in its history, was confronted with the criticism that it was a class organization. The *Morning Albertan* commented in an editorial: "The *Albertan* has no faith in this Non-Partisan League because it is a class organization with membership limited to certain of our people engaged in certain occupations. It stands to make dangerous class divisions."[4] In the same issue, however, there is a report of a meeting of the People's Forum at which Irvine spoke on the aims and purposes of the Non-Partisan League. In response to the question whether its membership was confined to any one class, he is reported as replying, "No, the only requirement is that a member earn at least 65 percent of his living by the sweat of his brow." One might naturally take this to be not a statement of the formal requirements for membership but rather an assertion that the League existed to forward the interests of the working people of Alberta, whether farmers or urban workers. As the farmers' movement developed, the class bias charge was often repeated, and on many occasions Irvine in effect replied that government in Canada already was class government, and that the traditional parties, Liberals and Conservatives, both represented big business, while the interests of the majority class of working people went unrepresented.

There was no doubt that the NPL's main thrust was towards organizing farmers for political action and as a consequence the question of eligibility for membership arose. Irvine's own position as a leading member of the NPL was anomalous. He was not a farmer, nor did he, being a full-time Unitarian minister, earn his living by the sweat of his brow. But this may not have struck him or his associates in the light of the fact that he had often worked as a carpenter and that during much of the nine years before coming to Calgary, he had lived in lumber camps and rural communities, where he sometimes worked for farmers. After coming to Alberta Irvine had made contact with farmers all over the province, so that it is not surprising that many of them thought of him as an integral part of the farmers' movement.

Although the Alberta NPL soon opened its membership to all who subscribed to its principles, regardless of occupation, the membership continued to be drawn largely from the farming community. Since Irvine was equally interested in getting urban workers into political action, a few months after the founding of the Non-Partisan League, he and friends in the trade unions set about the formation of a Labour Representation League.

The Labour Representation League was initiated at a meeting of the Calgary Trades and Labour Council on 19 March 1917. The president, Elmer Roper, announced his resignation owing to his forthcoming move from Calgary to Edmonton, and Alex Ross, a bricklayer and mason, was unanimously elected president for Roper's unexpired term. The Council went on record in favour of forming a permanent Labour Representation League that would deal exclusively with politics. The LRL formally came into existence at a meeting in the Calgary Labour Temple on 9 April 1917. Alex Ross was in the chair and William Irvine was there representing the Non-Partisan League.

At a later meeting of the LRL, a comprehensive election program was formulated as follows:

Platform of Principles

Franchise extension and election reforms:
1. The extension of the federal franchise to every British subject of twenty-one years of age and over.
2. Satisfactory arrangements to be made whereby a citizen may exercise the right of the franchise, whether such person or persons be at the point of registration on the election day or not.
3. The abolition of property qualification for civic offices to all British subjects.
4. The abolition of all deposits for candidates seeking public office.
5. All election days to be fixed in legislative assembly and recognized as public half-holidays.
6. Proportional representation.
7. Direct legislation, including initiative, referendum and recall.
8. Civil service reform, all appointments to be made on merit.

9. Abolition of the Senate.

Public ownership and control of all the means of wealth, production and distribution:
1. Natural resources.
2. The means of transportation and communication, etc.

Proper regulation of workers' time and pay:
1. Abolition of child labour for children under sixteen.
2. Equal pay for equal work for both sexes.
3. Universal maximum eight-hour day.
4. Semi-monthly pay for all workers now on a monthly basis.

Taxation for revenue:
1. By a direct tax on unimproved land values including all natural resources.
2. By a sharply graduated income tax upon all incomes over $2,000 per year.
3. By a graduated inheritance tax.
4. By a graduated income tax on the profits of corporations.

Although the political platform of the LRL was more detailed and had specific reference to matters of concern to labour, nevertheless there was considerable overlap with the program of the Non-Partisan League. Both regarded the established party system and its operations in Parliament and legislative assemblies as fundamentally undemocratic, and both aimed not only at getting more farmers and workers into the legislatures, but also at bringing political decision-making closer to the people. Both proposed the initiation of legislative programs at the constituency level, the more frequent use of the referendum to settle important issues and procedures by which constituents could at any time recall their elected representative if they were dissatisfied with his performance. Finally, both organizations proposed substantial and far-reaching measures of public ownership.

The LRL selected two candidates to run for seats in the Alberta Legislative Assembly in the election of 7 June 1917. Alex Ross was chosen as candidate for Calgary Centre. Ross was a thirty-six-year-old bachelor who came to Canada from Scotland in 1906; he had topped the poll for the Calgary school board elections in December 1916. Irvine was selected for South Calgary.

Meanwhile, the Non-Partisan League was also preparing for the provincial election. The NPL was handicapped by the fact that Irvine's candidacy in South Calgary riding for the LRL fully occupied his time and rendered him unable to give assistance in the Non-Partisan campaign except in so far as the LRL might be regarded as part of the same movement. The NPL ran four candidates in rural ridings: Mrs. Louise McKinney for Claresholm, James Weir for Nanton, J.E. Hillier for Pincher Creek and John W. Leedy for Gleichen.

Alberta had been a province with its own legislative assembly since 1905. The new province was set up under the federal Liberal government of Sir Wilfrid Laurier and was dominated by Liberals from its inception. At the first election in 1905, the Liberals won twenty-three out of twenty-five seats and in 1909 they gained thirty-seven out of forty-one seats. One of the three Conservatives elected then was R.B. Bennett, who launched an attack on the Liberal government, alleging graft on the part of Premier A.C. Rutherford and some of his Cabinet ministers, in connection with the financing and construction of railways. Rutherford resigned and A.L. Sifton took over as premier. Under Sifton's leadership the Liberals weathered the storm and were again returned to office in 1913. The Liberals easily survived the fourth provincial election in 1917. However, thanks to Irvine and his friends in the NPL and the LRL, they were confronted with a more varied opposition.

Louise McKinney won her seat in the legislature and thus became the first woman in Canada, or indeed in the British Commonwealth, to do so. James Weir, who besides being a leading Non-Partisan was also second vice-president of the United Farmers of Alberta, won his seat. Alex Ross also won his seat for the LRL.* Irvine was not so fortunate and went down to defeat in a three-way fight. Dr. Blow, a Conservative MLA and a member of the local recruiting board, retained the seat, partly because of the unpopularity of Irvine's anti-conscription stand (compulsory

---

* He was subsequently re-elected in 1921 and became Minister of Public Works in the UFA Government.

military service was introduced three months later) and partly because of the intervention of another independent, John McNeil, a Calgary alderman.

W.M. Davidson, publisher of the *Morning Albertan*, was elected and seems to have been counted as one of the "progressives." An enthusiastic crowd gathered outside the *Morning Albertan* and a victory procession of progressives proceeded to the Labour Temple. The leading vehicle, drawn by ropes, contained Ross, Davidson and Irvine. The latter, as a defeated candidate, felt out of place in the victory parade, but his friends and supporters insisted that he be part of the celebration. On arriving at the Labour Temple, the three men were carried in, the successful ones sitting upright on the shoulders of their supporters and Irvine, who was the "corpse" in a reclining position. Irvine, called upon to speak, said that he was defeated but not beaten. The election of the other progressive candidates was a great victory for democracy and was due to the character and ability of the candidates and the issues at stake. As to his own defeat, he was satisfied about two things. First, the money of the Labour people that had been put up as a deposit had been saved, and secondly, that Alderman McNeil had lost his. A voice from the crowd interrupted: "He never lost it because he never paid it. Dr. Blow paid it!"[5]

In a subsequent statement, the Labour Representative League reported that the total cost of running their two candidates was less than $200.[6] The election budget of the Non-Partisan League for four rural ridings was almost equally frugal, amounting to only $1,109.[7]

Encouraged by the election of two of its candidates and the good showing made by Irvine in South Calgary, the Non-Partisan League reorganized itself for a new membership drive in the rural areas. The *Nutcracker*, a few issues before the completion of its first year of publication, with its circulation standing at 7,500, changed its name to the *Alberta Non-Partisan*, thus making itself the official organ of the League. The journal remained essentially unaltered; perhaps there was an increased reporting of Non-Partisan meetings and conventions, and of course the two new MLA's frequently reported their activities in the legislature in the pages of the newly named journal.

One report of a U.S. Non-Partisan convention at St. Paul, Minnesota, is of particular interest, since it emphasized the concerns of Irvine and the Alberta group. The *Alberta Non-Partisan* commented:

> This is the first attempt on a national scale to bring together the agrarian and industrial workers for mutual protection and the advancement of democratic principles. The tremendous significance of such a step is fully recognized both by those whose private interests would be jeopardized by the alliance and also by workers of both classes.
>
> These two groups of producers comprising as they do the great majority of any nation, coming together with the common aim of doing away with private profit, and seeking the democratization of government and industry, constitute the greatest force ever organized against the entrenched individualistic system. The farmer and the industrial worker meet on the common ground of producers, and with the common desire to secure a more equitable distribution of what is produced among those who toil to produce it.... A national program was endorsed by this great convention.... Resolutions demanding conscription of wealth, government ownership of basic industries, and for organization for increased production and equitable distribution, were passed.
>
> The Non-Partisans demanded that the government take over at once and operate flour mills, terminal elevators, iron, coal and copper mills, oil fields, packing houses, railroads, all means of communication, clothing factories, steel mills, armour plate mills, and shipyards, etc. Perhaps the most significant resolution passed by the Non-Partisan Convention was its endorsation of trade unionism. The resolution recognizes the true position of labour, sees the necessity for organization under the profit system, and heartily endorses the movement. If this results in the affiliation of these two great classes — which go to make up the real working class — things will move quickly in the United States.
>
> The Non-Partisan movement is the greatest of the hour. It is that organization which will bridge the intervening space

between what is and the true commonwealth of socialistic economists, hence it is both necessary and timely.[8]

Meanwhile, the ruling federal Conservative government of Sir Robert Borden had formed a coalition cabinet drawn from both traditional parties with the alleged purpose of more efficiently prosecuting the war. The Liberal party was split, with its leader, Sir Wilfrid Laurier, supporting those who opposed conscription. Québecois were dissatisfied with the Compulsory Military Service Act passed on 26 September 1917, and many resisted conscription.

The new Union Government called an election for 17 December 1917. The Non-Partisan League immediately plunged back into electoral activity, nominating three candidates for rural ridings and joining with the Labour Representation League in putting forward Irvine as their joint candidate in East Calgary. The joint program of the two groups is expressed in an editorial, almost certainly written by Irvine, in the *Alberta Non-Partisan*:

> There is no better test of the honesty of the Union government movement than will be furnished by the Non-Partisan and Labour Leagues of Alberta. These institutions have been actively engaged in fighting the two old parties, and were organized with a view to obtaining representation for the workers in the House of Commons as well as to overthrowing the old party system....
>
> What will be the attitude of the Union government towards those Non-Partisan candidates who will run in Victoria, Bow River, Macleod and East Calgary? Will the Union government oppose these men? If so it will be positive proof that the Union government is not sincere in its professed desire to get rid of partyism. The Non-Partisan and Labour Leagues were advocating this essential reform long before the Ottawa aggregation ever thought of it. On what grounds then can a government professing to be non-partisan, oppose true non-partisan candidates representing the farmers and the industrial workers?
>
> The impression is general that the Union government is nothing but a name in so far as true non-partisanship is con-

cerned and that it is a fusion of the financial interests of Canada to maintain their profits in spite of the demands of war. The Non-Partisan candidates therefore throw this challenge to the directors of this Union government scheme.... If the Union government be honest it will NOT run men in these ridings where Non-Partisan candidates have been nominated; we will be convinced in our suspicions as to the character of the Union government if it does.

The Labour and Non-Partisan Leagues have taken the only possible attitude on the Military Service Act, consistent with their democratic ideals and the necessity of the hour. The press has deliberately or ignorantly misrepresented the position taken especially in the case of the Labour League.

In the program that was endorsed at the Labour Temple, this question received complete attention.... The aims for which we will prosecute the war are stated as: peace without annexation, universal disarmament, a league of nations to maintain the peace of the world, and Canadian representation on the peace conference.

The attitude of the Labour League as set forth in our program is the most thorough and the most fearless ever taken by any organization in Canada, and will be seen to meet the difficult situation adequately. The high-handed and autocratic methods of the administration which passed a law conscripting men without conscripting wealth calls for the strongest condemnation. We therefore state that we are opposed to the PRINCIPLE of conscription of men ALONE, without a referendum of the people.

This does not imply that the present Act should be repealed. We recognize that all the machinery for voluntary enlistment has already been abolished, and that the Conscription Act is being enforced....

The Labour League therefore declares itself for the most courageous and democratic and the most adequate policy ever advanced in Canada, i.e., Universal Conscription. It stands for conscription carried to the logical conclusion and not a class conscription imposed by a class government to save its wealth while it takes human life.

Our policy is therefore constructive and not retroactive.... The position of Labour on the Military Service Act is therefore clear and unmistakable — either the government must give us Universal Conscription or else we demand a referendum on the present Act. There will be no objection to the conscription of men providing that all wealth is conscripted in the manner set forth in the Labour program. If this is not done we insist on a referendum.[9]

The election was fought under very difficult conditions in the winter months of November and December. The win-the-war and conscription issue aroused passions and prejudices unfavourable to the Non-Partisan and Labour Representation Leagues. Irvine in particular was a target for chauvinism. His Union opponent was Major D.L. Redman, who had been wounded in battle in 1915 and invalided home. R.B. Bennett was one of Redman's most active supporters, and on several occasions Irvine and Bennett engaged in public debate of election issues. On one occasion, the people of Acme arranged for a debate between them. Bennett arrived first, paid the rent on the hall, and refused to allow Irvine in. Irvine knew no one in Acme, so he returned to his hotel room. Bennett proceeded to give his speech to the assembled citizens. However they had come to hear a debate and they insisted that Irvine be sent for and that the debate take place. Afterwards, Bennett went back to Calgary in the same train with Irvine and took him to dinner. An odd sort of friendship developed, each respecting the other's abilities while detesting his political opinions. It is said that Irvine got 50 percent of the votes in Acme; if so, he certainly did not do nearly as well elsewhere, for Redman had no difficulty winning the seat with more than two-thirds of the total vote.

The Non-Partisans were disappointed but not discouraged by the result. They felt that the campaign had secured for the League much needed publicity and that it had demonstrated the ability of the farmers to manage and finance their own campaigns, to put worthwhile candidates in the field and to mobilize a number of enthusiastic and willing workers. They anticipated success in the postwar period.

After the electoral activity of the latter half of 1917, Irvine continued to work for the expansion of the Non-Partisan League but otherwise he reverted to his normal busy schedule, which involved a Sunday morning and evening sermon or lecture to the Unitarian Church, and participation in the People's Forum on Sunday afternoons. On Wednesday evenings he held a sociology class, which was described by one of the participants as "an endeavour to discover the laws governing progress with the object of bringing dynamic forces under the control of human intelligence." He continued to edit the *Alberta Non-Partisan*, which steadily increased its circulation, and his support for the labour movement was unabated. For instance, he was one of two main speakers at a mass rally of retail clerks held in the Calgary Labour Temple. The clerks, mostly women and girls, were entitled by law to a minimum wage of $9 per week, but many were being paid less, and efforts to organize a clerks' union were hampered by employers. One of the largest of these — the Hudson's Bay Company store in Calgary — had dismissed the secretary-treasurer of the clerks' union. Irvine made a telling speech on organization that drew a hearty response from the audience. He said in part:

> We are on the threshold of a new age which is getting away from individualism. We are getting the idea of collective effort — an education in how to get along together ... stay by it, build up. The day is not far off when no employer will dare fire any man for trying to get his fellow men together. Remember you are taking part in the great forward movement of the great proletariat.[10]

However, he soon acquired an additional work burden. As a result of the election of 1917, much publicity had been given to his stand that there should be no conscription of men without conscription of wealth. This, as we have seen, provoked newspaper attacks and the charge, or at any rate the insinuation, that Irvine was pro-German. Some local super-patriot wrote to the Unitarian headquarters in Boston repeating these slanders. Without further inquiry, church officials stopped payment of Irvine's salary. The Unitarian church in Calgary never doubted his integrity and the members continued to attend church. There was congregational polity and Irvine could not be deprived of his pastorship unless the congregation voted to do so. This they did not do and in fact they never even suggested taking a vote on the matter. However, it was a comparatively small congregation and it could not afford to pay its pastor a salary, so Irvine took a job as a carpenter at the CPR roundhouse, and according to his account he earned more than he had from his church salary. Nevertheless, his services to his Unitarian congregation were undiminished, as were his editorial and political activities.

The year or so following the conclusion of the war was a period of social conflict and governmental repression in Canada. Men were returning from the armed forces dissatisfied with the society they found awaiting them. There was considerable unemployment, due to the ill-planned "free enterprise" transition from wartime to peacetime industry. People were inspired or disturbed by accounts of the Russian Revolution. Most reports of what was happening in the newly formed Soviet Union were distorted and inaccurate. The *Morning Albertan* wryly commented that in a period of six months it had reported the death of Lenin, by assassination or otherwise, a total of sixteen times! Small socialist and working class groups throughout Canada actively sympathized with the Bolsheviks, but a large section of the conservatively minded business community was terrified that Bolshevism might come to Canada and was eager to suppress any incipient signs of its growth.

During the war, the federal government had passed an Order-in-Council prohibiting publications deemed to be against the national interest. This legislation continued in operation after the end of the war, and one particularly flagrant example of its use or misuse occurred in January 1919, when a person in Toronto was prosecuted for possessing a book entitled *A History of Canadian Wealth*[11] by Gustavus Myers, an American journalist in the muckraking tradition. Published in 1914, before the outbreak of the war, it exposed how wealth had been acquired in Canada and how it had become concentrated in the hands of large corporations and wealthy individuals.

To the embarrassment of the government, it was discovered that the book was on the shelves of public libraries across Canada (there were two copies in the Calgary Public Library). There was widespread protest across the country, and in Calgary a large meeting sponsored by the Calgary Trades and Labour Council passed an almost unanimous resolution demanding from the Dominion government the release of all those imprisoned for exercising freedom of speech, or for possessing copies of books blacklisted by the chief censor.

Irvine, speaking at the meeting, said that he had read *A History of Canadian Wealth* after borrowing it from the Calgary Public Library. He said he could not recall any passage in the whole book that was at all seditious, but the government had taken advantage of its wartime Order-in-Council to ban literature which it thought was against the interests which it wished to protect and defend. He urged that the ban be removed.[12] Ten months later however, the Government was still at it, and the *Morning Albertan* reported that police were seizing books, including *A History of Canadian Wealth* and all the publications of Charles H. Kerr Company, Chicago, the American publisher of translations of the works of Marx and Engels and other socialist writers.

During this period of censorship and repression, the label Bolshevik was frequently used for those who offered any criticism of the established order, and Irvine was a frequent target for this kind of attack. He dealt with this humorously in a short column in the *Alberta Non-Partisan*:

The Bolsheviki Menace

There are many varied opinions as to what the "Bolsheviki" really are. In Russia, the Bolsheviki are a political organization of the workers who have seized the government and industry through revolution, and have since deprived all those who do not work of votes and property income. The revolution has been accompanied by many excesses, probably by fully as many as the French Revolution.

In Canada and the States it appears to be the style to call anyone holding opinions opposed to your own Bolsheviki. The term has been applied to leaders of various organizations, even though these same organizations do not believe in overthrowing the existing social, political and economic order by violence but by constitutional means through the ballot.

A writer in a popular magazine tells of an American captain in France who addressed his men on the Bolshevik menace saying: "These Bolsheviki are dangerous. If anyone of you sees one of them I want you to grab him and bring him to me right away." A couple of days later, one of his privates (who hailed from the lumber camps and had IWW tendencies) visited him with something tightly clutched in his hand. "I've got one of 'em, sir," he said. "One of what?" asked the captain. "One of them Bolsheviki," returned the soldier, opening his hand and showing a small red insect. "As soon as I seen it, I knew it wasn't a cootie or a bedbug, and so I brought it to you."[13]

Another radical movement with which Irvine's name was constantly but erroneously associated was that of the One Big Union. At a Western Labour Conference in Calgary in March 1919, 265 delegates representing the official trade union bodies of western Canada voted unanimously to launch a new type of industrial union to be called the One Big Union, and they embarked upon a campaign to draw away the membership of the existing trade unions, which were in part organized on a craft basis and also had close affiliation with trade unions in the United States. J.S. Woodsworth succinctly gave the rationale for this action, in terms appropriate to the largely rural community of Alberta which stressed the common objectives of farmers and urban workers:

> But what about the One Big Union? Well, before you condemn this organization you ought to think of what it really means. The United Farmers of Alberta are in reality organized into one big union, the Manufacturers' Association constitutes essentially one big union. If the industrial workers are to possess any common strength they too must be united. . . .
> Surely it would seem to be reasonable to get the farmers, irrespective of whether they raise horses or wheat or cattle, together into one organization. And that is precisely what the labour people are attempting to do and they are being opposed by the American organizations and the govern-

ment. Even responsible government officials have not hesitated to make the most serious and unfounded charges against industrial workers, who after all are merely fighting for their British rights.[14]

There was, however, another important aspect of the OBU movement that Woodsworth does not mention here, namely their rejection of political action in the sense of running candidates for office. Most delegates to the Western Labour Conference believed economic and social change could best be effected by the use of the workers' industrial power through the strike weapon. Irvine crossed swords with the OBU on the choice between industrial and political action. In an editorial he summed up the controversy as follows:

> There is much need for clearer cut expression as to the difference both in end and method between industrial and political action. We are not certain as to which will lead to the goal of emancipation and democracy. Each view has its exponents and its philosophy and it is likely that both will play a part.... We admit that there are grave doubts about the political road being the way out, just as there are doubts of the industrial movement of modern times leading to the goal of the workers.[15]

Irvine's friends in the labour movement in Calgary were divided between supporters and opponents of the OBU. R.H. Parkyn, R.J. Tallon, A.G. Broatch, Walter Smitten and Harry Pryde were all OBU supporters, while Alex Ross, Fred White and John Barnecutt were opponents. However, his OBU friends were also for the most part in favour of political action. The members of the Socialist Party of Canada, which was influential in the OBU movement, frequently made their voices heard at the People's Forum, and Irvine was often tagged by association with the OBU label, although his commitment was firmly on the side of political action.

The Western Labour Conference was shortly followed by the Winnipeg General Strike. It began on 1 May 1919, with strikes in the building and metal trades, but by 15 May it had become a sympathetic general strike of all organized labour in Winnipeg, with the support of many unorganized workers and a number of veterans' organizations. It was a well-organized and peaceful strike, without violence until the arrest and threatened deportation of ten of the strike leaders. On 21 June, a peaceful and indeed silent parade held to protest the arrests was attacked by special police and Royal North West Mounted Police armed with baseball bats and guns. One man was killed and thirty injured.

J.S. Woodsworth, who had returned from Vancouver on 8 June and addressed a meeting of 10,000 strikers called by the Reverend W. Ivens' Labour Church, later took over the editorship of the *Western Labour News* when Ivens was arrested. Ivens had made the paper the voice of the strikers. The authorities were determined to silence that voice, so they arrested Woodsworth when he became editor. The next day, 25 June, Fred J. Dixon, a Labour MLA took over the editorship and was also arrested. On 26 June, after forty-two days, the strike came to an end, broken by the arrest of its leaders on charges of seditious conspiracy and by the depletion of its funds.

Woodsworth and Dixon were charged with seditious libel and released on bail two days after the end of the strike. Many months later, Dixon came to trial, ably defended himself and was acquitted. Woodsworth was never called to trial; the case was quietly dropped. Seven others charged with seditious conspiracy were not so fortunate, receiving prison sentences ranging from six months to two years.

As the charges indicate, the government was determined to regard the strike not as the normal outcome of a prolonged and unsatisfactory labour dispute, but as an attempt to bring about the revolutionary overthrow of the government. This attempt, they imagined, was inspired by the Socialist Party of Canada and the OBU and was planned at the Western Labour Conference in Calgary. As a matter of fact, the OBU had hardly had time to organize itself before the strike broke out and the new union did not come into existence until the strike was over. R.B. Russell was the only direct connection between the Western Conference and the Strike Committee and he opposed proceeding with the strike. He was also the only member of the Socialist Party of Canada and supporter of the OBU on the interim committee of five men appointed to conduct the strike. Of the other strike leaders arrested, only Johns and Pritchard were active in the organization of the Western Labour Conference. Johns was absent from Winnipeg throughout the strike; Pritchard was there for only a few days and played no active role. Ivens, Queen, Heaps, Bray and Armstrong were not at the Conference. Of these, Armstrong was the only member of the Socialist Party of Canada.

Yet to many, the strike appeared more dramatic and significant than it in fact was. When the General Strike was only a week old, Irvine wrote:

> The great strike in Winnipeg brought on by all crafts in sympathy with the metal workers is portentous. It gives evidence of a solidarity in the labour ranks hitherto unknown, and it clearly defines the struggle of the future as between the workers as a class and organized capital.
>
> It is not only a test of solidarity, but it will be a test also of what may be expected from direct industrial action in the way of emancipating the worker. If the Winnipeg strike proves successful in accomplishing its end it will give the encouragement necessary at this time to the industrial actionists represented in the OBU, and will be the precursor of that strike which is contemplated as the means of upsetting the capitalist system.[16]

But a different view of the strike was expressed some six months later by J.S. Woodsworth in an interview with Irvine.

> Many of my friends of former days have been asking me about the Winnipeg strike, whether it was not in reality an attempt at a revolution. I want to say that I had a splendid opportunity of knowing the strike from the inside, and that there was in my judgement absolutely nothing to warrant such a charge. The workers were banded together to secure higher wages and the principle of collective bargaining — a principle that has been conceded in England for a great many years, but which has hitherto been denied by the manufacturers of the United States and Canada.[17]

Woodsworth's account of the strike is the more accurate one, but

it is understandable that a strike beginning with bread-and-butter
issues and spreading to a sympathetic general strike could at the
time be seen as the prelude to a revolutionary situation.

The government, however, was determined to vindicate its own
view that the strike was part of a vast conspiracy planned and set
in motion by a small group of revolutionary fanatics, and it
planned to make the trial of the strike leaders a public demonstra-
tion of this thesis. Perhaps its prime purpose was to divide, dis-
credit and ultimately destroy the trade union and labour movement. To this end, they set the Royal North West Mounted Police
in motion on 1 July 1919. Calgary, the scene of the Western Labour Conference, and therefore regarded as a hotbed of radicalism,
was one of the targets. The *Morning Albertan* reported the event as
follows:

> Police officers in the principal cities of Canada yesterday
> celebrated Dominion Day by making raids upon the houses
> of prominent labour leaders, acting on warrants issued at
> Winnipeg. It is stated that the raids were made to round up
> evidence of a systematic Bolshevik plot in the Dominion,
> and to gain evidence which might strengthen the Govern-
> ment's case against the strike leaders at Winnipeg. Cities
> where labour homes were raided were Calgary, Victoria, Re-
> gina, Montreal, Brandon and Saskatoon.[18]

It is surprising that Irvine escaped the attentions of the police,
since he was a close associate of most of the labour leaders. However, all of those raided were members of the OBU and because
Irvine had differences with them on questions of political tactics
and strategy, it may have been that the police thought he was not
an appropriate object of their attention. This did not prevent
Irvine from protesting the police actions in the *Alberta Non-Partisan* and elsewhere. In fact, throughout the next twelve months, he
was frequently involved in meetings in support of the strike
leaders.

The first of these issues was the government's amendment to
the Immigration Act allowing for the deportation of British subjects not born in Canada. The amendment passed through the
House without debate in twenty minutes and within the hour

had been accepted by the Senate and given Royal assent. Seven of the strike leaders had been born in Great Britain and were thus made eligible for deportation without a hearing in a court of law. It is significant that Irvine was able to get support for his protest of the measure at a UFA political association convention. The convention instructed its resolutions committee to prepare a resolution demanding that trial by jury be upheld in Canada and that the amendment to the Immigration Act under which it was proposed to deport the strike leaders be repealed. Irvine was added to the committee for the purpose of helping to draft the resolution. When the resolution was finally put it was carried with only four dissenting voices.

Some months later when the first of the strike leaders, Bob Russell, was convicted and sentenced to two years in prison, Alex Ross, who was the chief labour opponent of the OBU in Alberta, said that this could only be regarded by labour as a challenge. He said that it was the first time that an active member of a labour union had been convicted for advocating a sympathetic strike. He declared that the strike, whether sympathetic or otherwise, was labour's only weapon, and every effort must be extended to protect a right that had been acquired after years of struggle. Ross urged that trade unionists, whether they agreed with Russell or not, should organize a forty-eight-hour strike in protest.

The Calgary *Herald*[19] hastened to point out that sympathetic strikes had been made illegal by Order-in-Council on 1 October 1918, and that therefore Ross was calling upon organized labour to break the law, and that as a consequence he should resign as MLA. Undaunted, Ross brought his proposal to the Calgary Trades and Labour Council, which passed a resolution recommending to the Alberta Federation of Labour that it should request the Trades Congress of Canada to organize a protest against the denial of the right to a sympathetic strike. The protest was to take the form, if necessary, of a general strike for a specified time. This resolution was passed with only a small dissenting vote. A few days later however, the AFL, apparently with little spirit left for a further fight, turned down Ross's resolution in favour of a nationwide strike, and contented itself with registering a strong verbal protest.

The final act in the drama came in March 1920, with the conviction of six more strike leaders. A large citizens' meeting was called in Calgary, representing not only all branches of organized labour but many business and professional people. Irvine was one of a number of speakers. He protested that the law was made by a class and used by that class for the promotion of their own interests. A resolution demanding a fair trial for the strike leaders was carried by a unanimous standing vote.

The following Sunday, Alderman A.A. Heaps of Winnipeg, the only one of the group of seven strikers to be acquitted, spoke to an audience of 1,500 in the Grand Theatre in Calgary. The meeting was held under the joint auspices of the People's Forum and the Calgary Defence League. Irvine was chairman and introduced Heaps as "a brand snatched from the burning." Heaps, on the occasion of his acquittal, had said to his friends and supporters, "I do not feel elated over my acquittal. I would rather have been convicted along with the rest."[20] At the Calgary meeting, speaking of his six fellow defendants, he said, "If I am innocent, they are innocent."[21] He claimed that the fact that the government did not carry out its intention to deport the strike leaders, including himself, without trial, was due to the intervention of the British Trade Union Movement, which had taken up the matter at its Southport Conference and had made representation to the Canadian government. He also told how the trial had revealed the role of the Royal North West Mounted Police as an anti-labour agency, which instructed its members to infiltrate and collect information on the activities of labour unions.

For some eighteen months of the period just described, Irvine had carried the heavy burden of working at the CPR on weekdays and serving the Unitarian Church at weekends, with his many other activities somehow squeezed into the time that was left. During this period, the *Alberta Non-Partisan* converted itself into the *Western Independent* and became the official organ of the newly formed UFA political action association. On 8 December 1919, Irvine gave his farewell address to the Unitarians and resigned his pastorate to devote his time exclusively to the editorship of the *Western Independent*. The Unitarians gave a farewell reception to the Irvines and the board of congregation presented them with a handsome silver tea service and a purse. Many years later, Irvine said of his Unitarian congregation:

> I am happy to say that they were the finest group of people any man ever had to work with. As I remember there were one or two more interested in the welfare of the Conservative party than in the Unitarian Church, but these were fine chaps too and I respected their opinions.[22]

After Irvine's resignation, the church continued without a pastor, relying upon guest speakers and, judging by the topics announced for Sunday sermons, it had a much reduced concern for social issues.

Irvine never again spoke in the Calgary Unitarian pulpit, although after the People's Labour church was formed in April, he was a frequent speaker there. In fact, Irvine himself and a number of his Unitarian friends including Rachael Coutts, Marion Carson, Edith Patterson and Alderman Broatch helped to set up this new church within three months of his resignation from his pastorate. It seems likely that one of Irvine's motives for resigning was not only to free himself for more work on the *Western Independent*, but also to assist the growth of labour churches, which had already been established in Winnipeg and Brandon by his friend J.S. Woodsworth, in conjunction with William Ivens and A.E. Stewart.

The People's Labour church in Calgary flourished for several years, essentially performing the function the Unitarian church had performed under Irvine's leadership, with perhaps a wider congregation drawn from labour leaders and others with radical and progressive politics. It was part of the upsurge in labour politics which developed across the country, stimulated by the Winnipeg Strike and the support for the strike leaders, particularly in the west.

The OBU also experienced a temporary surge forward. By the end of 1919 it had 101 locals and a membership of 42,000, but a year later it had only fifty-one locals and membership had declined to 5,000.[23] There was a similar temporary increase in labour electoral activity. In July 1920, four of the strike leaders (three of them still in jail) were elected to the Manitoba Legislature. But even before that, Irvine and his friends were getting ready for labour to enter the political field in Alberta and to make connections with other labour groups across Canada. The first attempt was made in April 1919, when the Calgary and District Branch of the Independent Labour Party was formed "for the purpose of effecting a democratic political organization for the education of the people in matters political and economic and for the securing of representation, on all representative public bodies, for those who toil."[24]

Less than a month later, however, a meeting was held in the Calgary Labour Temple, and the name was changed to the Calgary Branch of the Dominion Labour Party. The constitution worked out at the previous meeting was adopted, and Harry Pryde was elected president and Mrs. Corliss, Miss Patterson, Miss Coutts, Deachman, Broatch, and Smitten were officers and executive members of the new association. O.L. McPherson, the president of the UFA political association, was present and said that conditions were favourable for united action between the farmers and labour.

It is clear that internecine warfare was going on between labour groups across Canada, and Irvine and his friends were trying to find the name most acceptable to labour people in Calgary. At a Calgary Trades and Labour Council meeting four nights later the struggle continued. By a vote of eleven to ten, the Council decided that it, not the Dominion Labour Party, should be the body to select labour candidates for the forthcoming election. There was an angry discussion and the Dominion Labour Party was accused of trying to disrupt organized labour, and it was alleged that it was composed of members of the OBU and the Socialist party.

Despite this dissension and the barrage of criticism directed against it, the Calgary Dominion Labour Party survived and eventually ran candidates at all levels of government, often with conspicuous success. The fears of some members of the Trades and Labour Council must have been allayed because early in November 1919, a joint meeting of the Calgary branch of the Dominion Labour Party and the Calgary Trades and Labour Council was held. At the meeting, the following resolution was passed:

That we congratulate the farmers in the riding of Cochrane on being the first farmers' organization in the province to challenge the control of the old political parties; further, we wish the farmers every success and hope this will be a start towards the overthrow of the old political parties and their profiteering friends.[25]

This occasion must have warmed Irvine's heart, for it exemplified the unity he most desired. This unity was reinforced early in 1920, when a conference was held between the executive of the UFA political association and the Alberta executive of the DLP, with a view to promoting political co-operation between organized farmers and organized labour.[26]

On 5 July 1920, disaster struck the *Western Independent*. A notice appeared in the *Morning Albertan* on 21 July:

Owing to the mailing list, forms and matter to hand for the last edition of the *Western Independent* being destroyed in the big fire at the Western Print Works on July 5th, it was impossible to complete and send out the usual issue. The *Weekly Albertan* is being sent to all *Western Independent* readers this week and a full explanatory statement will be given in the next week's issue.

The *Western Independent* never again appeared in its original form. The *Weekly Albertan*, which picked out the highlights of the previous week's news in the *Morning Albertan*, was chiefly distributed to rural areas. The two middle pages of this weekly were given over to the *Western Independent* until that paper was re-established. Plans to reissue it as a six-page broadsheet failed, because a fall in farm prices led to a decrease in financial support. A plan to purchase an independent newspaper, the *Western Farmer*, and incorporate it with the *Western Independent* also failed, and finally the Alberta Publishing Company took over both and incorporated them as the *Western Farmer and Weekly Albertan*, with a special two-page section of the former *Western Independent* continuing to be published for several years under the heading "Independent Notes and Notions."

With the virtual demise of the paper he and Ford had produced for four years, and with no ministerial appointment, Irvine was faced with the prospect of working at the CPR, while continuing his political activity. There are indications that he must have been near exhaustion; in any case, he sought a change of scene for himself and his family.* Through his many connections with the farmers' movement across Canada, he obtained a position organizing co-operatives in Moncton, New Brunswick. Before leaving he was given a remarkable farewell:

> Citizens of all creeds and political faiths gathered to bid him godspeed in a new field of labour. Numbers of public men of the city, leaders of the organized farmers and a strong representation of the labour forces of Calgary, gathered in the Labour Temple last Friday at a farewell social in honour of the Reverend William Irvine. The social was given under the auspices of the People's Church. The large hall was filled to its capacity. It was a remarkable demonstration of the respect and esteem in which Mr. Irvine is held by citizens who have been associated with him during his life in Calgary.[27]

Three days later, the Trades and Labour Council also gathered to say goodbye. Irvine gave them some farewell advice:

> The first task of the Trades and Labour Council should be to organize labour in Calgary 100% strong. Labour organizations make the mistake of saying what they will do first and organizing afterwards. It is foolish for labour organizations to set an objective before organization along class lines is complete. The present split in the labour world will not last long. Unity will come soon, but it will only come along class lines by organizing 100%.
>
> I came to Calgary as a radical religionist. I believed that religion, to be of any value, should be closely in touch with humanity. It should find its way into business and into po-

---

* He and his wife now had four children — Ronald, born 1912; Harry, born 1914; James, born 1916; Vera, born 1918; his last child, Eric, was born in 1922.

litics. Some people thought I was an atheist, but if I am an atheist, I hope everyone will soon be one. I came to preach social religion believing in the uplifting of the masses to the point where it would be possible for them to live Christian lives. I received much support from your ranks and I am grateful for it.[28]

Irvine, born and raised within sight and sound of the sea, had not seen it for thirteen years when he arrived in New Brunswick at the close of 1920. His first view of the Bay of Fundy moved him to write a poem. Although, naturally enough, it is written within the literary conventions of the time, or perhaps in a slightly earlier Tennysonian vein, it is still a genuine and revealing expression of his feelings and state of mind:

Through all the years your song is still the same,
An angry roar, a moaning dirge,
A murmur
Which tells the world of your rebellion
Against the forces that have hedged you in
To spend your strength in futile rendering
Of efforts checked by law on every hand,
Till nothing's left you but that dreary murmur,
The wall of great ambitions loath to die.[29]

Irvine's image of the ocean in this stanza as frustrated, defeated and powerless is typical of what would otherwise be a conventional poem. Clearly, it reflects his own sense of defeat and fading hopes at the age of thirty-four. In his other writings, in his speeches and in his ordinary conversation Irvine rarely if ever expressed such moods of pessimism.

It was not long before Irvine was playing a vigorous role in farmer and co-operative circles in the Maritimes. The *Morning Albertan* continued its interest in Irvine and kept Calgarians posted on his activities with news reports and articles by Irvine himself. One such piece, entitled "The Maritime Farmers' Co-operative," gives a fair idea of the kind of work Irvine was doing:

The function of the central office is to buy collectively. It is really a wholesale house which buys directly from the manufacturers. The co-operative buying agency saves by buying in large quantities and saves on freight, but the wholesale profit is also saved for the farmers.

The Maritime United Farmers' Co-operative Company is a whole system which consists of a community co-operating to form a store, and then a community of stores co-operating to form a great system of commerce that will do all business at cost of production plus cost of handling. In this co-operative chain it is impossible for one of the stores in the chain to fail unless the whole chain is broken. . . .

Pretty soon this Co-operative will become the chief or perhaps the sole distributing agency for the Maritime Provinces. . . . People are beginning to see that it is even more important that they take a hand in the management of their business affairs than it is to elect a representative to Parliament. It is just as foolish to leave the manufacturing and distributing of the necessities of life to the caprice of a profit hunting individual as it would be to leave our government in the hands of a kaiser. It seems as if a real democracy in industry and commerce might be reached through the co-operative ideal.[30]

Yet, despite his enthusiasm for the possibilities of co-operation as a means of changing society, Irvine could not refrain from participating in politics. A by-election occurred in the New Brunswick federal riding of York-Sunbury. The Union Government candidate, Richard B. Hanson, K.C., was opposed by a United Farmers' candidate, Ernest W. Staris. Irvine campaigned for the Farmers' candidate and engaged in debate with a Dr. Edwards, who was assisting the Government candidate. The *Morning Albertan* presented the event to Calgary readers under a banner headline:

> *Great Triumph for Wm. Irvine in N.B. Campaign.*

After a triumph over Dr. Edwards, M.P. for Frontenac, in a meeting in the by-election in York-Sunbury, New Brunswick, William Irvine, formerly of Calgary, was carried shoulder-high through the streets of Fredericton, New Brunswick the other evening by enthusiastic followers of the Farmers' Party. Mr. Irvine has been campaigning for the farmers in New Brunswick for some time. The by-election in York-Sunbury is very tense and the farmers are gaining strength each day. They expect to carry the riding. The meeting at which Mr. Irvine scored a triumph over Dr. Edwards was described as the pivotal point of the contest.[31]

However, a few days later, the Prime Minister, Arthur Meighen, who had replaced Sir Robert Borden when the latter resigned the previous year, took part in the campaign. Meighen told the voters that a lawyer was better than a farmer in Parliament and apparently he convinced many people, for R.B. Hanson won the seat by 1,000 votes. Nevertheless, the farmers' candidate made a good showing with approximately 6,200 votes to his rival's 7,200.[32]

Before leaving for New Brunswick, Irvine had finished writing his first book, *The Farmers in Politics*, published late in 1920. A review of it by Alex Ross appeared in the *Morning Albertan* on 3 January 1921:

> It cannot be compared with any other book written by a Canadian author because it deals with economic problems, a subject usually associated with old developed countries. So he has the distinction of being one of the first Canadian authors to diagnose our social ills and to indicate a remedy.

The publication of *The Farmers in Politics* and the good reception it received may have played a part in motivating the *Morning Albertan* to offer Irvine a full-time post on its staff as an editor and columnist. Irvine, no doubt weary of his seven-month exile in the East, accepted. On 8 June 1921, the *Morning Albertan* ran a photograph of Irvine on its front page under the caption "Returns to Alberta" and praised him as "perhaps the finest exponent in Canada of the principles of the farmers' political movement." Irvine was back in Calgary in time to participate in the political campaigns which led the Alberta farmers to victory at both the provincial and federal levels of government.

FIVE

The UFA Enters Politics

Historians and others who have written and commented on the United Farmers of Alberta and the movement it represented have almost invariably given pride of place to Henry Wise Wood, president of the UFA for fifteen years from 1916 to 1931. Although Irvine is frequently mentioned in this connection, he is usually allotted a secondary role even though there is good evidence from which to argue that this is an unjust assessment.

Henry Wise Wood was born in 1860 in Missouri. His father was a prosperous slave-owning farmer who joined the Confederate forces to fight against the Union Government of Abraham Lincoln. At the conclusion of the Civil War he resumed farming and ranching apparently without any decline in his economic position. Henry went to rural school, then to a private school and later to Christian University at Canton, Missouri. At the end of his second year of college he married and concluded his formal education, but continued to read widely with an enquiring mind and a determination to formulate a philosophy for himself. In this effort he was in part influenced by his active membership in the Campbellite Christian Church, which is said to have been undogmatic and democratic in its teachings and organization. Wood took over the management of his father's farm and soon became a successful and respected rancher. He played little part in politics but was an interested observer. It is said that the difficulties and eventual failure of the farmers' populist movement during these years were the bases for his strong conviction that farmers' organizations should keep out of politics.

By the early 1900s, he wanted to establish his family on a farm of his own and eventually, in 1905, he moved to Carstairs, forty miles north of Calgary, where he gave up his original idea of ranching and became a wheat farmer instead. He was moderately successful and soon became a respected member of the community. He joined the newly formed UFA in 1909 and by 1915 he had achieved the rank of first vice-president in that organization. On the death of the president, James Speakman, he became acting president, and eight weeks later, at the annual convention in Calgary in January 1916, he was elected president of the UFA.

He soon acquired a position of extraordinary dominance in the UFA. This was partly due to his honesty, integrity and devotion to the organization. Wood was satisfied with his modest salary of $2,000 per year as head of the UFA and when in addition he became president of the Alberta Wheat Pool in 1923 at a salary of about $4,000 per year, he refused to continue drawing his salary from the UFA.

A tall man with a large bald dome-shaped head, his physical appearance suggested wisdom and he was not averse to enforcing this impression by the frequent use of his middle name, Wise. Wood arrived at his opinions slowly and cautiously, but once formed he stuck to them tenaciously. Surprisingly, in view of his strong religious inclinations, the thinker who influenced Wood most, and provided many of his fundamental ideas, was Herbert Spencer, a British philosopher and sociologist widely read in North America around the turn of the century. His key idea was the biological theory of evolution, particularly in the Darwinian version of adaptation of species through natural selection. Like Darwin, he thought that some forms of life were better suited to the environment than others, and therefore they bred more and stronger offspring than weaker species. Spencer more or less accepted the traditional concepts of virtue and vice and maintained that the evolving processes favoured the virtuous over the vicious, and that therefore human conduct by an inevitable process of natural selection was subject to moral improvement over the generations. He was strongly opposed to socialism because, at least in the Marxian version, it envisaged social change occurring as a result of class conflict, and he was also an agnostic who thought religions were mostly false and indeed absurd. Wood accepted the biological underpinnings of Spencer's social theory, but his interest was confined to the social dimension of this evolutionary theory and he had no qualms about providing it with a religious basis: in an early presidential address to the UFA he declared that democracy was the will of God.[1]

Despite the injection of this strong religious theme, Wood remained close to the Spencerian thesis that competition is bad and co-operation is good; that the evolutionary process is gradually eliminating one and advancing the other, so that inevitably a non-competitive, harmonious, co-operative society will emerge. However, Wood also borrowed, in modified form, the Marxian thesis of class conflict. When speaking to the People's Forum on the topic "Co-operation is the principle which is to save society," Wood told his audience that "the useless and deleterious classes would be eliminated in the great reorganization process."[2]

Despite his earlier observations and reaction against politics in the United States, Wood was not originally opposed to involvement in electoral politics. In 1911, the year he became a Canadian citizen, he worked unsuccessfully for the election of a Liberal candidate in Calgary. After his election to the UFA in 1916, he allowed his name to be placed in nomination as Liberal candidate for West Calgary and spoke so eloquently on his own behalf that he was only narrowly defeated by the Liberal Association's candidate.[3] These were passing aberrations however, and he soon arrived at the conviction that party politics and the parliamentary system were ways of frustrating democracy and keeping a ruling minority in power.

This raised the question: what, in a developed co-operative society, would replace these traditional processes of government? Wood's answer was that each producing occupational group should organize itself to protect its interests and to get a fair deal in relation to other groups, and that in the finally attained Co-operative Commonwealth, a truly democratic government would be composed of delegates sent from all the participating groups and the whole apparatus of general elections and parties would be rendered redundant. If one then asked: how can one help to bring this about? Wood's answer was, by organizing your group and by education that showed the merits of co-operation and the evils of competition.

J.S. Woodsworth, in a series of articles in the *Western Independent* section of the *Weekly Albertan and Western Farmer*, pointed out that the implications of Wood's theories were radical and were akin to those of the OBU, although they were couched in a different terminology. In fact, Wood's ideas outran his inclinations, for he was in practice a cautious and conservative man. Even on something as relatively non-political yet dear to the hearts of farmers as the setting up of a wheat pool, he dragged his feet. When Colonel J.W. Wood, publisher of the Calgary *Herald*, and others brought in Aaron Sapiro, an American promoter and evangelist for the wheat pool idea, in an effort to get it going and invited Wood to join forces, Wood found reasons for delay:

> The invitation was angrily spurned by Wood, who had decided that it was too late in the year to organize a wheat pool to handle the 1923 crop. Wood, that July, could think of a dozen reasons for backing away from organizing a pool for 1923. The farmers would be in the field with their binders once they got their hay off. There would have to be negotiations with the bank. Deals would have to be made with the elevator companies.[4]

In matters involving political action, Wood was even more cautious and reluctant, and here his version of the Spencerian theory of evolution came to his aid. The process of change was inevitably coming about according to natural law and divine plan. It would be rash and indeed impious to try to hasten the processes before the time was ripe. Thus radical ideas were accommodated to conservative actions. Wood fought incessantly against the farmers entering the political field. In later years he recalled, "The thing I feared most was the organization going into politics. I kept it out as long as I could."[5] Nevertheless, it is clear that Wood was slowly being forced to let the UFA enter the political field. The pressure to enter politics is generally attributed to a UFA rank-and-file, grassroots movement. This is probably true enough, but leadership was provided by the Non-Partisan League, and especially by Irvine, through his editorship of the *Alberta Non-Partisan,* through discussions held under the auspices of the People's Forum and the Unitarian Church, and through many meetings addressed by Irvine and his associates all over rural Alberta.

Irvine did not consider the struggle as one between the UFA and the Non-Partisan League, and he did not much care which organization led the farmers into politics, provided somebody did. His views were expressed in an editorial early in 1918:

> The policy of the farmers has been to remain outside the sphere of politics in any direct sense, entrusting its political achievements to its indirect influence. This is the weak spot in the organization. While its influence is strong, yet politicians and governments alike play with it. Parties cater for the vote but please themselves later as to legislation. To change from one party to another does not help, for neither party can give the justice demanded by the UFA, Grit and Tory alike being owned by the exploiters whom the farmers united to fight. Not only so, but when the monied interests are endangered, both parties will unite to defend them, as was done at the last election...
>
> ... The problem of Canada is the distribution of the products of human toil. Those who now are in control of our storehouses will not relinquish their privilege through indirect influence, they must be ousted by direct political action, and if the UFA does not see its way clear to undertake this task, it must be done by another organization, and the United Farmers will miss one great opportunity for service which it might accomplish with comparative ease.[6]

A year later, with the UFA still hesitating to take the plunge into politics, Irvine proposed that the UFA convention pass a resolution supporting the NPL in its political activities:

> We do not seek this in the interests of the League, but in the interests of the UFA. We will fight the battles of the movement whether the UFA co-operates with us or not, but we believe that both organizations would greatly profit were the UFA to clear the air by the passing of some such resolution. If it did nothing else it would make clear the separate func-

tions of both movements, and pave the way for mutual helpfulness and co-operation instead of the present indifference and incidentally would solve the problem of "What to do about Politics?" which is growing in both magnitude and intensity in the ranks of the UFA.[7]

The eleventh annual convention of the UFA met in Edmonton on 22 January 1919, attended by between 700 and 800 delegates, a somewhat smaller number than in previous years, due to the Spanish flu epidemic. There had also been a crop failure the previous summer which had depleted the farmers' resources. Nevertheless, it was an enthusiastic meeting that at last took the historic step making it possible for the UFA to enter politics. The resolution put forward by the board of directors and supported by Wood was only one of eleven resolutions on political action that had been submitted to the convention, but it was the one selected for debate and was passed unanimously (the UFA's eventual policy on political involvement can be found in Appendix A). It did not make the UFA a political party nor did it adopt the Non-Partisan League as its political arm, as Irvine had suggested, but it gave the UFA members in the various districts the right to call conventions for the purpose of taking independent political action, and if at least 10 percent of the local organizations so desired, they would receive assistance from the central office of the UFA and from the executive committee. Wood was apparently hoping that if political action was left to local initiative nothing much would come of it, and the UFA would not need to involve itself further in politics.

The decision of the convention received a somewhat less than enthusiastic response from Irvine:

> The UFA has at last come to the decision that political action is necessary....
>
> For this paper and the movements it represents, the endorsation by the UFA of the basic principles of the Non-Partisan idea is a matter for self-congratulation. It means that our educational efforts have not been without fruits, and that the cause of independent political action has been fur-

thered. Having welcomed the decision of the Alberta
Farmers to enter politics, and being deeply interested in the
political welfare of the western farmer, we might be permit-
ted to point out what seems to us to be weakness in the
methods of procedure as indicated in Mr. Wood's resolution.
Each local is left to take whatever action it sees fit. This we
venture to say is not organization, it is a planless plan which
spells defeat. What is this but sheer individualism in politics? There is no means of co-operation provided in this
method. How would it do to leave each local to take whatever course it desires in the UFA organization? Seemingly
not very well, for a constitution has been carefully provided
for the direction of each local, and machinery created which
makes each local an organic part of a co-operative whole. If
this be necessary and profitable in the UFA, how can a political movement get along without it? It seems to us that this
method lacks the idea of organization and the co-operative
principle has been entirely omitted.[8]

The following months involved intense political activity, with
Irvine and the Non-Partisans playing a critical role. After two
years, they numbered more than 6,000 members and their paper
had a circulation of 10,000. Ninety-five percent were also UFA
members and they acted as a ginger group within that organization of 19,000. Irvine and other leading members of the League
were determined to avoid if possible the emergence of two rival
political organizations among farmers. In order to promote unity
between the NPL and the UFA, a joint committee made up of
three members from the executive of each organization was
formed. They met 10 May 1919. H. Greenfield, W.D. Trego and M.
Sloan represented the UFA, and S.T. Marshall, J.W. Wilford and
Irvine the Non-Partisan League. The proposals to be made by the
NPL to the forthcoming local conventions were discussed and
with minor amendments were recommended by the committee.
The committee, however, had no authority to decide anything
about the terms of the amalgamation of the two political organizations and it was left to the constituency conventions to decide
whether to accept or reject the findings.

As a result of this meeting, the NPL issued a statement to its members advising them to amalgamate with the UFA, in order to better and more speedily achieve the aims for which the League had been formed:

> We would further advise that our members who are delegates at the conventions called by the UFA introduce resolutions on the following important matters, which we think embody the fundamental principles of the Non-Partisan movement. In the event of these resolutions being defeated there might exist a necessity for the League to continue. But if they be adopted by the convention, all that we stand for will be safeguarded in the one big agrarian movement for political expression and democratic government.
>
> 1. That this independent political organization is in itself a proof of our objection to the old party system of government, and that the chief aim of this movement shall be to change our form of government from the party system to a business administration, with members elected under the proportional system of voting, and subject to direct legislation including the initiative, referendum and right of recall.
> 2. That this convention make provision for provincial political action as well as federal.
> 3. That all finances involved in the farmers' political movement be met directly by the members, that proper account be kept of all funds and a statement issued annually.
> 4. That a separate department or subsidiary office be created under the UFA auspices to function as the central office of the political organization.
> 5. That the *Alberta Non-Partisan* be used as the official organ of the farmers' political movement; and that representatives be appointed as directors of the policy of the paper.
> 6. That in the interests of education, and also for the prevention of bureaucratic methods — so liable to grow up in any organization — the political program adopted shall be passed clause by clause at each constituency convention.[9]

Oddly enough, this statement does not raise the issue that became one of the chief bones of contention at all the local conventions, namely the question whether or not the UFA political associations would be open to non-farmers as well as farmers. Irvine set forth his views on this matter well before the conventions got under way:

> ...The farmers must either remain an industrial organization, run on industrial lines for industrial action, or they must take their troubles into the political field. But if they narrow their political appeal to their industrial limit, they will never gain political power. To say that the only way to have a voice in the new political movement is to come by the UFA door will mean one of two things, i.e., either the industrial lines of organization will have to be rubbed out, or there is no political future for the people of Alberta.
>
> The UFA should have stayed with the UFA work, and left the NPL to do the political work. The UFA door should either be shut against political action, or open to all who are interested in politics. If it remains shut against the town and city workers then political action is not being taken at all, but just another form of industrial action is being taken.[10]

The question was debated at practically all the local conventions and in many cases Irvine, Weir and Louise McKinney were invited to put the case of the NPL. Wood was also a frequent platform guest, and on several occasions Wood and Irvine and the two MLAs engaged in vigorous debates. Wood had been forced to bring the UFA to the point of political action, but the speed with which the local organizations set about forming political associations doubtless alarmed him, and he determinedly set about trying to minimize the influence of the Non-Partisan League.

Irvine clashed with Wood at many of the regional political conventions that occurred throughout the summer. The outcome of these conventions was a provincial political meeting in Calgary in July 1919. Here the directors of the district associations and the central executive of the UFA discussed matters of political organization. As suggested by resolutions from a number of locals, a provincial political association was formed under the presidency of Oran L. McPherson, a young farmer from Bow River. McPherson was in sympathy with Irvine and the Non-Partisan view-point and keen on co-operation with other groups, particularly labour.

Two months earlier, the Western Independent Publishing Company, Ltd., had been formed in order to sell shares to raise capital so that the *Alberta Non-Partisan* could become a weekly paper instead of a bi-monthly. It was now arranged with the UFA political association that the new paper, to be called the *Western Independent*, would be its official organ and that Irvine would continue as its editor and J.H. Ford as its business manager. The paper appeared in its new guise in October 1919. In his first editorial Irvine made it clear that:

> It is a farmers' paper, financed by the stockholders who are farmers on a plan that is democratic and co-operative. It is backed by the UFA political association as the official organ of the movement.
>
> The policy of the *Western Independent* will be determined by the spirit and outlook of the farmers' movement. It will seek to determine the viewpoint of organized farmers, particularly relating to matter political, and will be in the front line of subsequent political contests against the old line parties.[11]

Irvine's call for unity within the farmers' political movement and the emergence of the *Western Independent* as the official organ of that movement did not affect his loyalty to the labour movement. Earlier, on the eve of the UFA's decision to enter politics, he had written:

> The decision of organized labour in Alberta to take political action is significant and indicates a change in the policy of labour in its efforts to secure its aims. After years of industrial organization and effort this body has come to the conclusion that political action is essential to ultimate success, and thus labour enters the political field to make a bid for power as a means towards the expressed aim of industrial organization. This we believe is the logical step, and if the organized farmers who meet in Edmonton next week take

similar action, and co-operate with labour in this regard, a new day will have dawned for Canada.[12]

On the day the *Western Independent* made its debut, Irvine left for Ontario to work for the farmers' organization in that province during the political campaign preceding the October 20 election. The campaign was run largely on local initiative and with not much help from the executive of the United Farmers of Ontario. This call for assistance was an indication of Irvine's growing reputation as an effective speaker and proponent of the farmers' movement. The campaign was a success, for the United Farmers gained forty-three out of 111 seats and they were able to form a government under E.C. Drury, with the support of twelve Labour members. This government survived until June 1923.

The victory gave new impetus to the Alberta farmers. The Non-Partisans had weaned the UFA from the view that their political concerns lay solely in the federal field and it is significant that the first UFA candidate was elected to the provincial legislature. After a hard-fought and bitter campaign, Alex Moore won the Cochrane constituency by a margin of 145 votes against the Liberal candidate, E.V. Thompson, in a by-election on 3 November 1919. The Conservatives had obligingly vacated the field, making the election a two-way struggle between the UFA and the ruling Liberal party. Premier Stewart, and almost all his cabinet ministers, campaigned in the constituency. With the exception of the *Western Independent*, all the press opposed the UFA candidate.

The Cochrane by-election also had ideological repercussions. Wood took the opportunity to appear at an election rally at Crossfield, where he gave an address devoted to expounding his philosophy of co-operation and group government and tried to apply it to the current situation. The gist of his remarks was that farmers should organize as an exclusive economic group and if elected to legislative bodies or Parliament, maintain their individuality in relation to other groups. These proposals precipitated the somewhat hypocritical charge from Liberals and Conservatives that Wood was proposing class government and class legislation. To which he replied that this was not so, since other groups would be represented in the assembly and would share in the responsibility for passing legislation.

For Wood, this move to spread his doctrine was not so much a serious attempt to solve political problems as an attempt to maintain his control over the UFA. Later, when the UFA was successful in both the federal and the provincial field, he strongly urged the group idea for the UFA federal MPs because it helped to retain the UFA members within his orbit. On the other hand, in the UFA-dominated provincial legislature where he was still very influential, he did nothing to further the application of his political theories but instead took steps to minimize the political role of the UFA. His first major move was the dissolution of the political association and the taking over of its functions by the central executive of the UFA at the twelfth annual convention of the UFA in January 1920, where it was claimed that the work of the association could very well be accomplished by the central office.

A recommendation had been made to the UFA central executive to the effect that the *Western Independent* continue as the official organ of the farmers' political movement, since the paper had served the farmers well. J.H. Ford said that he would have preferred the paper to stand on its own feet, and that it would continue publication in any event. No doubt Ford saw the writing on the wall, for in fact, the *Western Independent* in the next few months continued to try to get itself adopted as the organ of the farmers' political movement without avail. The UFA executive led by Wood was adamant and eventually cut off all financial assistance and endorsation for the paper.

The chief act of the convention itself was to reverse its long-standing constitutional ban on *direct* UFA involvement in electoral politics, and this was done by passing Resolution 31, which made no direct reference to politics or even to a change in policy. It reads in part:

> RESOLVED that the powers and duties of the board and executive of the UFA continue as in the past, recognizing no other authority than this convention in all educational, social, economic and other propaganda work of whatever character; and further, that they advise and assist all federal district boards in whatever way may be necessary to carry out all legitimate work of the said districts.

The resolution was passed with Wood's blessing, but this reversal of his previous stand was made more palatable to him by the subsequent endorsation of his stipulation that the UFA would enter politics as an economic group and not as a political party.

The twelfth convention gave every appearance of being a great triumph for Wood, and in some respects it was. However, this concealed the fact that, in a period of not much more than two years, Wood had been forced to lead the UFA in a way that went against his deepest convictions. Historians of the period often write as if Wood defeated the Non-Partisan League, but this is treating the matter as if it were a contest for leadership, and it was only one-sidedly so. For Wood, the important thing was that the UFA as an industrial organization should survive under the leadership of Henry Wise Wood, and if the UFA had to enter politics in order to insure this, then so much the worse, but so be it.

The Cochrane election victory made Irvine decide that it would divide the growing farmers' movement to insist on opening its membership to non-farmers. He added to this the notion, largely accepted by farmers but only reluctantly by Wood, that the UFA should co-operate with labour groups to overthrow the old-line parties and establish a co-operative commonwealth. By the time the question of group government came up for discussion at the convention, Irvine had gained a reputation for being able to explain lucidly the ideas which some complained Wood expressed obscurely. A resolution submitted by Wood's own local organization at Carstairs read:

> This Convention endorses the principle of economic group organization for political purposes as explained by the president of the UFA and by the editor of the *Western Independent*.

Irvine told the Convention:

> I believe that democratic groups cannot hold together without a cement — and the only cement the farmers have is the organization which they have created. One year ago I was in favour of the open door. Your organization convinced me that I was wrong.[13]

The resolution was carried by a large majority, and both Irvine and Wood were loudly cheered. Irvine was content that the farmers of Alberta had at last unequivocally entered politics, and Wood was content that he was still the acknowledged leader of the UFA.

Years later, Irvine recalled conversations that he had had with Wood after the battle was over:

> I think Mr. Wood had, in fact he told me he had afterwards, some idea that I was trying to get the leadership of the farm movement. That was something which I had never dreamed of. I didn't know enough about farming to lead anybody. I wouldn't have thought of taking the leadership from farmers who knew their business when I didn't know it. It would have been ridiculous. But at any rate, he knew better after a while and he smilingly told me that he had thought for a while that that was what I was after, but he found out that I wasn't after anything for myself in particular, I was just doing things that I felt I had to do.[14]

William Irvine was undoctrinaire and a pragmatist. He was undoctrinaire in that although he had a set of basic principles and purposes that he was not prepared to compromise, yet his mind was prepared to entertain different ideas and ways of seeking his goals. He was pragmatic in the sense that he adopted or abandoned ideas according to whether they would help or hinder him in his aims. However, he also believed that it was necessary to have carefully thought out social and political views and commitments.

Although many people were astonished by the variety of ideas that Irvine entertained at any one time and by his ability to change them quickly when necessary, they nevertheless appreciated the clarity and facility with which he expressed these ideas in speech and writing. Thus, from such diverse sources as his early-found socialism, the politics of the U.S. Non-Partisans, the ideas current among western Canadian farmers, and finally from the ponderings of Henry Wise Wood, he was able to construct a point of view amounting to a social philosophy which was in large part adopted by the UFA.

Irvine's initial attempt to put this philosophy in a more or less coherent form was his first book, *The Farmers in Politics*. A good deal of its content had already been expounded in speeches to both urban and rural audiences, and some of it was derived from his editorials and articles in the *Alberta Non-Partisan* and its successor, the *Western Independent*. It was essentially a book written for the occasion of the rise of a farmers' political movement in western Canada, and its purpose was to explain and assist that movement. Irvine wrote in his preface:

> Ruskin divides all books into two classes — the books of the hour and the books of all time. In as much, however, as any writing dealing with a movement still in the process of development can have vitality for only so long as the movement itself is one of current interest, this book has no hope of belonging to Ruskin's latter category, and the writer's fullest hope will be realized if he has succeeded in writing what he acknowledges must necessarily be a book of the hour.[15]

Nevertheless, this "hour" lasted nearly fifteen years, and when nine years later Irvine published his second book, *Co-operative Government*, it consisted of a collection of addresses given throughout Canada in the intervening period on themes not differing substantially from those in his earlier book. The distinctive feature of the second book was the extent to which Irvine's nine years of parliamentary experience had confirmed and reinforced his original opinions on the party system. *The Farmers in Politics* to some extent belies its name, since about half the book is given over to a discussion of "the great awakening of the common people of which the farmers' movement is only one phase."

Like Wood, Irvine purported to find the philosophical foundations for his social philosophy in the theory of evolution as expressed by Herbert Spencer, and like Wood, he added to and adapted the Spencerian account in order to make it compatible with the rest of his thinking. As a pastor, he used the concept of evolution as a means of secularizing religion, since it enabled him to dispense with the notion of a supreme being and creator. The deterministic implications of evolution with regard to social change were both used and evaded by Irvine. He believed that a socialist society or a co-operative commonwealth was on the evolutionary agenda and was bound to come about in the course of time, and he borrowed from G.B. Shaw the conception of an unconscious life-force working in co-operation with man's conscious efforts to produce a better society. There are other more philosophically and scientifically respectable ways of getting around this deterministic dilemma, but the Shavian doctrine served Irvine's purposes, enabling him to be both evolutionist and activist. Put simply, his position was that there are laws of social development which people can consciously help or hinder.

More fundamental than Irvine's evolutionary views was his perception that in capitalist society there is a class struggle going on between those who produce and those who profit from or exploit the work of others:

> Labour is organizing against a system which metes out a bare existence to the thousands who produce the wealth, while the few who control the means of wealth production roll in the fatness of the land. It stands opposed to a system which produces jobless men, and in favour of the inauguration of a new order in which all may have work and in which all will be able to reap the benefits of their toil.... A matter which involves the very life of the people can no longer be left to the caprice of individuals in search of profit. The movement everywhere is towards the nationalization of basic industries, aiming at democratic control and the principle of service.[16]

Irvine then had to decide by what method he would seek to change the social order. He was faced with a choice of three possibilities: to work towards armed revolution against the oppressors; or to work towards the building and strengthening of industrial organizations, such as the OBU, for the urban workers with the ultimate aim of using this power to bring capitalism to an end through such weapons as the general strike; or, thirdly, to organize workers and farmers politically to seek election to legislative bodies where they might eventually change the economic and social structure through democratic means.

Irvine rejected revolution, partly from a natural aversion to violence, and partly from the conviction that revolutions come about because of long delay and failure to bring about needed social changes by other means. To Irvine, the occurrence of a revolution in Canada was a remote possibility — so remote that it left would-be revolutionaries with nothing to do of any social relevance. It was on these grounds that he joined issue with the adherents of the Socialist Party of Canada.

The second alternative, that of so-called industrial or direct action, had more attraction for Irvine, but it offered only one real weapon, the general strike, which was of little use to farmers. Furthermore, like the sting of the bee, the strike hurts both the giver and the receiver and is difficult to sustain. Irvine thought the strike was an efficient weapon for limited and short-term objectives, but was not effective in bringing about radical social change. After the failure of the Winnipeg Strike, the possibility of successful direct action in Canada seemed unlikely.

Irvine was strongly in favour of building organizations that united and stood for the interests of industrial workers, and he was equally in favour of building farmers' organizations to fight for farmers' interests, but he doubted their ability to bring about major social changes. For these reasons he was at odds both with his OBU friends and with H.W. Wood before the farmers entered politics.

This left Irvine with the third alternative: political action through the ballot box, although this is perhaps a misleading way of labelling his choice, since it suggests a narrowing of his interests to the political, and this certainly was not the case.[17] There is no doubt that Irvine was committed to bringing about a truly democratic society in which all people would participate equally in making the decisions that controlled their lives, and he was also committed to doing this by democratic means. Many people have thought and many still think that in Canada there have existed since Confederation the political institutions and traditions to enable us to freely bring about whatever social changes the majority desires, and that consequently the circumstances in which we live at any given time are the result of our free choice. It may not, they say, be the best world that we can imagine, but it is the best of all *possible* worlds.

Surrounded by this climate of opinion, Irvine was a heretic in so far as he did not believe that our political institutions were really democratic, nor did he believe that Canadians lived in what has been called an "open society," responsive to the need for far-reaching changes and improvement. So if political action was to be effective, then new democratic tools must be forged and used by those who wished to change society.

His first target was the party system, which he considered corrupt and a tool of the wealthy:

> In fact it may be said that partyism became an investment for big interests in Canada, dividends being paid in the shape of legislation and privileges to those in a position financially and morally to make the investment. Business interests no longer content themselves with financing one of the parties — they donate freely to the campaign funds of both, and so make doubly sure of purchasing government influence, no matter which party happens to be elected. Thus our governmental machinery has grown to be the most farcical of institutions, being used by the wealthy as a means of attaining financial advancement, and applied to the masses for the purpose of dividing them foolishly against themselves, dividing them in fact to such an extent as to render them politically helpless. Between the parties, any difference of an economic nature has long since ceased to exist. In organization, in lack of principles, and in practical misgovernment, the Tory and Liberal parties are identical....[18]

Irvine's first response to this situation was to work with the Non-Partisan League and the Labour Representation League, to get farmers and workers elected. These organizations tried to distinguish themselves from political parties in various important ways. Those who were elected gave their supporters the right of recall at any time when the majority were dissatisfied with them. They also proposed to give their constituency associations the right to initiate legislation, and they pledged themselves to vote on every legislative issue according to its merits and never on grounds of expediency or mere partisan opposition. Above all, campaign funds would be raised exclusively from the individual donations of supporters in the constituency. These were all measures aimed at greater participation on the part of the electors and closer relations between the electors and their legislative representatives. Irvine and his farmer and labour friends hoped eventually to swamp the legislatures with MLAs and MPs pledged to these principles, and in so doing not only to gain majority representation for those classes now practically unrepresented, but also to make the party system irrelevant.

Two things made Irvine begin to rethink his position in 1919-1920. On the one hand, the Non-Partisans in North Dakota, after their initial successes, were beginning to crumble under the attacks of their political enemies and were being increasingly deserted by the voters; and the UFA decided to go into politics but only as an organized economic group excluding non-farmers.

In the circumstances, it was not difficult for Irvine to come around to the UFA point of view (see Appendix A). Only on the question of closed membership had Irvine differed with the UFA, since his criticism of the party system, of the class nature of legislative assemblies and of their "unbusinesslike" procedures, were shared by most UFA members. Although the NPL and the LRL were both formally open to all who agreed with their principles, one consisted largely of farmers and the other largely of labour.

He had criticized the closed-door policy on the grounds that it was undemocratic, so naturally his acceptance of that policy led him to re-examine his concept of democracy, which he defined as the intelligent self-direction of an organized people. Irvine thought that democracy was not something born fully formed but something that must grow and develop:

> The lowest possible democratic unit is the group. The birth of a group is the birth of democracy. That group, like the child, must learn to move as a unit, must become conscious of itself, and must learn to talk and express itself. When the

group learns to speak it will not be the voice of an individual, it will be the voice of democracy. The opinion expressed by a group will not be the opinion of an individual but a true group opinion. As a group advances in its thinking powers, it will become conscious of itself in relation to other groups, and will find its fuller life in a group of groups, and from that group of groups will come the consciousness and expression of a whole people, or, in other words, a democracy.[19]

It is clear in the above passage that Irvine was laying the basis for co-operation and unity between farmers' organizations and labour organizations and that he was seeking ways to transcend the possibly divisive and isolating effects of the closed-door policy.

Irvine next raised the question on what basis can groups be organized. His answer was that they cannot be organized around ideas, as these divide people as much as unite them and often avoid the basic issues. He went on to argue that economic interests are always stronger and more determining in an organization than ideas:

It cannot be truthfully denied that economic questions are fundamental. The first question to every person is, "How am I to live?" But this is not the only question. There is another and even greater "Why am I living?" If one has to live merely to secure bread in order to live while more bread is secured, then death is preferable to life. But "How am I to live?" is still and must remain, the first question. If an answer is not found to this, answer to the second there can be none. Without bread one does not make enquiries about that for which one *should* live. . . .

But it is artificial to distinguish between life itself and life worth while. The materialistic and idealistic schools must be brought together and unified on a basis that will uphold life as a whole. . . .

The United Farmers happily find a synthesis for the seeming antagonism between these two philosophies. They began with the price of wheat, but they do not stop at that.[20]

Irvine's claim is that what holds people together most securely is common economic interest, associated perhaps with a common economic way of life. On this secure basis groups of people can together devise policies for furthering their common interests. This provides the only sound foundation for democratic thought and action. Once this is established it can be built on in two ways. An economic group may go on to concern itself with non-economic values and work out a program for non-economic goals, as did the UFA, partly through the activities of its auxiliary, the United Farm Women. Secondly, two or more economic groups may co-operate on grounds of common interest, as Irvine constantly worked at getting farmers and labour to do.

Irvine's assumption was that we live in a fragmented society divided by competition and exploitation. The task was to build a holistic society by eliminating competition and exploitation and replacing them with co-operation, equality and social justice. The foundation of this co-operative commonwealth would be composed of economic groups held together by common interest, but the structure built on this foundation would rise far above its base.

In seeking models for his co-operative commonwealth, Irvine critically examined contemporary syndicalist and socialist thought:

> Syndicalism is based on industrial groups. Its group formation is its virtue. But its teaching in respect of the State, which by its opponents is held to be objectionable and impractical, is not a necessary corollary of group organization. Syndicalism aims at the overthrow of the State; it seeks to invest each syndicate or group with full control of all that pertains to the life of the syndicate. There is no provision made for the unification of the syndicates so as to regulate the interlocking and common interest of all.... Its logical outcome would be anarchy. The Syndicalists, while creating members of one body, refuse to allow the bodies themselves to federate.
>
> In contrast to the Syndicalists are the Bolsheviki with their Soviets. It would appear that industries and professions

form the basis of the Soviet system. But here again, we find a departure from the logic of the group idea. From the industrial basis the Syndicalist works towards a stateless civilization, while the Bolshevik, from the same basis, arrives at a rigid state control. Every step which the Soviet system takes from the industrial group leads further away from the people toward autocracy, until it culminates in a dictatorship. The industrial system centralized in this dictatorship becomes a bureaucracy which may in time become as intolerable and inefficient as private ownership under Czarism.

The Syndicalist theory and the Soviet State both start from the same basis, and reach diametrically opposed results. Neither system has followed the natural co-operation which underlies the group organization. . . .

The Guild Socialists also advocate a group system which is, perhaps, the sanest and most practical of all European theories of social improvement. . . . The guild is to have democratic control of the industry, but according to guild socialism there must be also a central control or state for the supervision of all industries for the common good, and to prevent strife arising between one industry and another. But this central body or parliament is to be elected in a manner similar to that in vogue at the present time. This is the weak spot in Guild Socialism. The parliament should be the elected representatives of the various guilds, and thus preserve the opinions, and represent the interests, of each democratic unit in the State. . . .

The co-operation which brought individuals together in a group must be applied between the groups until the highest form of co-operation is reached, namely a fully organized co-operative state.[21]

Despite the fact that Irvine's references to Marx were often critical, influenced as they were by the sectarian view of the Socialist Party of Canada or the actions of the Bolsheviks in Russia, nevertheless there were similarities between some of his basic ideas and those of Marx. They shared the same view about the fundamental importance of the economic base and of its relation to the ideological superstructure. Marx saw the industrial working class, motivated by class interests, as the agent of social change. Irvine did not quarrel with this view, but found in Canada in the 1920s a relatively undeveloped and divided working class. The farmers, on the contrary, forming between 50 and 60 percent of the population, were well organized, had developed a philosophy of co-operation and were about to take political action against their class enemies: the bankers, industrialists and corporations. The farmers seemed endowed with all the qualities Marx allotted to the proletariat. A major difference, of course, was that Irvine did not envisage the farmers using their potential power to establish class rule as a prelude to the eventual construction of a new society. However, just as Marx thought the interests of industrial workers transcended class interests and were the interests of society as a whole, Irvine thought the same goal would be accomplished in Canada by farmers' organizations. He illustrated this viewpoint in a detailed discussion of the national policy of the Canadian Council of Agriculture.

The bias of Irvine's thought was clearly democratic with its roots deep in the history of the socialist, labour and co-operative movements. Some writers, perhaps misled by Irvine's attacks upon the party and parliamentary systems, have thought that his intent was anti-democratic, and in fact it has been absurdly suggested that he had affinities with fascism. Paul F. Sharp, with direct reference to Irvine, says: "What the UFA really meant was 'group representation' similar to the 'corporate state' though without the elements of coercion and dictatorship which Mussolini applied to it in Italy."[22] The *Oxford Companion to Canadian History and Literature* includes a biographical sketch of Irvine which must set some kind of record for inaccuracy, errors of fact and of interpretation. It says: "In *Co-operative Government* (1929), for which Wood wrote the foreword, Irvine discussed the failure of democracy and advocated a modified form of the Corporate State, the basic fascist idea."[23]

In neither *The Farmers in Politics* nor in *Co-operative Government* did Irvine attack democracy. What he did was to attack Canadian political institutions for not being truly democratic. Group government as described by him was not an alternative to democracy but a form of genuine democracy described in the earlier book in 1920 and not changed in any way in the later work. The purpose of fascism was to destroy socialism, working class movements, the trade unions, and any other movement or organization that threatened capitalism. Its whole purpose and spirit was alien to that of the farmers' movement in Canada in the years in which the UFA came to power.

Irvine declined to give a detailed account of the structure and workings of a group government, tending to take cover behind his evolutionary theory:

> The new form of government cannot be constructed beforehand by any individual. Suffice it to say that the group government which will result from the new forms of political organization must be moulded to fit the new conditions. It will be a natural outgrowth of group representation, and will have to accommodate itself to its group environment. Governments in the air are castles in Spain. I shall not therefore occupy space with worthless detail while there are general principles involved that may be considered with more profit.[24]

Although we may accept this lack of detail about the ultimate makeup of group government, there remains the more serious difficulty about the nature of political action when economic groups are first elected to legislative assemblies (for a discussion of C.B. Macpherson's views on UFA social theory, see Appendix B). Suppose farmer and labour groups are elected in sufficient numbers to form a majority and there are also elected representatives of the Liberal and Conservative parties. How are the latter to be treated? Are they to be regarded as economic groups and given their proportional share in the government along with labour and farmers? Or are only bona fide economic groups to form the government?

Although Irvine did not elaborate upon these questions, his thinking would lead us to speculate as follows. It can be assumed that in a certain sense the two traditional parties represent eco-

nomic interest groups and in fact they largely represent the same
ones; nevertheless, they have been elected by people of various
classes and do not conform to the notion of an economic group. A
number of different possibilities exist. Farmers' organizations, because of their (at that time) dominant proportion of the population and their superior organization, win a majority of seats in
Parliament. They provide good government and also seek to implement a program similar, let us say, to that of the Non-Partisans in North Dakota in 1917. Encouraged by this, labour groups
in industrial areas elect a labour contingent to Parliament and
they are given a proportionate place in the government. Slowly,
the traditional parties are squeezed out and more and more economic groups seek representation. Finally, the economic groups
who now control Parliament bring before the legislature constitutional changes by which representatives are elected directly from
their own economic groups. Presumably, enough economic
groups will have been formed so that everyone has an appropriate group to which he or she may belong. Some such evolutionary process must have been in Irvine's mind, and since the existing processes of government came about in some such fashion,
there is no reason to suppose they might not radically change in a
like manner. Certainly Irvine does not distinguish clearly enough
between group government as finally attained and the initial processes by which it would establish itself. He is vague about the
period when farmers, workers and other productive groups face
bankers and industrialists within a group government. Would
not the exploitative and profit-seeking groups resist the transition
to a co-operative commonwealth as well as the interim measures
of nationalization on the agenda of the producing groups? The
path to the co-operative commonwealth, if the farmers had resolutely followed it, might have been less smooth and evolutionary
than Irvine envisaged.

SIX

First Years in Parliament

The Farmers in Politics was published on the eve of the most crucial year in UFA history and it brought Irvine back on the political scene in Alberta six months before his actual return from New Brunswick.

The first skirmish in the election campaigns in Alberta in 1921 occurred in March when A.L. Sifton died, leaving the federal constituency of Medicine Hat vacant. At this time there was no inkling of the coming provincial and federal general elections. Nevertheless, the farmers went into the political fray with great enthusiasm.

Seven hundred delegates filled the Empress Theatre at Medicine Hat and chose Robert Gardiner, a forty-two-year-old bachelor who emigrated from Scotland in 1902 and farmed first in Saskatchewan and later at Excel, Alberta, as their candidate on the second ballot. Wood, who did not take part in the nomination proceedings, was the guest speaker in the evening. He expressed his conviction (which he reiterated throughout the election year) that any attempt by the farmers and organized labour to form a joint platform would weaken both organizations. Many farmers did not agree with Wood. Harry Simpson of Hanna, writing in the *Western Independent* section of the *Western Farmer*, argued in favour of farmer-labour unity:

> ... we are both of the exploited class. As we perfect our organizations and are able to place our representatives in Parliament, we will see that we have a common enemy (the exploiter) and when we get strong enough between us to

control Parliament and thoroughly understand our present economic system of exploitation by the few, it will rest with ourselves how long that enemy lasts.[1]

J.S. Woodsworth, who was visiting Alberta, spoke at Gardiner's election rally in Medicine Hat, urging labour support for the UFA candidate, since "the two main democratic forces were found in two main groups — labour and farmers." The Medicine Hat UFA district association also went on record in favour of co-operation with other groups:

> We invite other organized democratic groups which have no candidate in the field to co-operate with us in the election of our candidate and ask our people to reciprocate in districts where candidates are reversed.[2]

The Dominion Labour party of the Medicine Hat constituency endorsed Robert Gardiner's candidacy and urged all wage-earners to do likewise. They emphasized their co-operation by sending a copy of their resolution to the executive officers of the UFA.

In an article on the Medicine Hat election, Irvine pointed out that in the House of Commons farmers with only fifteen Members were grossly under-represented and that labour was not represented at all: "It means that Canada is suffering now from class legislation — it means that less than 20 percent of the population dominates in their own interests the whole economic life of the country."[3] Alex Ross and Irvine went to Medicine Hat to speak to a crowded hall at which they claimed that Labour was 100 percent solid for the farmers' candidate; and on UFA Sunday Irvine gave two sermons at Stavely, which was one of the first rural centres to support the Non-Partisan League in 1917. When 27 June, election day, came around, Gardiner was elected to the House of Commons by a sweeping majority of 9,764 votes, while his Conservative opponent, Colonel Nelson Spenser, lost his deposit.

Unexpectedly, four days before the by-election, a provincial election was called for 18 July. Earlier in the year there had been rumours that Premier Stewart had asked several prominent UFA members, including Wood, if they would accept Cabinet positions

with the Liberal government. Wood was not open to such proposals and when the election was called, forty-four UFA constituency associations fielded candidates. The manifest enthusiasm of
the Albertan farmers was not entirely shared by Wood, who told
a UFA convention at Medicine Hat: "If I had my way we would
put about 20 of our best men in the legislature at this election and
leave the responsibility of governing on the shoulders of someone
else."[4]

The Dominion Labour party in Calgary nominated three candidates: Alex Ross, Fred White, and Bob Parkyn. Irvine, who was
present, withdrew his name from nomination and concentrated
his energies on working for the three labour men. When the election results came in, the UFA had captured thirty-nine of fifty-
nine seats, the DLP won four, the Liberals were reduced to thirteen, and there were two Independents and one Conservative.
Two labour men were returned from Calgary, Alex Ross, who
topped the poll, and Fred White. The two pioneering Non-Partisan MLAs elected in 1917 disappeared from the scene. James Weir
did not contest his seat in Nanton and it went to D.H. Galbraith,
also a former Non-Partisan who ran for the UFA. Louise McKinney did contest her Claresholm riding but was narrowly defeated
by C. Milner, who ran as an Independent. There is little doubt
that she would have retained the seat if she had sought UFA
nomination. However, there were still women in the legislature,
for Irene Parlby,* president of the United Farm Women's Association, was elected in the Lacombe riding and became Minister
without Portfolio in the UFA government, thus becoming the first
woman to reach Cabinet rank in Alberta, and the second in the
British Commonwealth.

Under the impact of the shattering defeat of the government's
candidate in the Medicine Hat federal constituency and the triumph of the UFA in the provincial elections, the Union government split into its component Liberal and Conservative parts, and

---

* Irene Parlby, along with Henrietta Edwards, Emily Murphy, Nellie
  McClung and Louise McKinney, appealed to the British Privy
  Council in 1929 and established that women were "persons," in
  the use of that word in the BNA Act. Nellie McClung was also
  elected to the legislature in 1921 but on the Liberal ticket.

the Conservative Prime Minister, Arthur Meighen, on 1 September, announced a forthcoming general election that was subsequently called for 6 December. The Dominion Labour party held a nomination meeting in Calgary in mid-September. Irvine won the nomination on the first ballot with 117 votes, against the twenty-six votes received by the other two candidates. His nomination was for either the East or West Calgary riding and the decision as to which one was to be made at a joint meeting of the UFA political associations from the two ridings and the executive of the Calgary Dominion Labour party.

The result of this joint meeting on 8 October was a unanimous vote, after long and frank discussion, in favour of giving the DLP its choice of the two ridings, while the farmers agreed to take the other. Delegates from the labour group expressed their appreciation of the spirit of co-operation shown by the UFA delegates and chose the East Calgary riding, in which they estimated 75 percent of the labour voters resided. The West Calgary UFA delegates then endorsed Joseph T. Shaw, a Calgary lawyer, war veteran and prohibitionist, as an Independent candidate. The UFA agreed to support Irvine as the labour candidate in East Calgary, while labour agreed to support Shaw as the farmers' choice in West Calgary. It was further agreed that each of the candidates was responsible to the group that had selected him and that there was to be no co-operation in platforms but only in voting. This distinction did not make much sense, since Irvine's platform combined the UFA and labour programs, and farmers could hardly agree to vote for a candidate whose platform they found unacceptable. However, the UFA plan of co-operation between organized democratic groups, as approved at the previous UFA convention, precluded the formal setting-up of joint platforms.

Irvine started his campaign by addressing an enthusiastic overflow audience of more than 1,000 people in Paget Hall, where many were turned away. His speech was concerned mainly with an attack upon the old party system, but he made passing reference to Meighen's election proposals for protective tariffs:

> The tariff is an issue for Mr. Meighen and his masters, the manufacturers and the financial interests, but is not the issue of the common people. The issue for them is the election of

representatives they can depend upon to do their will in democratic legislation. Mr. Meighen and his friends tell us we want class government. Was there ever any greater class government than we have today with the government representing only the big interests? Mr. Bennett tries to frighten the farmers by telling them I want to free the land. There are a hundred million acres of land in this country held by speculators. The farmers believe in taxing those speculators until they either sell or cultivate the land. I want to see the land brought down to prices where it will be within the reach of the people who will use it. That is what I mean when I say that I want to free the land.

The one issue is this, that we should select and control our own representatives and through them legislate as well as vote....

The greatest danger in Canada now is the reactionary class government in power. We are at the threshold of a new age... in which our political life will be based upon the human well-being of society.

R.B. Bennett says that the Liberal party is dead. Could there be anything more dead, too, than the Conservative party? It was buried at the last provincial election. Let us now finish the job and bury the other party.[5]

Irvine revisited Acme, in the rural part of the East Calgary riding, where he had debated with R.B. Bennett in 1917. The audience remembered the incident and showed by their applause that they had not approved of Bennett's unfair tactics at that time. During the campaign it sometimes seemed as if Bennett was Irvine's opponent rather than Smith, the sitting Conservative Member, or his Liberal competitor, Marshall. Actually Bennett, now Minister of Justice in the Meighen government, was the Member for the adjoining riding of West Calgary and engaged in a close battle with J.T. Shaw, the UFA-endorsed candidate.

The *Calgary Herald*, running true to form, was Irvine's chief critic, and it tried to recreate the political atmosphere that contributed to Irvine's defeat in the same riding in 1917. This time it attempted to demonstrate that he was a supporter of the OBU. The *Morning Albertan* sprang to Irvine's defence, giving him strong support and frequently reporting his invariably successful meetings in this campaign on the front page. He also got a strong endorsement from W.M. Davidson, the paper's editor and an Independent Liberal MLA.

Irvine was under attack from the left as well as the right, and members of the Socialist Party of Canada sometimes made themselves heard at his meetings, attacking him and the Dominion Labour party for seeking "peaceful penetration" of capitalism instead of revolution. However, workers showed considerable support for Irvine. He held two large lunch-hour meetings in the CPR Ogden Locomotive Workshops, where he had formerly been employed. They were the largest meetings of their kind ever held in the workshops, and each occasion drew receptive audiences of 300 to 400 men.

Irvine's campaign successfully united farmers and labour in a common political effort, as did Ted Garland's in Bow River. In general, this was the case throughout Alberta, although there were one or two cases of disunity. In Lethbridge, for example, labour tried to rally farm labourers and sheep herders to support the Liberal party!

On election day, 6 December 1921, the farmers scored another triumph. Of the twelve Alberta federal ridings, eleven went to UFA candidates, and Irvine was victorious as the labour candidate with UFA support, receiving a majority of 1,898 votes over Smith, the Conservative candidate. R.B. Bennett expressed regret at Smith's defeat and described Irvine as a destructive and dangerous influence. Bennett had still more to regret, for about two weeks later he lost West Calgary by sixteen votes to UFA-supported candidate Joseph Shaw, on a recount.*

William Irvine spoke from the balcony of the *Morning Albertan* offices to an enormous crowd, and this was followed by a torchlight parade of his labour supporters through the streets of Calgary. Across Canada, the progressive farmers had elected sixty-

---

* Bennett and his supporters were considerably embarrassed by the fact that as a candidate running on the Meighen protectionist issue, he had distributed thousands of "Vote for Bennett" buttons that had on their reverse side the name of the American manufacturer.

five Members to the House of Commons. William Irvine and J.S. Woodsworth, who had been elected in Winnipeg Centre, were the only representatives of labour.

On Wednesday, 8 March 1922, Canada's first session of its four-teenth Parliament was convoked. Ted Garland, the UFA Member for Bow River, recorded his impressions of his first day in Ottawa:

> When I got down to Ottawa, the first man I met was Bill Irvine. Then I met Agnes Macphail, then I met Henry Spencer.* And we decided it was a lovely Sunday, and that we'd all get out and have a look at the Experimental Farm. So we all four went together on a streetcar. We had a little walk and it was a beautiful place.... It was lots of fun and when we got back to town after spending most of the day there, somebody said maybe we should go and have something to eat. And do you know, we went through our pockets and we didn't have enough money, between the four of us, to go and have a good meal. Yet we had a feeling — I think it was shared by the others — that here we had arrived in Ottawa as Members of Parliament and why didn't they have a brass band out at the railway station to greet us?[6]

As a result of the election, Mackenzie King was able to form a Liberal government, but it was in a precarious position, being short of a bare majority by one vote. Against 117 Liberals, there were ranged 117 on the other side of the House, made up of sixty-five Progressives, two Labour and fifty Conservatives. Well before the new Parliament met, King was trying to improve his position. He approached T.A. Crerar who, because of his previous parliamentary experience, had been endorsed as the leader of the Progressives, and offered Cabinet posts and more farmer-oriented

---

* Agnes Macphail was the newly elected United Farmers of Ontario Member for Grey South East, the first woman member of the House of Commons and later a member of the Ginger Group. Spencer was UFA Member for Battle River, and later a member of the Ginger Group.

policies in exchange for Progressive support in the House. It is uncertain whether what King proposed was fusion with the Liberal party, or whether the Progressives were to retain their separate identity, but Crerar did convey King's proposals to a special meeting of newly elected Progressives from the Prairie provinces, in Saskatoon on 20 December 1921. There was strong opposition from a sizable minority of the members, especially the Albertans, and eventually, because of increasing opposition from Progressive members, the idea was dropped.

Garland, who was at the Saskatoon meeting, recorded the shock felt by the more radical Progressives at the proposal:

> At that meeting in Saskatoon, Mr. Crerar said to us that he had been offered a Cabinet position by Mr. King and that Mr. King's idea was that he would rather have Mr. Crerar representing the moderate element of political thinking than Sir Lomer Gouin from Quebec, an extremely conservative Liberal, very high in business circles and a very wealthy man whose influence Mr. King was a little afraid of. Mr. Crerar wanted us to endorse his acceptance of a Cabinet position with the Liberal government before we went to Ottawa. In the opinion of our UFA group this was a terrible thing. The result was that at once we began to draw away from him — and that was the *beginning* of the later separation of the UFA group completely from the Progressive caucus. It took a couple of years to do it, but we finally withdrew because we couldn't stomach this thing. Now what happened after that was that when we got to Ottawa, we found that Sir Lomer Gouin had been installed as the Minister and Mr. Crerar had not — we had not given the necessary endorsation. Mr. King was not prepared to accept Mr. Crerar unless he could carry the sixty-five Progressives with him in a block — to have him alone was no particular help to Mr. King.[7]

As the second largest political group in the House, the Progressives were entitled by long-standing tradition to take on the task of being the official opposition. They decided not to do so, but to let the much smaller Conservative party take that role, led by Arthur Meighen. Their decision was said to be based upon their awareness of their lack of parliamentary experience. W.L. Morton agrees that this was a factor, but alleges there were deeper reasons. He says that one section of the Progressive party, represented by Crerar and the Manitobans, hoped to recapture the Liberal party for rural democracy and low tariffs, against the protectionist Liberals from Quebec and Ontario. This aim had suffered a setback with the failure of the King-Crerar negotiations, but there was still hope for an eventual coalition, Morton argues, if the Progressives refrained from forming the official opposition: "To commit the Progressive group, however, to opposition while coalition with the Liberals was still in view, would be to render the hope all but impossible."[8] He goes on to say that the decision was supported by the mainly Albertan section of the Progressives for quite a different reason, namely that they wanted to destroy the system of party government and replace it by some form of group government.

There is no evidence for Morton's second supposition and it seems highly implausible, for to have pursued this policy, it would have been necessary for the Progressives not only to refuse to be the official opposition, but also to seek some agreement with the other parties that would eliminate the role of an opposition as such. They could better have proceeded toward the goal of group government by becoming the official opposition and then playing the role in a new way.

Henry Spencer, talking about the situation years later, gave no indication that the Albertans were influenced by their theory of group government in this matter:

> We had the right to be the official opposition — we were the second largest group. Now Crerar at that time advised us not to be. I think now that that was a great mistake, that it would have been a great thing for us to be the official opposition.... But to let a minority — a third group — take over the official opposition and to let us be moved further down the House, I think was an error. But Crerar's argument was that most of

us were new members and it would be better to sit in the
House and get experience.[9]

Irvine's comment on the same situation was somewhat more
trenchant:

If the Progressive party had formed an opposition in 1922 as
their numbers entitled them to do there would have been no
cushy place for Crerar, and subsequently Forke, to go to.
Also they could not have formed an opposition without a
definite political philosophy, which they lacked. They had
nothing to warrant being the government. They had nothing
the Liberals didn't have, and I think Crerar, knowing he had
nothing, did what he could to go into the Government because otherwise he would have been snowed under. Finally,
the Progressives were all Liberals and did not wish to em-
barrass the party of their forefathers and of their first love.
As for group government, not one of them had ever heard of
it at that time.... Wood's idea of group government had
nothing to do with the breakdown of the Progressive
party.[10]

Here Irvine was excluding the Albertans from the "Progressives." After all, they were elected as UFA members and only
became Progressives by association with the larger group of
farmers from Manitoba and Ontario. He would also have ex-
empted from his strictures the four or five Progressives who
shared the largely Albertan attitudes and who were later associated with the Ginger Group. His remarks were then directed at
a group of nearly fifty farmer members who were motivated by
direct dissatisfaction with the economic policies of the Liberal
party (and, of course, the Conservatives) and had not advanced
from there to a broader criticism of Canadian society and the political system.

Irvine and the other radicals were somewhat dismayed when
they first encountered this rather inert majority. It must surely
have given Irvine occasion to question his view that people are
more firmly united by a common economic interest than by an
idea. In working with farmers' associations across Canada he had

been impressed by the enthusiasm with which they had organized for political action (in contrast with the relatively meagre performance of labour) and had failed to notice that a movement sparked by common economic interest does not necessarily give rise to a system of ideas essential to the maintenance and effectiveness of a people's movement.

Irvine's first session in Parliament must have driven this lesson home. It was expressed in homely language by Ted Garland, when asked to recall his impressions of his Progressive colleagues in the House:

> They were all fine chaps and nice fellows. We quickly realized of course that fellows like Bob Gardiner, Bill Irvine, Henry Spencer, Woodsworth, myself and a few others were different. . . . We grew together, we thought the same way. Our economic background may not have been identical but our economic thinking was, and we felt that some of the other members were not quite as . . . radical as we hoped they'd be. Good, well-living men, like Bob Forke, Tom Crerar and others — we didn't regard them as very strong and our confidence in them wasn't very strong for that reason. · Now there were some others in the House that did very well and worked very hard, but there were also some who weren't worth a hoot. From the very beginning it was clear that there was a crystallization of these forward-thinking minds — the group that afterwards, years later, become known as the Ginger Group.[11]

Both Irvine and Woodsworth were invited to sit in the Progressive caucus. Woodsworth gave their reason for refusing: "We refused this because we believe our policy is not identical with that of the farmers and if we went over with them our hands would be tied."[12] But Spencer recalled that they both attended the UFA caucus and that after a few meetings Woodsworth was too busy to do so. Spencer adds that Irvine worked with the Alberta group continuously and that they always used the room shared by Irvine and Shaw as a general caucus and conference room.[13] It was natural that Woodsworth should devote himself chiefly to labour, since not only was he elected as a labour representative but most if not all of his social and political work had been with urban workers. The contacts he had with farmers' organizations arose mostly out of his association with Irvine. Irvine, although he had been elected as a labour candidate, had had considerable farmer support and had had close relations with the UFA group, and he maintained this connection in Parliament and served both as a representative of labour and as a radical catalyst within the farmers' group.

Many of the Progressives were reluctant at first to make their voices heard in the House. Irvine had no such inhibitions and delivered his maiden speech at the first opportunity, the period set aside for debate on the address in reply to the Speech from the Throne. He spoke for one hour and forty minutes, and immediately established himself as one of the oratorical stars of the House of Commons.

Irvine argued that the parliamentary system should be changed to meet contemporary needs. The two-party system arose out of circumstances in which there were two opposing interests, but now there were more than two groups in the House and their existence was not accounted for in terms of government and opposition.

> We have a system of voting which makes it very difficult for us to receive the proper expression of the will of the people at the ballot box.... the Government represents about 41 percent of the popular vote.... They represent, in my opinion, the financial interests of this country primarily.... Then we look to the group which forms the so-called Official Opposition, and I think we may say that they also when in power represent the big interests....
>
> The third group is composed of representatives of the organized farmers....
>
> But that brings me to the consideration of the group for which I have the honour to speak this afternoon — the labour group. We are very small, and for several reasons. We are small because the great body of labour has not yet been swung into political action; we are small also because the system of voting by means of which the present government holds power with 41 percent of the total votes polled has

prevented us through its gerrymandering from receiving the labour vote that has been cast; then again, we are small because of the way we are accustomed to measure things by so many tons avoirdupois. . . . However, I wish to state that the Hon. Member for Central Winnipeg, Mr. Woodsworth, is the leader of the labour group — and I am the group. But even if we are small, I should like to say, without any presumption whatsoever, that a small living seed, however small it may be, is greater than a dead trunk, however bulky it may be. . . .

If this Parliament is to function in the highest interest of our people, it must find some way of modifying itself to correspond with the changes, which I have referred to as having taken place in the constituencies outside. Our Parliamentary system prohibits us from taking, as groups, any real active part in the government. We have a parliamentary system which presupposes only two parties. . . .[14]

Earlier Woodsworth had spoken about the growing unemployment in Canada and the lack of adequate housing for many working people. Irvine took up this theme and argued that one of the root causes of economic depressions lay in an inadequate credit system.

The greatest charge I have to make against the present government is as regards the issue of credit money. It is not necessary to say that the banks today have a monopoly of the issuing of financial credits, and the credit is usually issued in the interests of the shareholders and not for the benefit of the country. It is also issued with an adherence to the gold standard and not on a proper economic basis. The volume of credit is created and issued by the banks irrespective of demand or ability to produce. Thus we in Canada today are really at the mercy of Wall Street, whether we realize it or not. We are manipulated by them, from booms to slumps, at their convenience.[15]

After considerable elaboration on this theme, Irvine urged that in view of the fact that the Bank Act was coming up for revision at the next session of Parliament, the government should set up a committee to investigate the nature of the credit system and its bearing on Canada's industrial troubles.

This was the first of many eloquent speeches made by Irvine and he soon became one of the most active of the private members in the House. A short while later he was involved in the first of many occasions when he and Woodsworth defended the rights of labour, and Irvine's example drew some of the more radical of the UFA members into the debate. Ted Garland recalled that:

> The very first speech I made in the House of Commons was on behalf of the coal miners in Cape Breton who were involved in a strike and were in desperate circumstances, and our sympathy went out to them so much that several of our members felt impelled to get up and plead their case. And I am proud of that today, though at the time I thought: "Well, here I've come to represent farmers in western Canada, and the first thing I do is speak about miners in eastern Canada." But they were the victims of the same economic system and the same injustices, the same monopoly controls.[16]

Irvine had initiated the debate by moving the adjournment of the House for the purpose of discussing the serious crisis in the Nova Scotia coal mines, and in support of his motion he proceeded to give a complete summary of the situation and of the Liberal government's inaction and refusal to intervene. The British Empire Steel Corporation had cut the wages of its miners by 37½ percent. When the workers resisted, a conciliation board, which favoured the company position, recommended a cut of 32½ percent. The miners rejected this offer and decided to "strike on the job"; that is, to reduce production to correspond to the reduction in wages. The poverty of the workers made it impossible for them to strike in a regular fashion but their work slowdown aroused accusations of "loafing on the job" and being part of a "red element" and "un-Canadian," from the Minister of Labour, James Murdock, and the Liberal government. The miners pleaded for a Royal Commission to be established to investigate their grievances and Irvine supported this request in his speech. He was deeply touched by the plight of the undernourished, powerless miners. Woodsworth reminded the House that the position of the UFA was that the coal mines, as an essential industry, should be nationalized.

Irvine intervened several times during King's speech with rather pointed questions. He wanted to know in what way government action to settle the trouble in Nova Scotia would be countenancing sabotage: "If it is sabotage for the men to say 'We will give so much work for so much money,' is it not sabotage for the company to say 'We will give so much money for so much work'? What is the difference?"[17] T.A. Crerar brought the debate to a close by saying he had serious reservations about the wisdom of appointing a Royal Commission, and suggesting instead that the conciliation board be reconstituted. Mackenzie King, embarrassed by the critical reaction to the government's policy of inaction, hastened to accept Crerar's proposal.

Irvine had gained his point, namely to force the government to pay attention to the plight of the miners. However, the situation in Cape Breton did not come to any easy, short or happy conclusion. The conciliation board was reconstituted, but was so ineffective that the situation became even more explosive. Police were used to control the desperate miners and the minister of defence authorized the use of troops at the Dominion Coal Company. By the spring of 1923, the miners were demanding a 20 percent increase in wages, an eight-hour day, and a check-off system. The president of the British Empire Steel Corporation, addressing a closed meeting of the Sydney, N.S., board of trade, declared that it was up to them to drive the radicals out of Cape Breton or he would withdraw his capital and allow the grass to grow on the streets of Sydney.[18] He did not carry out his threat, but a year later the secretary of the United Mine Workers, J.B. McLachlan, circulated a letter to various unions describing the brutality of the Nova Scotia police in the course of their strike-breaking tactics. McLachlan was arrested and charged with "spreading a false tale." When the "tale" turned out to be true, he was convicted on the charge of sedition and sent to the penitentiary. The federal government, to save itself embarrassment, released him on parole.

The troubles in Cape Breton continued throughout the Twenties and Irvine, Woodsworth and their associates kept bringing these conflicts to the attention of the House of Commons. They established themselves as the real representatives of the working people and the defenders of labour. It is not surprising that years later, in 1938, the Cape Breton miners, District 26 of the United Mine Workers of America, were the first organized labour group to affiliate en bloc with the CCF.

Woodsworth's and Irvine's claim to be the representatives of labour, although amply justified by their actions in the House of Commons, did not go unchallenged. Liberals and Conservatives both claimed that they were not class parties and that they too represented labour. Sometimes their eagerness to prove their labour sympathies bordered on the ridiculous, as in the lengthy debate, in June 1923, on a motion to amend the law to allow both the importation and manufacture of oleomargarine in Canada. James Murdock, the Minister of Labour, in the course of arguing for the necessity of oleomargarine in the diet of the unemployed and their families, suddenly remarked: "I am rather surprised to note that the Labour party in this House is conspicuous by its absence tonight, as I think this is one of the most important questions concerning labour that has been dealt with for some time."[19] When informed that Woodsworth and Irvine were serving on the banking committee in progress at that time, he remarked: "They ought to be looking after the feeding committee."

Shortly afterwards Irvine took his seat in House and at the earliest opportunity he rose to reply to the Minister of Labour:

> ... Let me inform the Minister that I, as a representative of labour am more interested in giving to the people real good fresh butter instead of margarine, and if the best the Minister can offer them is this substitute, I am not sure that he will get a very great following from the ranks of labour. I assure him that if he does not change his attitude considerably he will have to grease labour with something better than oleomargarine.... I have discovered that on all big questions in which labour interests are really involved the Minister of Labour has not been quite so outspoken as he has been on this comparatively paltry subject. When it comes to a question of protecting the miners of Nova Scotia, he sends them guns rather than butter.[20]

As might be expected, this last sally of Irvine's brought forth vigorous protests from the Liberals and as a result the Speaker admonished Irvine to confine himself more closely to the issue. However, Irvine had already made his point and disposed of the pretensions of the Minister of Labour to be a guardian of the interests of labour.

In 1924 Irvine again clashed with the Minister of Labour, this time over the eight-hour working day. As far back as 1909, Mackenzie King, then Minister of Labour, had spoken in favour of a private member's bill calling for an eight-hour day on all federal works. He then asserted: "So far as this question has a bearing upon ameliorating the ordinary everyday life of the working people, I submit that we should in this Parliament, so far as we have the power — and we have certain powers in regard to contracts let by the government — we should do all that we can to further that end."[21] Nevertheless King proposed that the bill be sent to committee for revision. This was done and, as perhaps King intended, it never re-emerged.

Fifteen years later, J.S. Woodsworth moved an amendment to the final report of the Select Standing Committee on Industrial and International Relations. The amendment required that for all federal government works the hours of labour should be limited to eight a day and forty-eight a week and, secondly, that legislation should be enacted to bring under Dominion control such works as were advisable for the purpose of limiting the hours as above.

Woodsworth pointed out the need for acting speedily on this legislation, since there were Canadians still working twelve to thirteen hours a day, seven days a week. The Minister of Labour, supported by a number of other Liberal members, argued for proceeding slowly on any such legislation. After several repetitions of arguments of this kind, Irvine intervened vigorously:

> The amendment is in itself a very small concession to the demands of labour throughout Canada. I have been amazed at some of the things said by some hon. members in objecting to this amendment, and much more amazed at the attitude of the Minister of Labour, Mr. Murdock, who has had, I think, thirty-six years of training in the front line of labour

struggles, as he says, and there he has been initiated and understands their movement very well. Now when he gets to be a cabinet minister he promptly forgets all about that; contents himself with telling labour how much he used to fight for them.[22]

Irvine refused to accept the Liberals' argument that implementation of the eight-hour day would encroach on provincial jurisdiction. He argued that the principle had already been adopted by Parliament and that it remained simply for it to be applied to public works over which the federal government had absolute jurisdiction. He resisted the position that this would create a disturbance in local conditions and result in two "classes" of workers by insisting that the federal government was obligated to implement this policy regardless of provincial reaction or the resistance of workers who were not going to benefit from it. However, in spite of the efforts of Irvine and others, Woodsworth's amendment was defeated. It was not until 27 March 1930 that the eight-hour day was introduced for all direct employees of the federal government, by an Order-in-Council passed by the Bennett government.

Since 1906, the question of old age pensions had been raised in the House from time to time, but without leading to any definite action. In 1924, after repeated urgings from some of its own members as well as from Irvine and Woodsworth, the government decided to appoint a special committee to look into the matter and to report back to the House. Irvine was named as one of the twelve committee members, presumably representing the more radical element in the House. At least one other committee member, Joseph Fontaine, a Liberal from Hull, was strongly in favour of old age pensions.

After considerable research into the pension systems of England, Australia, New Zealand, and other countries, and a study of information obtained from thirty-one municipalities across Canada, the committee presented the following recommendations to the House on 1 July 1924: that pensions of $20 per month be granted at the age of seventy to all British subjects of twenty years' residence in Canada, and all naturalized citizens of at least fifteen years' citizenship who had completed twenty-five years of residence; that the maximum of $20 be lessened by private income or partial ability to earn; that the costs be shared equally between the provinces and the federal government; and that the government initiate the action by communicating with the provinces to ascertain their willingness to join the scheme on a voluntary basis. The committee estimated that approximately 98,850 people might be eligible and that if all received the maximum pension the federal government's share would be about $12 million.[23]

The committee's report was submitted for information and not for action and was not debated in the House. In response to a query as to whether or not the report was unanimous, the chairman replied: "It is a unanimous report of the members present at the final meeting; all the members of the committee were not in attendance." This concealed the fact that Irvine had opposed the idea that pensions should be contingent upon federal-provincial co-operation, and had moved a minority report in the committee calling for immediate federal implementation of the old age pension. His minority report did not get a seconder and was therefore not presented to the House.[24]

It was not until May of the following year that the matter again came before the House, presumably in response to some prodding from Irvine, Woodsworth and other members. This time the Minister of Labour moved that the report of the special committee of the previous year, along with communications received from the provinces, be referred to another special committee for examination and report. Questions elicited from the Minister the information that British Columbia had strongly favoured the proposal, that Quebec had refused to have anything to do with it, and that all the other provinces were giving it their somewhat unenthusiastic consideration. Clearly the government was using its old tactic of making federal and provincial relations an excuse for inaction.

Despite Irvine's protests that nothing would be accomplished by this procedure, the members of the previous committee were reappointed to the new special committee and the matter delayed while they discussed the report they had drawn up themselves the previous year. A few weeks later the special committee reported that generally it had found the provinces unwilling to co-operate and that since in the opinion of the Department of Justice pensions were a provincial rather than a federal matter, the government could do nothing more than continue to consult with provincial premiers.

Irvine immediately castigated the committee and the governments for their delaying tactics:

> I wish to express my personal disapproval of the report of the committee.... I think that this committee has been working on a wrong line. It has been endeavouring to arrive at some scheme of old age pensions that would embrace the voluntary co-operation of the provinces.... but I do not think that any member of this House will anticipate that all the provinces of Canada will agree to such a scheme anywhere this side of the next thousand years.... If hon. members will go over the replies which have come to us from the premiers of the various provinces it will be found that nearly all consider old age pensions entirely a federal matter and will have nothing to do with it. [They] point out the injustice which would come to the provinces which would not come into the scheme, and consequently if we are to pay any attention at all to the advice of the provinces, we will abandon the scheme suggested by the committee, and proceed at once with a scheme which would be entirely federal....
>
> We have been told by the chairman of the committee, Mr. Raymond, that the committee does not consider that Canada can stand the financial pressure involved in raising the money required to carry out the old age pension scheme; the committee however thinks it could be done if the provinces came in. It is surely clear that it would take the same amount of money whether the provinces came in or not, and the taxpayers of Canada are not so foolish as to imagine that they pay any less if they pay part of it through the municipalities, part of it through the provincial government and part of it through the federal government.... On the other hand, to say that we cannot afford it is a confession which I, as a member of this House, do not wish to concur in. I believe we can afford it, but if it be so that we cannot afford it, let us frankly say so and not continue making a pretence that

we are on the way to obtaining old age pension legislation by referring the whole question to a conference.[25]

Irvine moved that the committee reconsider a purely federal scheme. After further heated debate, the House voted on his amendment, which was heavily defeated by 139 to 17. A considerable number of the Progressives voted against the amendment, including, notably, Forke and Crerar.

On 9 February 1923, with less than a year of parliamentary experience behind him, Irvine introduced his first private member's bill, which recommended abolition of the death penalty in favour of life imprisonment. Irvine's motion was accepted and the bill had its first reading, following which there was, as is customary, no debate. In spite of repeated efforts, Irvine was unable to get a second reading and the bill expired undebated with the end of the parliamentary year. It was not until 10 April 1924 that Irvine's bill got its second reading. However, now its time had come and it was debated at length in the House. Irvine, in his introduction of the bill, and later in his reply to critics, took up about an hour and fifty minutes of the allotted time and made one of the major speeches of his career.

> I think you will agree with me that the time is sure to come, if it has not come already, when we shall lay aside this method of dealing with criminals, not so much in the interest of the criminals — indeed I am not going to plead in the interest of the criminal classes at all — but in our own interest we ought to abolish [the death penalty] because it is degrading and demoralizing to humanity; it is an outrage upon the finest sensibilities; and, in addition, it fails to do that thing for which we impose it, it fails to deter people from the commission of any crime. . . .
>
> In the minds of those who have not given very much thought to the subject, capital punishment is still believed to be to some extent a deterrent and it is on this ground that we tolerate it at all. . . . I think it is due to Canada as well as to this Parliament, that if the nation is going to continue to occupy the position of the avenger of blood with regard to criminals, there ought to be no doubt whatsoever about the efficacy of the system in securing the civilized end for which

we retain it. I want the Minister of Justice, if he opposes this argument, to bring the proof — not belief merely, not mere opinion, but I want him to bring the proof — that capital punishment has hindered one single criminal from committing a crime.... Nothing short of absolute proof can be accepted as an excuse for Canada retaining the death penalty and placing our nation in the position of an executioner.[26]

The Minister of Justice, Ernest Lapointe, was unmoved by Irvine's appeal. He claimed that his personal rejection of the death penalty was outweighed by his sense of duty to protect the public. Meighen and King concurred.

Irvine received substantial support from Agnes Macphail, W.C. Good, Robert Forke, T.A. Crerar, and two prominent Liberals, E.J. McMurray (Solicitor General) and George P. Graham (Minister of Railways and Canals), but it was not enough to outweigh the opinions of the Liberal and Conservative party leaders and popular sentiment. When the division was called, twenty-nine voted for the abolition and ninety-two for the retention of capital punishment.

As we have seen, even before his election to the House of Commons, Irvine was acutely aware of defects in the parliamentary system and in parliamentary procedure. He thought these were inherent in the party system and constituted roadblocks to genuine democracy. Early in his career in the House he launched attempts to bring about reform. On 12 February 1923, he moved the following resolution: "That in the opinion of this House, a defeat of a government measure should not be considered as a sufficient reason for the resignation of the government unless followed by a vote of lack of confidence." He went on to marshal an impressive array of arguments in support of his proposal:

> Parliament today, I maintain, is dominated by the Cabinet through the party caucus, and much of our boasted democratic liberty is pure theory. Theoretically, the Cabinet is responsible to Parliament, and Parliament in turn, is responsible to the people. The actual condition, however, is that the Cabinet is responsible to those who appoint it, and as the Cabinet brings forward its policies and ensures support of them by a prearranged majority, it is not in any real sense

responsible to Parliament. Of course Parliament is allowed to discuss the policies of the Cabinet, but an effective majority has been arranged for. The policies of the Cabinet have been already drawn up, they are outlined in the Speech from the Throne, and will be carried through in the manner and to the extent desired by the Cabinet, provided that the majority party is strong enough numerically to outvote the rest of Parliament.

It is contended that such a party, namely the majority or government party, represents the voice of Parliament because it is a majority. Again theoretically, this is perfectly true, but practically it is not true.... Under the conditions that exist today, members of the majority party may be compelled to vote contrary to their best thoughts and their declared principles. A system which puts a member of parliament in that position is defective both from the point of view of the mentality and morality of Parliament. The practice of Cabinet control by threat of election has a tendency to confuse the issues upon which members are called upon to decide, and it has the effect of placing them in a position which, to say the least, is at times very uncomfortable and very embarrassing....

It is commonly understood to be the practice in Canada that if a government is defeated on a matter of policy, or on a measure considered by the administration to be of importance, that such a defeat is tantamount to a vote of no confidence [which brings] the possibility of defeat and... a general election. But it has the effect also usually of defeating the measure, no matter what merit there may be in the measure, because in such a case the salvation of the government is considered first by the majority party and the measure afterwards.... This practice is not at all an aid to responsible government... it is rather a hindrance to that desirable end, for we find by this practice the principle of responsible government has been inverted. Today the individual members of the government party are responsible to the Cabinet, instead of the Cabinet being responsible to the individual members of the party. What chance has the courageous individual, who is prepared to stand up for the principle in which he believes — what political future in a party has such an individual?[27]

The ensuing debate lasted four and a half hours. Irvine received substantial support for his point of view, not, however, from either the Prime Minister or the Leader of the Opposition. Mackenzie King was alarmed by the implied threat to cabinet authority, saying it paved the way to anarchy. Meighen, although taking a calmer view than King, nevertheless wanted no diminution of government or Cabinet authority and thought that Irvine's proposal would deprive the government of its power to provide leadership. When the vote was taken, Irvine's resolution was defeated 103 to 52.

Irvine, from time to time, persisted in his attempts to make parliamentary procedure more democratic or at least more efficient. In the last year of the fourteenth Parliament he succeeded in getting Mackenzie King's and the House's agreement to set up a special committee to consider the advisability of revising the rules of the House, but the usual processes of delay brought Parliament to an end without receiving a report from the committee, and indeed it was not until March 1927 that the report was heard.

In his first four years in Parliament, Irvine had established himself as an effective thinker and speaker on all the major questions of social policy current in his day, and indeed he had shown that he was far ahead of his time in many respects. During this period, he and Woodsworth had gathered themselves a small but vigorous band of the more radical Progressives who were to constitute what was aptly termed "The Ginger Group."

The term "Ginger Group" began as a nickname to designate a group of members elected to Parliament in 1921. Although the name did not appear in the press until July 1924, it is possible and indeed likely that it was used in conversation before then. In such circumstances, it is not surprising that there is a certain amount of vagueness and ambiguity about its usage.*

---

* Members of the Ginger Group at first showed a reluctance to accept or use the nickname, perhaps because there is an earthier

We can better understand the goals of this group by looking ahead to 1935. Of the fifteen MPs who could be included in the Ginger Group, eight were in Parliament from 1921 to 1935 or later. They were Irvine, J.S. Woodsworth, G.C. Coote, R. Gardiner, E.J. Garland, D.M. Kennedy, Henry Spencer and Agnes Macphail. Throughout this time, these people shared the same radical outlook. They worked to change the structure of society and of government and to replace it with a variety of socialism akin to guild socialism. They wished to replace private ownership by public or co-operative ownership and to make government more democratic by making it more responsive to the popular will. Finally, they thought of themselves as defending the interests of urban workers and farmers against those who exploited them. For fourteen years they were a radical presence in the House of Commons and eventually they helped to create the CCF, which carried on the struggle after 1935.

The original coiners of the term "Ginger Group," whoever they were, were probably not fully aware of the significance of the people they so labelled, but they were aware of a radical and, to some, disturbing element in the fourteenth Parliament. Five of the eight mentioned were UFA MPs, while Agnes Macphail represented the Ontario farmers and Woodsworth and Irvine were, of course, labour members, although after 1926, Irvine too represented the UFA. To these core members of the Ginger Group we must add seven others: Joseph Shaw, an Albertan Independent; W.C. Good and Preston Elliott, Ontario farmers who did not serve in Parliament beyond 1925; Milton Campbell from Saskatchewan and W.J. Ward of Manitoba, who served only until 1930. These five played a somewhat temporary role in the Ginger Group, but two other latecomers stayed longer and played much more significant roles. They were A.A. Heaps, who sat as a labour member for Winnipeg North from 1925-1940, and Angus MacInnis, also a labour man (and son-in-law to J.S. Woodsworth), who served from 1930-1957.

---

meaning than the more usually mentioned one of adding to the piquancy of food. No doubt they knew of the unscrupulous practice of making a jaded nag look more lively and spirited by applying ginger or a similar substance to its rear end.

At the beginning of the fourteenth Parliament in 1922, the original members of this likeminded group were, except for Irvine, Woodsworth and Shaw, part of the sixty-four Progressives.* As we have already seen, from the very first they began to have doubts about the political acumen of their "progressive" colleagues and became increasingly dissatisfied. Their views are reflected in the pages of the *UFA*, the official organ of the Alberta farmers' organization. Irvine and other members of the Ginger Group were frequent contributors. An editorial in the tenth issue already discerned signs of disintegration in the Progressive group in Parliament, and quotes the comments of the Ottawa *Citizen* with approval:

> The United Farmers of Alberta had to enter politics largely owing to the failure of the orthodox parties to respond to the awakening public spirit of the province. But Alberta is obviously ahead of the procession in Canada. The Progressive members, with few exceptions, from other parts of the country, are little if any ahead of the Liberals in their political thinking. Nor do they manifest any marked desire to venture far ahead. Unless there is an awakening of public opinion before next session in the constituencies that elected Progressive representatives to the House of Commons, the government can have the support of sufficient Progressive members to keep them in power on Premier Mackenzie King's own terms.... Progressive party knocks at the door of the Liberal caucus may be heard all around the corridors before the end of another session. The exceptions may decide to stay out, satisfied to remain as private members for another ten years or so, until public opinion in Canada is ready for something more effective than the ins and outs and ups and downs of tariff politics. In the meantime, the independent progressives are resisting the organization of another party machine. They seem to be right. It would be

---

* Shaw, who ran as an Independent with UFA support, is sometimes counted as one of the Progressives, bringing the number up to 65. However, it is doubtful if he ever attended the Progressive caucus and he seems to have been more closely associated with Irvine and Woodsworth.

nothing more than the fifth wheel to a coach until there is a more apparent difference between Progressive and Liberal politics.[28]

At a meeting of the Progressives in Winnipeg in November 1922, Crerar pushed hard for the building of a party machine but was thwarted by the Albertans, who were supported by Agnes Macphail. They were opposed to the formation of a central organization to direct political activities, and in consequence of their action the conference unanimously agreed that any such decision must be left to the proper organization in each of the provinces concerned. They were not, however, opposed to parliamentary co-operation. In order to co-ordinate the parliamentary activities of the members from each of the provinces, an executive committee was set up, each representative on the committee to be elected by and answerable to the members in his own provincial unit. Each provincial group was to be represented by one member, with the exception of Ontario, which was granted two. T.A. Crerar promptly resigned as leader of the Progressives and ceased to play any further active part.[29] Robert Forke, a farmer and MP for Brandon, Manitoba, was elected chairman of the parliamentary executive committee and in this capacity took over Crerar's duties as leader.

The *UFA* in an editorial approved the position taken by the Albertans at Winnipeg, and again quoted the comments of the Ottawa *Citizen*:

> The Progressive party would be very little different from the Liberal party, unless it were inspired with the Alberta point of view and opposition to forming any such party is strongest among the Alberta members. . . . In the Alberta group indeed, there is evidence of a real desire to make fundamental progress. It is based too on a better understanding of economic and social questions and is backed by a more awakened electorate.[30]

Forke turned out to be little different from Crerar as a leader. He too was a western agrarian liberal who hoped to improve the agricultural and tariff policies of the Liberal Government and was more concerned with keeping the Liberals in power than with pushing for social change.

Although formally Irvine and Woodsworth were outside the struggle going on among the Progressives, they were nevertheless heavily involved. Irvine maintained close ties with UFA members. He was a frequent contributor to the UFA journal, and in the winter of 1923 he had given many weeks of his time to a membership drive among the farmers of Alberta. It is not surprising, therefore, that Woodsworth took action which sharpened and brought to a head the differences in the Progressive group. In the debate on the budget in April 1924, he exercised his right as leader of the labour group to move an amendment to the budget to reduce tariffs on the "necessaries of life, including foodstuffs, clothing and building materials." He moved that the subsequent loss of revenue be made up by: "(a) The readjustment and extension of the income tax to bear more heavily on unearned incomes; (b) A direct tax on unimproved land values, including all natural resources; (c) The institution of a graduated inheritance tax on large estates."[31]

After some inessential changes, the amendment eventually came up for debate, and although very similar to a resolution introduced by Forke a year before, because of fears that a government defeat on this issue might lead to the resignation of the Liberal government, the majority of the Progressives opposed it. Following a lively debate, the House divided on 16 May 1924: Woodsworth's amendment was defeated by 204 to 16, with the majority of Progressives voting against it. However, it is significant that thirteen of the sixteen supporting the amendment, namely Campbell, Coote, Elliott, Gardiner, Garland, Good, Irvine, Kennedy, Macphail, Shaw, Spencer, Ward and Woodsworth, comprised all of the Ginger Group elected at that time.

The dissidents were further alienated by J.F. Johnstone of Saskatchewan, who was the Progressive whip from 1922-25. Formerly a Liberal MP, he clearly retained his Liberal sympathies. When the radicals opposed paying out of public funds the expenses of a group of MPs to attend Wembley Exhibition in London, England, they were outvoted by their Progressive colleagues and discovered that J.F. Johnstone was to be one of the recipients of this public bounty. They were also perturbed by the rumour that Johnstone (who did not run in the 1925 election but returned to the House as a Liberal a year later) was secretly plotting for an arrangement of western constituencies that would promote Liberal electoral success at the expense of the Progressives.

At last, in June 1924, six of the dissidents (Campbell, Gardiner, Garland, Kennedy, Macphail, Spencer) wrote a letter to Forke in which they withdrew from the Progressive caucus and asserted their independence. The source of their discontent was twofold: a fundamental policy disagreement on economic matters and a rejection of the party system that was co-opting Progressive support to keep the Liberals in power at the expense of the Progressive constituency.

Shortly afterwards, four more Progressives, W.C. Good, P. Elliott, W.J. Ward, and G.C. Coote, joined the six. They advised Forke by letter that they were

> ...in a large measure in agreement with the statement of principles and viewpoint issued by the seceding members. In the second place, as regards the work of Parliament, we have been for a long time in active and regular collaboration with most of the seceders and believe it is our duty to continue that collaboration. For the remainder of the session, therefore, we think it better to discontinue our attendance at the Progressive caucus.[32]

It is important to note that in the first letter there is considerable emphasis upon disagreement on matters of policy as well as disagreement about political structure, while the second letter makes the point that the group had been in existence for a long time and thus disposes of the misleading suggestion made in some press reports at the time that a new group had been born with the publication of the first letter.

Other contemporary press accounts make the connection between the ten seceding Progressives and Irvine, Woodsworth and Shaw, albeit in a scurrilous fashion. Two articles in the *Financial Post*,[33] for example, asserted that Woodsworth and Irvine, with the assistance of Shaw, had seized control of the ten Progressives and were manipulating them in the interests of the "international communist conspiracy." These charges were absurd and malicious, but they do indicate that the anonymous author was aware that the so-called Ginger Group included not only the ten Progressives but also the two labour members and an Independent.*

Some historians have linked their usage of the term "Ginger Group" to particular interpretations of contemporary political movements, and in doing so have limited the group to the ten seceders from the Progressive caucus.[34] It has been contended that what lay at the heart of the dispute within the ranks of the Progressives was largely, if not entirely, a difference about political structure and that the ten seceders were "doctrinaire" (and indeed wrong-headed) opponents of the party system and adherents of the UFA theory of group government. The remaining Progressives were for forming a party structure and party discipline similar to those of the Liberals and Conservatives, to better exert influence and gain power within the parliamentary system. One might wonder why this interpretation of the split should be linked to the narrow definition of the Ginger Group. Woodsworth, Shaw and Irvine were at this time all proponents of group government and indeed Irvine was co-author of the theory and its most articulate exponent. It is also claimed that the secession of the ten brought about the disintegration and, within a few years, the demise of the Progressives as an independent political force.

The facts do not support this interpretation. At the seventeenth UFA convention, January 1925, the five UFA members who had seceded from the Progressives were faced with five UFA members who had not (L.H. Jelliff, D.C. Kellner, W.T. Lucas, A. Speakman and D.W. Warner). The issue of constituency autonomy had already been publicly discussed at the constituency level and discussions had taken place in private among the Alberta UFA MPs. The split between the UFA federal members was healed when they unanimously agreed upon a resolution that provided the basis for agreement among them and which was endorsed by the Convention:

That while differences of opinion will naturally arise on

---

* At the time of the split, the term Ginger Group was used to designate the six (or ten) dissidents, since after all it was their particular actions which were under discussion at that time, but this should not be allowed to obscure the fact that a wider group of people was involved.

specific questions, it is essential that the elected UFA representatives, having in mind the guiding principles of the organization, shall maintain their solidarity as a group.
And that recognizing their responsibility to the organization and to the farming industry, they shall at all times be seized with the important duty which devolves on them of co-operating in finding practical methods whereby they can further the aims and objects of the organizations.[35]

The enthusiastic acceptance of this resolution by the convention delegates was interpreted by the *Morning Albertan* and the *Manitoba Free Press* as the end of the Ginger Group. However, reports of the group's demise were premature. The next day the convention passed a Declaration of Principles of Political Action and this document (see Appendix A), while it makes explicit and to some degree clarifies the basic principles of the UFA, does not introduce any major change and certainly none that would disturb the UFA Gingerites. One clause clarified the question of constituency autonomy:

That each elected member who has been nominated by the UFA organization in any constituency, shall be known only as a UFA representative and shall be expected to attach himself to no other legislative group or party, and further, that each UFA member is responsible directly to his own UFA constituency organization and the organization is responsible to the UFA as a whole.[36]

There is no ground for thinking that the Gingerites would regard the last sentence of the above as compromising their beliefs. It was an invariable practice of the UFA to debate and decide questions of both principle and policy at annual conventions.

What the UFA Gingerites got was, in fact, an overwhelming endorsement of their action in leaving the Progressive caucus, and their five non-seceding colleagues were persuaded, indeed by implication instructed, by the convention to follow suit. The five UFA Gingerites were authorized to go back to the House of Commons free of any obligation to enter the Progressive caucus and with encouragement to co-operate with the Gingerites of other provinces and of the labour group and, if and when desirable, with the Progressives or any other group. They were reunited with their colleagues in pursuing exactly the policies and tactics that they had previously embarked upon. It is difficult to view the decisions of the seventeenth UFA convention as anything but a complete, albeit tactful, endorsation of the Ginger Group.[37]

The Ginger Group did not die but neither did it kill the Progressive group in the House of Commons. The latter's death was self-inflicted. After the secession of the ten Gingerites and the subsequent withdrawal of all UFA members from the Progressive caucus, there was nothing to prevent the forty-nine remaining Progressives from organizing along party lines if they so wished. They would have been only one short of the strength of the Conservative opposition and they had nine months in which to prepare for a general election. However, at the election later in the year, they were reduced to fifteen members, with eleven others joining the Liberal government as Progressive Liberals. A year later they were reduced to seven. Defeat at the polls and desertion to the Liberal party brought about the demise of the Progressives. Meanwhile the Ginger Group maintained its strength and survived as a force in Parliament until 1935 when its name was still in common use in such papers as the *Alberta Labour News*. After 1935, since eight members had been for the first time officially elected as CCF members, the title CCF displaced the more informal nickname "Ginger Group." As Kenneth McNaught says in his biography of Woodsworth:

> The "Ginger Group" was, then, the product of the preceding years of discussion; the influence of the Social Gospel, the Society of Equity and the Non-Partisan League; the reading of Ernest Gronlind's *Co-operative Commonwealth* and Edward Bellamy's *Looking Backward*; the immigration of men aware of socialist writing and action in the United Kingdom; the experience of war and post-war problems, mortgage companies and banks. It grew out of all these things, and to suggest that suddenly in 1924 or 1930 it began to take on a socialist hue is to ignore a considerable background of socialist thought including the labour element.[38]

SEVEN

Social Credit and Bank Reform

Throughout his parliamentary career and earlier, Irvine was greatly concerned with public policies in relation to money, banking and credit. One of the stated objectives of the Alberta Non-Partisan League had been to secure public ownership and control of the banks. Although he rarely wrote on such questions in the *Nutcracker* and its successors, he published a number of articles by others on these topics. Irvine himself said:

> I was first intrigued into a study of money by observing the stupidity of the old theoretic gold basis. That fetish presumed that every paper dollar and all credit could be reduced to gold. This of course was, and is, a lie. To anchor the issuance of currency to gold is to say that unless someone finds a large lump of gold somewhere, a nation must not issue either credit or currency sufficient to move the real wealth of a nation — products of factory, fishery, mining and agriculture — to meet the vital needs of the population. I therefore read and studied every book written on the highly technical matters of currency and the function of banking. This matter had been brought into the UFA locals long before Aberhart ever heard of it.[1]

Irvine's first acquaintance with the social credit theory of C.H. Douglas probably came with the publication of a series of articles which appeared in the *Western Independent* section of the *Western Farmer and Weekly Albertan*, 23 March 1921. At this time Irvine was still in New Brunswick and would not return to Calgary until

three months later, but there is little doubt that he received the
Alberta paper and read the articles.

Clearly the function of the banks was a matter of much concern
to farmers and it is not surprising that, as we have already seen,
Irvine introduced into his maiden speech a proposal that a committee be set up to inquire into the credit system in preparation
for the revision of the Bank Act to take place in the next session.*
As prelude to this proposal, he embarked upon an exposition of
the nature of credit and spoke of

> ... the recognition of real credit as created by and belonging
> to the community ... and we ... look upon credit in this re-
> spect as being a correct estimate of the ability to produce and
> deliver goods as, when and where, required. You will re-
> cognize in that statement the famous Douglas definition of
> credit.... There are two factors employed in real credit,
> namely, needs to be satisfied and ability to produce; and
> both producers and consumers are necessary in the creation
> of such credit. On this basis treasury notes could be issued
> periodically to represent real credit as it expands or con-
> tracts. There could not be any inflation as was experienced
> during the war; that would be checked by the regulation of
> prices. Such a system might be arranged on the principle of
> decentralized control. It would not operate properly in a bu-
> reaucratic system such as would likely be developed by gov-
> ernment ownership....
>
> Government ownership might not do any more than
> transfer control from an efficient autocratic corporation to a
> less efficient and possibly bureaucratic state organization.
> But by a proper decentralized system of controlling credit on
> the basis that credit is created by the community, belongs to
> the community, and should be operated by the community,

---

* The commercial banks are called chartered because they operate
under the charter or licence granted by Parliament. Charters are
renewable normally every ten years when the Bank Act, which sets
out what the chartered banks can or cannot do, is revised by Parliament.

it might be possible for organizations such as boards of trade, the Manufacturers' Association, the United Farmers, the organized labour movement, the Great War Veterans' Association, and similar bodies to handle their own credit.... We should also require to have a national clearing house. In other words, a proper democratic system of credit should be organized, a system which would provide the greatest amount of local responsibility and control consistent with that measure of unity necessary to secure efficiency...if we had a commonwealth there would be, I presume, an annual dividend of surplus national wealth to be divided amongst its citizens. That of course would be very Utopian, so Utopian that we can scarcely even mention it. But the Douglas system, to which I have referred, and which I would commend the House to study, would make it practicable to receive our dividend in the commonwealth in the form of reduced prices....[2]

Passages such as the above have given rise to the belief that at this stage of his development Irvine had rejected socialism in favour of social credit and that this phase continued for some years until he turned to socialism in the Thirties. This interpretation arises because contemporary views of social credit are coloured by the phenomenon of William Aberhart, the fundamentalist lay preacher who, under the guise of social credit, promised every Albertan $25 per month, or because we have seen thirty-six years of Social Credit government in Alberta, or because we are repelled by the disturbing aberrations of C.H. Douglas's last phase. But all these things are only marginally related to the original theories on social credit that attracted Irvine and many of his friends in the 1920s.

No two people could be further apart in their approaches to life and thought than Irvine and Aberhart. While Irvine as a pastor in the Unitarian church was attacking fundamentalism, preaching social concern and expounding the theory of evolution as one of the greatest achievements of science, Aberhart, a high school teacher and lay preacher, was proclaiming the literal truth of the Bible and the falsity of evolutionary theory and most other science. Irvine's opinion of Aberhart was expressed years later in a letter to his friend and former parliamentary colleague, W.C. Good:

> Mr. Wm. Aberhart began to sound a political trumpet. He had already a Sunday audience who listened to a very primitive form of "fundamentalism." He had read a book. The author was a British actor who expounded the theories of one Major Douglas, who showed how easy it was to have abundance for all. There was abundance for all in Canada at the moment, only people did not have the money with which to buy and enjoy that abundance. Then he went on to say how easy it was to create money. He described the bankers' technique of creating money by writing figures in a book, and giving the borrower the right to write cheques to the extent of the figures in the book. It can scarcely be imagined by anyone who did not witness it, how easily this more or less spurious analysis slipped down the throats of penniless farmers. They knew that manufacturers and wholesalers had plenty of goods on hand which the farmers wanted. They could see that money in their pockets was the missing factor, as of course it was. Now here comes a "man of God", yea verily a prophet, who promises to create the necessary money with which to buy prosperity, who promises to pay $25 a month to every adult for all time, that such money will not create a debt and will never have to be repaid. This was a plausible plea backed by the authority of Holy Scripture and nailed down by the prophet of God.... There was no attempt to explain the real basis for the creation of money, and indeed, it would not have been understood by 90 percent of the Aberhart following if he could have explained it. The people leaped after the lure like hungry fish after an attractive fly. It is well to remember that there was an actual financial problem involved in the breakdown of the economic system. Aberhart neither understood the problem nor its solution. But he was enough of a politician seeking power to exploit the situation.[3]

The nostrum peddled by Aberhart under the name of social

credit was far removed from any policy Irvine advocated, and even C.H. Douglas himself, who, although flattered by the political success of his brainchild, remarked of Aberhart:

> It would not be possible to claim that at any time the technical basis of social credit propaganda was understood by him, and, in fact, his own writings upon the subject are defective both in theory and in practicability; but he did grasp, and his audience grasped, that in the subject of the provision of effective monetary demand lay the clue to the salvation of their difficulties.[4]

When Aberhart died in 1943, and the premiership of Alberta passed to his protege, Ernest Manning, the retreat from any kind of social credit theory accelerated, so that soon social credit became a meaningless label for what was an essentially conservative government, supported by the prosperity first engendered by a war economy and subsequently by an oil boom. Even Manning, towards the close of his twenty-five years as Premier, felt embarrassed by the meaninglessness of his party's name and proposed an assimilation with other political elements under the title "Social Conservatism." He noted that Albertans were voting for Social Credit provincially and for the Progressive Conservatives federally, and concluded that:

> This fact supports the conclusion that in the national field, the Social Credit party can make its maximum contribution to the furthering of its own ideals and principles and more importantly to the well being of the country as a whole, by doing everything within its power to encourage and assist in bringing about an effective reorganization of the Progressive Conservative Party of Canada.[5]

The decline of social credit in Alberta as a movement was hastened by the adherence of a group of Alberta social crediters to the last phase of C.H. Douglas's career when, just before the war, his monetary theories fell into the background and he adopted an extreme form of individualism incompatible with most forms of social co-operation, combined with a demand for the abolition of the secret ballot and an anti-semitic theory of world conspiracy.

Irvine himself felt nothing but revulsion and disgust for this aspect of Douglas and for those social crediters in Alberta who echoed him.

The origins of social credit were very different from its conclusion. It was originally an offshoot of guild socialism and most of C.H. Douglas's early writings on the subject first appeared in A.R. Orage's weekly review *The New Age*. Under Orage's editorship, this review had such celebrated contributors as H.G. Wells, George Bernard Shaw, Upton Sinclair, Arnold Bennett, and many other well-known writers. The paper had a small circulation but it was read by the intelligentsia of British radicalism and was a powerful influence on their thought. Under Orage's guidance it became the unofficial organ of guild socialism, which tried to find a middle way between the state socialism of the Fabians and the anarchism of the Syndicalists. C.H. Douglas, who was himself a guildsman, entered into collaboration with Orage to develop the theory of social credit which was conceived by them as a new and better means of achieving the ultimate aims of guild socialism. The Douglas-Orage Scheme, as it was sometimes called, aroused considerable controversy in the ranks of guild socialists, particularly from G.D.H. Cole, which eventually led to the social crediters splitting off from the main body. The chief impetus behind the development of social credit was the growing economic crisis and the accompanying maldistribution of income.

Douglas's monetary theory intrigued Irvine, and this was the only aspect of Douglas's theory that he ever mentioned.[6] In adopting this monetary theory, he did not switch from socialism to social credit, because he did not see the two as incompatible. He merely added a method of socializing credit to the particular style of socialism he had already espoused, which was akin to, but not identical with, guild socialism.

Irvine's scepticism about the merits of state ownership was not anti-socialist, but arose from his adherence to a certain kind of socialism, which seeks to express itself in popular and co-operative forms rather than in highly centralized institutions. That social credit was an addition to, rather than a substitute for, his basic socialist beliefs is shown by the fact that in his maiden speech in Parliament he expounded on the concept of group government and the co-operative commonwealth and concluded with this quotation from the manifesto of the British Labour party:

> We must be sure that what is presently to be built up is a new social order, based not on fighting but on fraternity; not on the competitive struggle for the means of bare life, but on a deliberately planned co-operation in production and distribution for the benefit of all who participate by hand or brain; not on the utmost possible inequality of riches, but on a systematic approach toward a healthy equality of material circumstances for every person born into the world; not on an enforced dominion over subject nations, subject races, subject colonies, subject classes, or a subject sex, but in industry, as well as in government, on that equal freedom, that general consciousness of consent, and that widest possible participation in power both economic and political, which is characteristic of democracy.[7]

At this time, Irvine's vision of a socialist society was one made up of co-operating groups of producers, with the elimination of the exploitive and parasitic classes, and the avoidance, as much as possible, of centralized bureaucracies. He saw social credit as a device for regulating the economy within the framework of the co-operative commonwealth. When speaking at a federal election campaign meeting in Edmonton in 1935 on behalf of CCF candidates Mary Crawford and Elmer Roper, Irvine is reported as saying:

> As the first step, the CCF would socialize the financial instruments of this country. But the CCF does not believe that social credit will be sufficient to solve all the problems. Mr. Irvine said that while he believed in social credit he believed also in social justice, which was infinitely more important.[8]

On the other hand, as late as 1945 he wrote: "Those who insist that a mere change in monetary policy will remove all the economic ills of society are no more in error than those who think that the evils can be removed without a change in financial policy."[9] Irvine's position on the relation of social credit to socialism was largely shared by his colleagues in the Ginger Group, although usually he was their most articulate spokesman on monetary questions.

In response to the deepening depression of the Thirties, a significant number of theorists were beginning to challenge economic orthodoxy, and Irvine and others were well aware of this. In 1935, he said in the House:

> I direct the attention of this House once more to the analyses and the mathematical demonstration of Major Hugh Douglas, of London, who I think has shown more thoroughly than any other economist of his time, the scarcity of money and the causes of that scarcity. But he is by no means the only one who has demonstrated that fact. Foster and Cutching have demonstrated it in the United States; Kitson, Keynes, Right Hon. Reginald McKenna, and numerous others have proved beyond a shadow of a doubt to every intelligent student of the question that there is not sufficient money in circulation at a given time to buy those goods on the shelves at the prices at which those goods are marked, and that while that is so, those goods cannot be distributed.[10]

Social credit grew in the minds of a few intellectuals in England, but it spread among all classes and to all of the English-speaking world and beyond. In England it sparked a movement among the unemployed, John Hargrave's Green Shirts, and it to some extent penetrated the labour movement, although officially rejected by the leadership. It found fertile ground in Alberta where, long before Social Credit came on the scene, there had been widespread discussion and deep interest in monetary questions. Interest in monetary reform was not confined to farmers but was strong among urban workers. The Alberta Federation of Labour demanded that advocates of Douglas's social credit should be given the opportunity of presenting their views to members of the legislature, and the railway workers formed a strong social credit centre at the Ogden workshop in Calgary.[11] Social credit was thought of as a genuine grassroots radical movement.

Immediately after the 1935 provincial election, when Aberhart's Social Credit party took fifty-six of the sixty-five seats, entirely eliminating UFA and labour candidates, the *Alberta Labour News*, which had supported the UFA-CCF, ran the following editorial:

> It would be hypocritical to say that Thursday's result causes us no disappointment. Labour's loss is a matter of serious regret and discouragement.... But an examination of the returns reveals very clearly the fact that it was not a knowingly reactionary vote. Indeed it was a radical vote. It was a vote that was seeking to find expression in the proposals that appeared to offer the most striking challenge to the present social order. The labour vote went Social Credit. It went that way because the people were seeking to find a more immediately effective means of voicing a protest against things as they are.
>
> Despite the fact that the labour and UFA candidates who were committed to the policies of the CCF were not elected, it was not an anti-CCF vote. Because the CCF was not organized for provincial purposes, a great many supporters of the movement felt no obligation to support candidates who as individuals were committed to the CCF. The electors were trying to hit as hard as they could at things as they are and they felt that on the provincial field the Aberhart movement offered the best opportunity to do it.
>
> What of the future? Well, the *Labour News* believes that many of the newly elected members of the legislature are sincere men who are honestly seeking to bring about a better social order. That being the case their future course is inevitable. If they continue the study of economic realities which they have started, they must come to the conclusion that the remedy for what ails us is not a new form of superficial treatment but the removal root and branch of the cause from which all our ills spring. And although Mr. Aberhart has expressed some opposition to the CCF philosophy, the *Labour News* here predicts that the Social Credit movement will move more to the left than to the right, and that many of the new members of the legislature will, if they take their task seriously, find themselves in the CCF camp before very long.[12]

This CCF attitude toward the social crediters as fellow radicals (albeit misguided ones) continued for several years and is expressed in a pamphlet produced by Irvine in 1939 entitled *Let Us Reason Together*:[13]

> Social Credit and CCF theory may well be forgotten momentarily, until it is clearly seen that the people who support these two organizations in Canada are the only people who really want to achieve fundamental economic change. Moreover, the people who vote for the representatives of these two organizations in reality want to reach the same general economic objective.... Meanwhile, however, the people who desire identical objectives are being divided into hopeless minorities. And this situation cannot be altered unless and until we arrive at that happy point when we are disposed to reason together.... It may be truly said that it was the hope of economic security too long deferred which drove those who supported the UFA to turn to Social Credit in search of a shortcut to their desires. It was the UFA, now out of action as a political entity, which helped to formulate the principles upon which the CCF was launched. The fact of the matter is that it was the people who formed the labour unions and who composed the organized farmers' movement who gave birth to the radical desires which now find expression even if inadequate in the Social Credit and CCF movements....

The CCF refused to join the Independent Party, which was the "Defeat Aberhart" coalition formed by the Conservatives and Liberals in 1937. Many influential ex-members of the UFA legislature actively participated in the coalition and the refusal of the CCF to join this negative crusade cost them the votes of many former UFA supporters in the election of 1940.

The Communist party also, at this time, considered Social Credit to be a movement on the left, and it went even further than the CCF in this regard. Orvis Kennedy, the Social Credit candidate in a federal by-election in Edmonton in 1938, was elected with the open support of the Communist party. The support was gladly received by the Social Credit leaders and enthusiastically acknowledged at a victory rally at which Social Credit leaders and

Communist leaders appeared on the same platform. The victory celebration took place at the committee rooms of the successful Social Credit candidate who was later to become the national organizer of the Social Credit party. Jan Lakeman, the Communist leader in Alberta at that time, was called to the platform to acknowledge the thanks tendered to him by the Social Credit leaders for his support. The *Edmonton Journal* reported the event:

> Others who addressed the cheering crowd at the Kennedy headquarters were N.B. James, MLA for Acadia, Leslie Morris, Toronto, national secretary of the Communist Party of Canada, Hon. E.C. Manning, provincial secretary, and Hon. Lucien Maynard, Minister of Municipal Affairs.... Leslie Morris, who said he happened to be in Edmonton working with Jan Lakeman in the campaign, declared that people all over Canada will view the Social Credit victory with pride and enthusiasm. "It's a national victory for all who stand for a free, progressive, democratic Canada," the Communist secretary said.[14]

However, when Aberhart died in 1943, and his lieutenant E.C. Manning took the reins of government, Alberta was beginning to bask in the sunshine of wartime prosperity, the Social Credit party was on the road back to orthodoxy and its radical ideology was beginning to wither away. The Independent party was also withering away, leaving the CCF as the only real political threat to the Social Credit government.

Manning accordingly entered the 1944 election campaign presenting Social Credit as a solid sensible free enterprise party guarding Alberta from the socialist excesses of the CCF. The CCF made a brave effort. It doubled its popular vote over that of 1940 to 70,000 and gathered in 25 percent of the total vote cast in the province, but it elected only two members to the Legislature. From now on the battle lines were clearly drawn and there could be no doubt that Social Credit had become a right-wing political party.

Meanwhile, Irvine had been reassessing the merits of social credit as an accurate analysis of the capitalist system. By 1934, he was aware that C.H. Douglas had moved away from any sympathy that he may have had with socialism, but Irvine still thought that Douglas's monetary theory could be used by socialists. In a letter to Irvine in which their mutual concern with social credit is discussed, W. Norman Smith urged Irvine to write to Douglas to clear up certain questions:

> The point is, one may accept the soundness of certain principles and yet not agree that *only* credit needs to be socialized. Douglas himself has stated that his proposals are not incompatible with nationalization of industry. That, I should say, is contrary to his taste but not invalidated by his theorem.[15]

By 1936, Irvine had read certain socialist critiques of social credit, particularly a pamphlet by John Strachey,[16] but it was not until 1939 that these changes in his point of view became publicly recorded and then, oddly enough, the arguments are set forth in his pamphlet, *Let Us Reason Together*:

> There can be no question that in spite of the common objectives of the two parties . . . the points of difference are fundamental. To begin with, official Social Credit holds as the very keystone of its economic edifice that the existing financial system always tends toward a deficiency of purchasing power. In fact, shortage of purchasing power is regarded as a permanent or chronic condition. While the CCF agrees that shortage of purchasing power is part of the phenomena of a trade depression and that there should be means of increasing consumers' incomes at such a time, we contend that this shortage is not permanent but rather a feature of a depression. For we note that during the boom time which usually precedes a depression, there is a surplus of purchasing power over prices — a fact which cannot be denied and which blocks the way to the conclusion that the financial system leads to a chronic deficiency of purchasing power.
>
> The CCF readily agrees with Social Credit that purchasing power should be increased in proportion to the increase in production. The only safe basis on which to issue new money is that of the actual wealth on hand in the form of goods, or on the wealth about to be created. With such a system of managed currency, which we have not got today, it would be possible to stabilize price levels.

Irvine goes on to demonstrate that Douglas's theory regarding the shortage of purchasing power does not fit the realities of contemporary economics:

> Everyone must know that the present producing mechanism has not been geared to serve the needs of consumers, but rather has been and is geared to the exclusive purpose of making profit for the owner. And it does what it was designed to do. The same mechanism geared by public ownership to supply consumers as the reason for its operation is what is required. Then all profits will be distributed as wages, and when all profits are thus distributed the money in existence will buy all consumer goods, and what is more the consumer will get the goods.... It will be seen then that the whole analysis of the modern economic problem by Social Credit is financial and the sole remedy proposed is financial. The CCF on the other hand, while not overlooking the part that finance must play in the rebuilding of an economic system in which poverty will not be known, sees the imperative necessity of going far beyond that if the ultimate objective is to be reached....

Only when more essential economic factors came under CCF control could financial policy be successfully worked out. Because of these and other important considerations, the CCF policy was:

1. To nationalize the financial institutions. For an instrument as essential to the economic life of the community as money is should be not only public property, but should be used by the public to mitigate the evils of capitalism during the transition period between capitalism and the co-operative commonwealth, and also used to speed up the transition.

2. That the creation of new money should at all times be made in the interest of the people as a whole and not as now, when it best suits the interest of those who monopolize the creation of money for private profit. We hold that bankers and governments can't both have the right to create and control money. If bankers have a monopoly of money they will create it when they like and for their own monetary advantage. If the government which is the people controls money, then

money will be made and used to serve the people, if, as, and when required by the people.

Social Credit is particularly hazy on this point of public ownership. It asserts that it is opposed to government or public ownership of financial institutions. But if the banks still retain their power to create money then a Social Credit government would have no more control over money and its creation than other governments have. If, however, a Social Credit government takes the power to create money into its own hands by commanding the bankers to do what the government wants them to do, then that is nationalization and finance would under such an arrangement become a government monopoly. But since the Social Credit party renounce and denounce nationalization and reiterate that bankers will still run the money system under a Social Credit regime, then we fail to see why there is any need of a Social Credit government since the banks are already in command of finance.

It is apparent that not only has Irvine made a reassessment of social credit but he has moved towards the acceptance of state ownership as a necessary part of a socialist or co-operative commonwealth.

In an address he gave in 1933, he speaks of the kind of property that should be taken out of private hands and made public:

.... property which brings to its possessor tribute from the labour of other men, property which is the source of rent, interest or profit.... This includes our abundant national resources, coal and oil deposits, timber and minerals, mines, mills and factories and the social credit resources of the country.... Under the co-operative commonwealth these things would certainly not be owned by private individuals. The object of socialism is to make the means of wealth production, distribution and exchange the common property of the people, to organize national industry under co-operative control as a public service for national benefit instead of private control for profit.... If it is good business to own and operate our school system, water supply, power plant and telephone exchange, why would it be bad business to have our milk or bread supplied under the same principle? . . . If it didn't sound so simple I would like to say that is all that socialism means — the operation of industry without profit, rent or interest as a public utility.[17]

Throughout his years of involvement with social credit theories, Irvine continued to hold a basically socialist position. He wanted to help build a co-operative commonwealth in which the producers of the country's wealth owned and controlled the means of production by one arrangement or another and where production was carried on to meet the needs of all and not for private profit. After his abandonment of the central tenets of Douglas's social credit, Irvine still maintained that an understanding of the workings of the financial system was essential for making the transition from a capitalist to a socialist society. When they were in the House of Commons, Irvine and his colleagues in the Ginger Group attempted to educate their fellow members by clearing away some of the mysteries surrounding money, banking and credit. It was not an easy task. As Irvine himself said: "Teaching economic sense to some people is about as difficult as teaching a hippopotamus to ride a bicycle."

During his first term in Parliament, the revision of the Bank Act and the reform of the banking system, including the socialization of credit, was Irvine's main although by no means his only endeavour. He had raised the matter in his maiden speech and a few weeks later he moved a resolution:

> That, in the opinion of this House, a representative Parliamentary Committee should be appointed to investigate the basis, the function and the control of financial credit, and the relation of credit to the industrial problems.[18]

Irvine was requested by the Prime Minister to hold over his resolution until the Minister of Finance was present in the House. Not surprisingly, it did not appear again that season. The fourteenth Parliament prorogued on 27 June 1922, and its second session did not commence until 31 January the following year.

Irvine took advantage of this interval to make his first visit home to Shetland after an absence of fifteen years. During his visit, he participated in the Labour party's campaign in the British general election on 15 November. The result of the election was the formation of a Conservative majority government in place of the previous Liberal one and the rise of the Labour party, for the first time, to the role of His Majesty's Opposition. Irvine also found time to meet and discuss monetary theory with Major C.H. Douglas.

Irvine returned invigorated to Ottawa to once again call for an inquiry into banking and credit. He resubmitted his resolution of the previous year and spoke at length in its support, adding some lively illustrative material:

> In the city of Calgary we require a new post office, not a political post office but a real post office. Political parties have, for some time, as an election talk, been promising to build a post office at Calgary.... We have the spot of ground on which we want to set the post office. We have in Calgary, or can secure, the material out of which the post office would have to be built. We have in Calgary the labour walking the streets, doing nothing, looking for an opportunity to build the post office. We are renting from private institutions offices for public purposes to the extent of $50,000 yearly. We therefore need the post office; but although we have the place upon which the post office would rest very solidly, the material out of which to build it, and the need which would save us $50,000 a year in rent alone, we cannot build the post office because, it is said, "We have no money."
>
> Let me give you a parallel illustration. I will take you out to a river bank and I will show you a tribe of Indians sitting on the river bank, disconsolate and distressed. I approach them and I ask the chief: "What is the matter?" "Oh," he says, "we cannot fish and we cannot hunt because we have no money." I say: "Man, you have lots of fishing tackle, and I see there are fish in the stream. You have lots of guns and ammunition, and I can see there is plenty of game in the bush. Why do you not fish and hunt?" "Oh yes," says the chief, with tears in his eyes, "we have lots of fishing material

and there are lots of fish; we have lots of ammunition and there is plenty of game; but you know we cannot fish and we cannot hunt because we have no money." We would promptly send that whole tribe to the asylum; but ... let us all go along with them, because we are doing precisely the same thing in Canada as that hypothetical tribe of Indians would be doing by taking such a stupid attitude as that.[19]

This time Irvine's efforts met with a measure of success. After some debate — in which he was supported by Spencer, Garland and Speakman — the Minister of Finance, W.S. Fielding, suggested an amendment to Irvine's motion by which the investigation would be carried out by the Standing Committee on Banking and Commerce. This Irvine and his supporters accepted, and the amended motion was passed.

The committee was a large one with a total membership of eighty-nine, although the quorum was set at twenty-one. Besides Irvine and Woodsworth, among the more radical of the members were Agnes Macphail, Spencer, Speakman, Coote, Good and Shaw. The committee had altogether some fifty sessions, spread over a period of 104 days, sometimes meeting morning, afternoon and evening, and frequently running concurrently with the sessions of the House of Commons. The committee gave Irvine practically a free hand in choosing witnesses to appear before it. Altogether there were some twenty-three witnesses and the report of the sittings took up some 1,036 pages of the *Journal* of the House of Commons for 1923.

The committee refused, however, to provide travelling expenses in the case of two of Irvine's witnesses from outside Canada, C.H. Douglas and Henry Ford. Douglas eventually came with expenses paid partly by contributions made by Irvine and his friends, and partly by probably more remunerative invitations to speak in the United States. Henry Ford at that time was interested in monetary reform and had written in his own newspaper, the *Dearborn Independent*, on this subject. For publicity reasons, Irvine and his friends wanted him to come to Ottawa and give his views to the committee. In order to persuade Ford to come, Irvine made a trip to Dearborn. He travelled by rail on his MP's free pass. In the smoking room on the train, a number of businessmen were discussing the work of the committee, and one of them remarked bitterly that there would have been no such investigation of banking if it had not been for that "ignorant son of a bitch Bill Irvine of Calgary." After they had practically exhausted the subject, one of them turned to Irvine and asked him what he thought about it. He replied, "Well, I'm that son of a bitch you fellows are talking about," and attempted to teach them some basic principles of banking with some degree of success. At Dearborn, Irvine met Ford only to discover that he had become preoccupied with the notion of running for President of the United States, and he had also, to Irvine's disquiet, developed a nasty strain of anti-Semitism.

On his return to Ottawa, Irvine worked tirelessly on the committee. Although there were a number of other active participants in the enquiry, Irvine was without doubt the chief interrogator. A professor of economics from the University of Saskatchewan was called as a witness because Henry Spencer once heard him give an address that seemed to be critical of the gold standard, but when Professor Swanson appeared before the committee and the chairman asked him: "Is it your view as a student of economics and banking that any instrument used for effecting exchange or in currency must have behind it some redemptive scheme?", Swanson replied: "Absolutely; and ultimately it must have behind it the standard of value of the country, namely, gold." When urged by the chairman to ask a question of this witness, Irvine said: "The professor has presented such orthodox views on that matter that it is not worthwhile. Perhaps it would be superfluous for me to have him reiterate what we have heard one hundred times already."

Irvine did in fact ask Professor Swanson a few more questions, getting the expected orthodox replies, so that he soon desisted. It was so unusual for Irvine to do so little interrogation of a witness that later one of the committee twitted Irvine on his restraint. Irvine retorted "Well, we got hold of a lemon and I did not want to squeeze it."[20] More usually, however, Irvine subjected the proponents of orthodox monetary doctrines to a relentless cross-examination, and the ignorance of several leading bankers about the financial system of which they were supposed to be the chief operators was repeatedly exposed.

A mixed group of monetary reformers also appeared, foremost among them C.H. Douglas himself, who spoke less persuasively than he wrote, and his presentation at Ottawa in April 1923 was no exception. There was also Professor Irving Fisher from Yale University, one of the most brilliant of American economists who, among other achievements, had applied mathematics to economics and was the inventor of the price index. Fisher held that the rate of circulation of money as well as the volume was important in terms of purchasing power, that both had their effects upon prices and should be used to control the ups and downs of the economy. Fisher, as the better-known J.M. Keynes acknowledged, was the progenitor of the theory that governments ought not only to create money but that they ought to ensure its use by spending it — at least in times of economic stagnation.

In response to a question from Irvine, Fisher said:

> I believe that a good banking system should serve the community not only in supplying loans in a decent way where anyone can get them who has the wherewithal, but also in preventing an upset in the merchant's calculations that comes from inflation or deflation.

In response to a statement by a previous witness that the remedy for hard times is economy and hard work, Fisher said:

> It is all right as far as it goes. But it is not *the* remedy. It is only *a* remedy and a small one at that. The source of hard times is the unstable dollar, inflation and deflation, the fact that debts are interfered with and people made bankrupt and concerns lose their profits, and have to discharge workmen, and you have unemployment and dislocation of business. If you can get rid of inflation and deflation you get rid of hard times.[21]

Despite the fact that the banking and credit inquiry gave Irvine and the other radicals a field day, it was in some ways a great disappointment to Irvine. The committee heard plenty of evidence, but never got down to sorting it out, discussing it, and arriving at conclusions which would be applicable, for instance, to the revision of the Bank Act. The committee in effect reported to Parliament that they had heard evidence and had examined witnesses, but that they were not able to complete their enquiry.

Irvine still hoped that the facts and theories brought forth would seep through and influence the MPs faced with a revision of the Bank Act, but this was not to be the case. In June 1923, the Bank Act came before the House of Commons for revision and renewal. The Minister of Finance was resolved to renew the Act virtually unchanged for a further period of ten years. Irvine complained to the House:

> The evidence taken before the committee ... in relation to the bill under discussion, has not been considered by that committee. I presumed that the evidence was taken in view to amending the Bank Act, but I discover now that it was merely taken as a gesture, seemingly to appease the public. But let me assure the public that whether the evidence was of value or not it has had no effect whatsoever upon the revision of the Bank Act, indeed it has not been considered at all in that connection.[22]

The only important revisions were proposed by the group of radical independents together with the labour group. These were voted down one after another by the solidly united votes of the Liberals and the Conservatives. The radicals tried to play for time by calling for a renewal of the Bank Act for one year only, in the hope that this would give the committee time to complete its deliberations. The amendment was made by Speakman and seconded by Forke; Irvine spoke to it at length, emphasizing the dangers of continuing for another ten years with an inadequate Bank Act. He foresaw an industrial crisis of unprecedented proportions if adequate safeguards were not implemented to protect investors in financial institutions. Nevertheless, all the amendments put forward by the radicals were voted down and the Bank Act was renewed for ten years.

Irvine's prophesy foreshadowed the crash of 1929, but there was a shorter reckoning when, within twenty-eight days of renewing the Bank Act, the Home Bank collapsed, and 60,000 depositors lost their savings. Irvine tried to bring home to the House the human cost of this failure, by describing the effect upon Blairmore, a small mining town in southwest Alberta:

> Approximately 500 accounts, aggregating $190,000, were lost in the Home Bank failure in Blairmore alone. Now fifty of those accounts were in the names of little school children. Just think of the lesson which comes to young Canada from that! A banking system that is heralded as the best in the world walks off with the savings of little children! ... Ten widows lost all their savings and insurance moneys in the failure, in this same town.... Surely we are not going to let this opportunity pass of coming to the assistance of these widows who have lost all their means through the incompetence of Parliament in years past — through the carelessness of the representatives of the people. But this is not all. At this same branch there were 190 savings accounts in the names of working girls and married women. Two hundred and fifty accounts were in the names of miners.... The Blairmore school district, which sustained a loss of $10,000, may be forced to close its schools, many workers that had saved some of their earnings through years of toil, and were depending upon these savings to carry them through periods of unemployment and other difficulties find themselves practically penniless and in distress....
>
> ... a Parliamentary committee should be appointed immediately to investigate the Home Bank failure, with a view to discovering any weaknesses in the Bank Act which may be amended to prevent a similar occurrence; to devise some means of protecting depositors generally, and to make recommendations as to the possibility of saving the Home Bank depositors from loss.[23]

Irvine in the course of this speech frequently reminded the government and the House of its delinquency in passing the Bank Act without substantial revision and argued that the banks could not be trusted to police themselves nor to report honestly on their own state of health: "A bank report in one month may prove the bank to be in a healthy state, while the next month it closes its doors, and the auditors discover that the bank has been in a bankrupt condition for a decade."

Irvine then referred to a pamphlet published by the Bankers' Association, in which it claimed that since the Bank Act was reviewed and renewed only a few months previously, everything in the banking system in the future would be on a sound basis.

> ...the Bankers' Association endeavours in this pamphlet to establish confidence on a false basis, and I have noticed also that a considerable section of the press, simultaneously with the issuing of this pamphlet, came out with editorials making a plea that the Bank Act, the dear Bank Act, should be given another trial. Now I recall an incident of my early boyhood. I remember seeing a couple of youths trying to get two roosters to fight; they succeeded, and one of the roosters was severely beaten. He ran to his own backyard around the barn, and got up on that old straw stack among the hens and he crowed and crowed as if he had been the master of all the henneries of the universe. Well, I would characterize this pamphlet as the cock-a-doodle-do of the Bankers' Association.

Irvine then demanded reimbursement to Home Bank depositors and an immediate amendment of the Bank Act to prevent another such occurrence.

Since the government and indeed the Conservative opposition were on the spot, the excellence of Irvine's oratory and the soundness of his arguments prevailed — the same arguments that a few months before had been characterized as those of "a Bolshevik financier who wanted to start a paper mill down in Ottawa to turn out bank notes."[24] Perhaps for this reason, Irvine's resolution was subjected to amendment and rephrasing by F.S. Cahill, a Liberal member who, instead of referring the matter to a special parliamentary committee, referred it to the Select Standing Committee on Banking and Commerce. Nevertheless, it was substantially the same as Irvine's, who withdrew his resolution and accepted the amended version, which was carried by a vote of 133 to 27.

A few months later, on 7 July 1924, J.A. Robb, the acting Minister of Finance, moved an amendment to the Bank Act that provided for the appointment of an Inspector General of Banks, and which gave him the power to inspect any bank, head office or branch, at his discretion and to make a thorough examination of all its affairs, his costs to be recovered by an assessment levied yearly on the banks. This was passed with little opposition.

Meanwhile, the Committee on Banking and Commerce had discovered that the Bank Circulation Redemption Fund did not operate as an insurance fund as had been assured. A bank that failed could only take out of the fund what it had put in, in order to redeem its banknotes, which had first claim on its assets. The Home Bank had about $2 million of its bank notes in circulation at the time of its bankruptcy, but as it had only $100,000 in the fund to fall back on, the depositors had to make up the difference. When the liquidation was finally completed, these depositors recovered only about 35 percent from the bank's assets, while another 35 percent was provided under the Home Bank Depositors Relief Bill, which cost the taxpayers $5,454,000.[25]

Henry Spencer tried to rectify this situation by moving that the fund be changed into an insurance fund, so that the depositors would not have to bear responsibility for the bank's paper money, and he further proposed that the banks carry the full cost of this protection, since, after all, they had the privilege of being able to print legal currency at a tariff of only 1 percent, while loaning it out at a lucrative 7 or 8 percent. Objections were raised to this proposal on the grounds that it was unreasonable to expect a well-run, solvent bank to pay for the mistakes of a failed bank, and Spencer's amendment was voted down.

A further opportunity to move towards bringing some sort of order and government control into Canada's banking system came when, at a session of the Select Standing Committee on Banking and Commerce, Irvine and others proposed that the Committee recommend in their sixth report to the House, "that the order of reference be enlarged so as to embrace the study and consideration of the purpose, organization and operation of some type of properly administered central or reserve bank."[26] The proposal was subsequently defeated in the House by a vote of 109 to 32. The radicals did enjoy some short-term victories, however. Because of their efforts, a government audit and strict government supervision of banking procedures had been established, so that the Home Bank failure was the last of its kind in Canada. By contrast, in the first years of the Depression, there were more than 4,000 bank failures in the U.S.

Around this time, Irvine was further involved in banking questions, but outside of Parliament. At the sixteenth annual convention of the UFA, a resolution was sponsored by George Bevington and others, calling for the UFA provincial government to make application for a Dominion charter to allow it to set up its own bank. To the surprise of some of his old friends, such as Bevington and James and Neil East, Irvine strongly opposed this resolution. He was reported in the *UFA* as follows:

> Mr. Irvine contended that a provincial bank, organized upon the same basis as the existing chartered banks, would give exactly the same financial results as these banks gave, because it would be bound by exactly the same conditions. Government ownership was a doubtful remedy for anything. While the provincial government might own the bank, the Dominion government would exercise control over its operation and would tie the hands of the provincial government. The bank would be under the necessity of operating under a Bank Act which was really a creature of the bankers.
>
> Mr. Irvine said to establish a provincially owned bank would be like placing a new engine on an old track — its destination would be exactly the same as that of any other engine, so long as the direction of the track remained the same. "For this reason I would fight your provincial bank as sincerely as I would fight your Bank of Montreal," he declared.[27]

Bevington made a spirited attack on Irvine's argument, but the convention sided with Irvine (and with Henry Wood, who endorsed Irvine's views in this case). Some of Bevington's criticism struck home; Irvine himself was later to use similar arguments in favour of nationalization. Others were based on a misunderstanding of Irvine's meaning, yet Irvine's main criticism of the proposed provincial bank stood, namely, that the provincial government did not have sufficient authority or power to really control and direct banking policy in the right direction. Ten years later, Irvine was to make a similar criticism of Aberhart's proposals and subsequent events proved him to be correct.

EIGHT

Defeat and Victory

The fourteenth Parliament terminated in June 1925 with the election to be held on 29 October. Irvine faced a difficult situation. Constituency boundaries had been changed since the previous election. In Irvine's case at least, the changes amounted to gerrymandering. He had been elected in 1921 on a combination of labour and farm support but the new boundaries cut off most of his rural support and left him with a potential 3,000 labour voters.[1] Furthermore, W.M. Davidson, the editor of the *Calgary Albertan*, who had been elected as an Independent Liberal to the provincial legislature, now decided to run for the federal house and was nominated as the Liberal candidate for Irvine's constituency, East Calgary.

As has already been noted, Davidson was a friend of Irvine's and the *Albertan* had given Irvine considerable support during the 1921 election campaign. Moreover, on 1 January 1925, the *Western Farmer & Weekly Albertan* (a rural subsidiary of the *Albertan*) announced that William Irvine MP had been appointed editor. There followed a glowing tribute to him which concluded:

> All that is necessary to attain success in this new venture is the cordial co-operation of all those who have the farmer's movement at heart and who will work for the abolition of all that breeds discord and envy within the nation and in our public affairs, and to adopt that spirit which will introduce "Goodwill among men." Let us hold ever aloft that ideal.[2]

However, there was not much goodwill expressed in the political attacks which the *Albertan* made upon Irvine during the election campaign, these being clearly inspired by the fact that he and Davidson were rival candidates. By 1 October, the names of William Irvine and J.H. Ford had disappeared from the masthead of the *Western Farmer and Weekly Albertan*. A hard, bitter struggle ensued between Irvine, Davidson and Davis, the Conservative candidate.

In the neighbouring constituency of West Calgary, Joe Shaw was having a hard two-way battle with R.B. Bennett. Shaw was again running as an Independent, but this time he had sought and had accepted the endorsation and support of the Liberals. In spite of Shaw's close association with Irvine and Woodsworth, he got strong support from the *Albertan*, which published a commendation from Woodsworth:

> As a labour man I regret that Mr. Shaw has accepted the Liberal endorsation, but I would not have the slightest hesitation in voting for him. Throughout the past four years he has consistently supported our labour program in Parliament and we have been able to work in very close co-operation.[3]

The farmers' paper, the *UFA*, commented with some surprise on the contrast between the *Albertan*'s treatment of Shaw and its treatment of Irvine, and remarked that Shaw must have found this unpleasant. Shaw, however, throughout the campaign, showed no signs of embarrassment on this score. Henry Spencer suggests that Shaw had some role in the anti-Irvine campaign and that he wanted to get even with his former roommate. It appears that on one occasion Shaw had voted with some of the Ontario Progressives and thus split the Ginger Group vote. An anonymous satirical verse purporting to explain Shaw's motives in doing this was circulated among the members, much to Shaw's annoyance. Later it leaked out that Irvine was the author.[4]

The issue of free trade versus protection was theoretically supposed to divide the Liberals from the Conservatives, although, as Irvine often pointed out, both parties acted on this question in much the same way when in power. Nevertheless, the Liberals were using it as the election issue and the *Albertan* repeatedly accused Irvine of favouring high tariffs. An incident in the House of Commons which was the pretext for this accusation was explained in a letter from S.J. Ewing, president of the East Calgary UFA constituency association:

> Irvine was absent from the House when a motion by Mr. Coote calling for a reduction in the tariff on automobiles and motor trucks was moved in committee at a late hour. Every Liberal member voted against this reduction. After the defeat of this resolution, Mr. Meighen moved a high tariff amendment. The government announced that the vote would be treated as one of confidence. Mr. Irvine then deliberately absented himself from the House. He gave as his reason for taking this course that he had lost confidence in the government and therefore could not support it by voting against the resolution, while he could not vote in favour of the resolution on account of its character. E.J. Garland, UFA MP for Bow River, whose free trade views are well known, was also absent from this division.
>
> I think it is due to Mr. Irvine that the public should be informed that he voted for tariff reduction upon every occasion upon which it was raised as a major issue and that he voted for reduction many times more than any Liberal member of the House, and also that he has never voted for protection.
>
> The fact of the matter is that Mr. Irvine, who says that the tariff issue is not fundamental, has supported every important move for tariff reduction in the last four years, while the Liberal members have failed to do so. From the standpoint of the western farmer, Mr. Irvine's record is infinitely superior to that of any Liberal member in Ottawa.[5]

In spite of the opposition of both of Calgary's daily newspapers, and the loss of most of the rural vote through boundary changes, Irvine made a good showing at the polls, getting practically all of the estimated labour vote, but it was not enough to surpass the Conservative candidate Davis, who won comfortably. Davidson ran a poor third and lost his deposit.

In West Calgary, R.B. Bennett, who had put an immense

amount of money into the campaign, triumphed over Shaw.*
Nine UFA members were elected from Alberta; fifteen Progres-
sives were elected from other provinces. A.A. Heaps of Winnipeg
Strike fame, became number-two labour man in place of Irvine.
Of the Gingerites, only Irvine and Shaw lost their seats, although
Good and Elliott from Ontario did not run. Altogether ten re-
mained among the twenty-six Independents.

The Progressives were reorganized on the basis of each provincial group being independent and retaining its identity, the House
organization being only for the purpose of co-ordinating efforts
on questions of legislation. H.E. Spencer was elected as secretary
and whip for the whole group and Forke was returned as House
leader. Together with the two labour members, they constituted
what were known as the Co-operating Groups. In this situation,
and with Irvine no longer in the House, it was Woodsworth who
provided the real, though informal, leadership.

The election had been disastrous for the Liberals, who were
reduced to 101 members out of a total of 245. King lost his own
seat and although still Prime Minister, he had to sit on the side-
lines until the safe seat of Prince Albert was found for him. The
Conservatives, with 117 members, improved their position but
failed to get a majority. If King was to form a minority government, he had to get support from the independent groups, who
now held the balance of power.

It is significant that in these circumstances King should turn to
Woodsworth and ask about the political price of his support.
Clearly he thought that Woodsworth's help would ensure that of
most of the Progressive and UFA members. It is also significant
that he used as go-between Charles Bowman, political editor of
the *Ottawa Citizen*, who had written sympathetically about the
Ginger Group.

Woodsworth sought King's pledge to amend the Immigration
Act, the Naturalization Act, and the Criminal Code, along lines
proposed by Woodsworth, and above all he demanded that legislation should be introduced immediately to implement old age

---

* Seven months later, Shaw became leader of the Alberta Liberals
and subsequently, with some difficulty, won a seat in the Alberta
Legislature, where he attacked the UFA as "class" government.

pensions and unemployment insurance. King met with Bowman, Woodsworth and Heaps, and finally agreed to these conditions, and at Woodsworth's insistence, he recorded his promises in a letter to Woodsworth.

During these negotiations, King offered first to Woodsworth and then to Heaps the post of Minister of Labour, which both refused. Forke, on the other hand, tried to convince the Progressives that it would be desirable for them to have one or two members in the Cabinet, but the members, particularly the Albertans, resisted this suggestion and insisted that there be no commitment to support the Liberal government except for a program of agreed legislation.

The Old Age Pension Bill passed in May 1926. Its provisions were that the federal government would pay to any province that agreed to co-operate half the cost, and that the maximum pension would be $240 per annum payable to British subjects of seventy years or over who had been resident in Canada for twenty years. Although passed in the House of Commons, it was vetoed in the Senate, where there was a Conservative majority. Perhaps King had anticipated this. It was reintroduced in 1927 and this time it passed the Senate.

Irvine had not been politically idle during the months between elections. A few weeks after his defeat at the polls he undertook to give six weeks of his time, without remuneration of any kind, to organizing work for the UFA. He expressed a preference for constituencies that he had not previously visited. Also he played an active part in the campaign preceding the provincial elections in June 1926, when again he travelled to many parts of Alberta. He was in great demand as a speaker and he must have made a considerable contribution to the UFA victory.

The UFA increased its strength in the legislature to forty-three out of a total of sixty-five seats. Although Alex Ross lost his Calgary seat, nevertheless six labour candidates were elected. They regularly voted with the Government and labour-farmer co-operation reached a high point, which must have been a matter of considerable satisfaction to Irvine. The *Alberta Labour News*, edited by Elmer Roper, welcomed the electoral success of the UFA and its growing influence.

When the 1926 federal election was called, it was natural that

Irvine should seek nomination as a UFA candidate. The chances of a labour candidate being elected were slim and he did not want to repeat the previous year's defeat in East Calgary. Wetaskiwin had recently returned UFA candidates to the Legislature in all of its provincial ridings, so Irvine, along with five other aspirants, sought the nomination there. The sitting member, J. Tobin, was a Liberal who had resigned his seat in the provincial legislature to try for a seat in the House of Commons in 1925. He soundly defeated his UFA opponent, Warner, and was one of only three Liberals to go to Ottawa from Alberta.

Irvine had the reputation of being a radical, which attracted some people but alarmed others. The apparently most favoured candidate for nomination was Dave Christie, a farmer from the Clover Bar-Leduc area, who was active in the UFA. The local UFA convention in Wetaskiwin was held 30 July 1926. Irvine won, seventy-six votes to seventy-five for Christie, on the third ballot.

Ironically, in his former constituency of East Calgary, a labour candidate had been nominated, H.B. Adshead. This time W.M. Davidson did not run and the *Calgary Albertan* gave the labour man a great deal of support. In this case the Liberals seemed to be wooing labour. They did not run a candidate in East Calgary, and much was made of the fact that Adshead had declared in favour of low tariffs. There was a third, Independent candidate, but he was not a serious contender, receiving only 176 votes. Adshead also had good relations with the UFA and had its support (for what it was worth in a largely urban constituency). He beat the incumbent Conservative Davis handily, having obviously received the combined labour and Liberal vote. He joined Woodsworth and Heaps in the House as part of the labour group, but he often voted against them and had a strong bias in favour of Liberal policies.

Despite the tensions created by a close nomination race, Irvine got wholehearted support from his rivals and was able to mount a strong campaign. Shortly before election day, Tobin, the Liberal candidate in Wetaskiwin, challenged Irvine to a debate. Although Irvine's advisors thought this only gave Tobin a platform he could not get on his own, Irvine, who never refused a challenge to debate, accepted. A few days prior to the joint meeting, some ex-Liberals told Cook, Irvine's agent, that the Liberals planned to disrupt the meeting. Irvine had the first twenty minutes, Tobin then had thirty minutes, followed by Irvine with ten minutes for rebuttal. The plan was to have six muscular Liberal supporters strategically planted in the audience so that before Irvine gave his rebuttal they could stand up and create a disturbance, thus preventing him from giving his reply.

Tobin had a pamphlet printed and distributed in which Irvine was denounced as a foreign intruder, a communist and a Shetlander! This was also the theme of Tobin's speech in the debate. As he delivered it Irvine sat and smiled. Cook was on the platform and had arranged his seat next to Tobin's. Beside each of the Liberal bruisers sat two husky UFA supporters. As Irvine was about to reply, Tobin stood up — a signal to the disrupters — but Cook pulled him down into his seat and as each of the Liberal "plants" started to stand, a strong man on either side held him in his seat. Irvine was then free to go ahead and demolish Tobin's "arguments," which he did effectively in ten minutes. On 14 September, polling day, Irvine won comfortably against both Tobin and the Conservative candidate. The urban votes, which were announced first, went against Irvine, but the rural voters turned the tide in his favour.

Irvine returned to a very much changed House of Commons:* Mackenzie King was in charge with a majority government, Meighen had lost his seat and had been replaced as Opposition leader by R.B. Bennett; Forke now sat on the Liberal bench as Minister of Immigration and Colonization, and although the UFA had maintained its strength, the farmers' independent representation in the House was much reduced and in consequence the co-operating groups wielded considerably less power than they did in 1926 or even earlier.

Now forty-one years of age, Irvine was to spend the next nine years primarily working with the Ginger Group. By establishing and sustaining an alliance between labour, UFA, Progressive and Independent members, the Gingerites were able to fight a number of important parliamentary battles.

One of these was the long drawn-out fight against the over-

---

* Liberals 119, Conservatives 91, Progressives 11, UFA 11, Independent 9, Labour 3.

capitalization of big companies such as Sun Life Assurance and Bell Telephone, which sought to increase their profits through the device of watering stock and asked for parliamentary sanction to make this procedure legal. Sun Life struggled for three years to get a bill to increase its capital stock by $2 million passed and did an immense amount of lobbying. Each year it got a different member to introduce the matter through a private member's bill, choosing sponsors from both the Liberal and the Conservative ranks. Finally, when Sun Life could not get its desired legislation through the House of Commons, it took it to the Privy Council. By the decision of this body Sun Life was given power to increase its capital by $2 million without hindrance from the federal government. It was also decided that the provinces had the right of control of life insurance in Canada.

By 1932, Sun Life was subject to attack from the press because of its speculative investment policy, as a result of which it was alleged to be close to insolvency. In the House of Commons, Prime Minister R.B. Bennett defended the insurance company on the basis that although its investments may have been unwise ("We all make mistakes," he said) yet they were legal and there were no grounds for parliamentary intervention. Thus a Privy Council ruling decided the matter and the House was prevented from having any further say.

Irvine was also involved in a parliamentary battle over the question of divorce. He supported a resolution making grounds for divorce the same for men and women. This bill never reached the House; however, in 1928, 1929 and 1930, Irvine and Woodsworth were concerned with the divorce laws from a different angle. Six of Canada's nine provinces had divorce courts established by law, but in the remaining three, Ontario, Quebec and Prince Edward Island,[6] divorce was only possible by means of a private bill that had to pass both Houses of Parliament. In the Senate each bill was considered by a committee and if accepted went on to the Commons for the prescribed three readings. These bills were handled in large batches, they crowded out the time available for the consideration of other legislation and were passed or denied virtually without discussion from the floor of the House. In addition, the committees involved were not conducted according to legal procedure, and they lacked the power to make binding decisions in regard to alimony and the maintenance and custody of children. The whole process was also very expensive and ensured that divorce was a luxury only the rich could afford. Irvine's position was that Parliament had no place granting divorces, which he thought belonged under the jurisdiction of the provincial courts, where proper attention could be given to the details of each case.

Meanwhile, the government refused to allow Bill No. 27 to proceed to a third reading. This bill had been introduced in the Senate with the purpose of empowering the Ontario courts to grant divorces in that province instead of having such cases brought to the Senate and eventually to the House of Commons. In April 1928, Irvine and Woodsworth decided to challenge the divorce procedures and to force the government to bring forward Bill No. 27 by demanding discussion of each divorce bill.

Discussion of the divorce bills continued until a few days later Woodsworth seized the opportunity of moving the second reading of Bill No. 27. The motion was not debatable and it was defeated by a vote of fifty-three to twenty-one; curiously enough, while Woodsworth and Irvine got the votes of seventeen Conservatives, they only got a minority of the votes of the co-operating groups. Campbell, Heaps, Lucas and Spencer would have voted for the motion but they were paired with absent members from other parties; others voted against Woodsworth's motion, including Ted Garland (because of his Roman Catholic religious convictions). Having forced Bill No. 27 to a vote and lost, Woodsworth and Irvine allowed the private divorce bills to go through without further delay.

In February of the following year, 1929, essentially the same bill, initiated in the Senate and now No. 38, was moved for second reading by Woodsworth, and again, after considerable debate, the bill was defeated, this time by ninety-nine to sixty-eight. Although bills to establish divorce courts in Ontario had twice been defeated by a vote in the House, Woodsworth and Irvine persisted in their struggle, and when the next batch of divorce bills came up in April 1929, they declared their intention of forcing a discussion and an individual vote on each one. This tactic effectively slowed down the passing of divorce bills and amply demonstrated the absurdity of this mode of dealing with the problem. After a few days Mackenzie King gave in and announced to the House his intention that Parliament pass legislation to free itself from dealing with divorce bills.

Woodsworth and Irvine accepted his informal assurances and allowed the House to revert to its assembly-line treatment of divorce bills. Almost a year later, 5 March 1930, when the government still had not moved on the matter, Woodsworth reintroduced Bill No. 20, which had now passed the Senate three times. On 11 March, a vote on the motion for a second reading was held. The actual result was the defeat of the bill by a vote of seventy-nine to seventy-eight, but owing to a clerical error the Speaker declared the vote to be a tie and then made his own casting vote against the bill. He revealed this to the House next day and declared his own vote to be invalid. After a series of skirmishes the bill was passed on 6 May 1930, a result due almost entirely to the pertinacity of Woodsworth and Irvine.

Their activities at this time were by no means confined to the House of Commons; they were both in great demand as speakers across the country, and this drained both their physical energies and their financial resources. They frequently travelled together and later Irvine recalled the spartan conditions they shared:

> We then had $4,000 a year indemnity. Two of us had to cross Canada. We were the only advocates of socialism that were available to make speeches and we got many demands and we felt that we had to take them and it was really an expensive thing. Although we had passes on the railway as Members of Parliament, you couldn't eat a pass and you couldn't sleep on a pass.... I don't remember ever having a sleeper in those days when we travelled all the way from Halifax to Vancouver. But those were the greatest meetings that we ever had, and I don't think that there was any part of my campaigning that I enjoyed nearly as much as when I did that, and I am quite sure that Woodsworth was in exactly the same position. But of course, Woodsworth was a frail man.... Woodsworth, I think, hastened his life's end a good deal by what he went through during twenty years in which

he campaigned throughout Canada under those circumstances. He was so constituted that if anybody offered to pay for a room for him, or was affluent enough to buy a berth for him, he wouldn't take it. He seemed to enjoy the hardship because of his anxiety to see things done to forward the socialist movement; and of course in the same spirit I agreed with him.

No collections were taken at our meetings in those days. We took collections of course at meetings during a campaign because it was one of our principles that we had to pay for the election of our candidates. When we went to those meetings of course sometimes we were entertained by our friends, but we had to bear all our travelling expenses.

In addition to meetings across the country there were always constituents to talk to within his own riding:

> ... the farmers' movement at that time was one of the best organizations that ever was in Canada. It was thoroughly democratic in all its actions, and those people came out and would question you for hours at a time on the details of legislation that had been passed, and it was extremely interesting.... I used to write a monthly letter to all the organizations and have my free time radio broadcasting. In between times I used to write for the *Alberta Labour News* something about Parliament and what was taking place there....
>
> I remember one night there was a blizzard — a real old time blizzard — and I had been driving Ted Garland down to a meeting in Saskatchewan, and just as I had dropped him the blizzard broke and I shovelled snow from about 6 o'clock at night, until nearly 12 o'clock the following day. I couldn't use up all the gas to keep my car warm and I didn't want to freeze to death, so I'd go a foot, maybe two yards on some occasions, then she'd block and I'd shovel her out again.... After that I decided that I'd never get caught like that again so I got a buffalo coat and a pair of those long-legged felt shoes and a fur cap and some fur gauntlets, so that I could lie down even in the snow and be warmer than in the car by myself that night....

From 1921-27, Irvine maintained his home in Calgary, building additions to it as his family grew. In 1927 he bought a farm in the Bentley district, about twenty miles northwest of Red Deer. A friend advised him that it would be a good idea for him to become a farmer and thus eligible to be a bona fide member of the UFA. Since UFA political candidates were not required to be farmers and members of the UFA, although most of them were, this was an unnecessary step, and it was also a disastrous one. Irvine could not run the farm himself, his brother Frank who was living with them at the time had little or no farm experience, and his eldest son, Ron, was a lad of fifteen.

Again, on the advice of a friend, he hired a man to manage the farm for him. The man he chose for this responsible job was an ex-convict. Irvine knew this and no doubt wanted to give the man a chance to rehabilitate himself. Irvine's farm "manager" sold the farm produce, pocketed the money, and left the bills unpaid. This left Irvine close to bankruptcy, which would have resulted in the forfeiture of his seat in Parliament. However, friends rallied around, and in 1932, Irvine disposed of his land and moved his family into the town of Wetaskiwin.

In the federal election in 1930, Irvine won his seat in a three-way race, with a reduced majority but with 424 votes to spare. This time the Conservative was the runner-up in Wetaskiwin, and across the country the Conservatives made gains, giving them 137 to the Liberals' ninety-one and an assortment of seventeen Farmer, Labour and Independent members. The UFA returned nine members, suffering only two losses. Of the Gingerites, only W.J. Ward from Manitoba was a casualty and since he was a rather lukewarm member his loss was more than made up for by the advent of Angus MacInnis, an Independent Labour party socialist from South Vancouver. Adshead reaped the wages of his Liberal inclinations and suffered defeat by a Conservative in East Calgary. The non-Gingerite Progressives had for all practical purposes ceased to exist in the seventeenth Parliament.

R.B. Bennett now had the unenviable role of Prime Minister during Canada's worst economic depression. Bennett chose as his Minister of Labour Gideon Robertson. Robertson had been a senator since 1917, and he had also been Meighen's Minister of

Labour during the Winnipeg Strike. Although he was the first trade unionist to become a Minister of Labour, he had earned a reputation for ruthlessness in dealing with labour problems. However, towards the end of 1931, Robertson died. Bennett had three Ministers without Portfolio in his Cabinet and the post might well have gone to one of them. Instead, Bennett approached Irvine, who replied that his actions as an MP were governed by the wishes of his UFA constituency association, and that any such offer should be communicated to them. In the event, Irvine received a letter on the subject which he took to the board of directors of the Wetaskiwin UFA constituency association, who told Irvine he should accept or not as he thought best, whereupon Irvine indicated his rejection of the offer by tearing up the letter in front of them.[8] Soon after, Bennett gave the portfolio to W.A. Gordon, who was already Minister of Mines and acting Minister of Immigration and Colonization.

Irvine and the other Gingerites, in addition to their political radicalism, also rebelled against the unthinking and often inconvenient conventions and traditions that prevailed in the House of Commons. Henry Spencer gives an account of one such rebellion:

> Sometimes in June and July the heat in Ottawa is terrific. One summer it reached 90° F in the House of Commons. The members had been in the habit of attending Committee meetings and working in their offices without wearing coats. Then they were expected to put on their coats and "cook" in the chamber. Some eight of us decided to test the rules and we appeared nicely and coolly dressed (minus coats) in the House of Commons chamber. Some Ontario members drew the attention of the Speaker to this innovation. The Speaker tried to overlook it but was again reminded of rule breaking and so we were invited to the Speaker's chambers.
>
> The Speaker said that we ought to try to copy Westminster as much as possible and there of course the Speaker wears a wig as well as a gown. George Coote then said: "If I move that you, Mr. Speaker, wear the wig, will you comply?" "No! No!" said the Speaker, "please not in this weather." When asked why he objected to *us* trying to keep cool, he

said "Well, it was when I saw Mr. Irvine address the Speaker, standing in the front row, less his coat and with his sleeves rolled up, it was too much for me."[9]

Towards the end of 1929, Irvine published his second book, *Co-operative Government*. It had a brief foreword by Henry Wood:

William Irvine has written this book, to which he has given the title "Co-operative Government." I haven't as yet had an opportunity to read it, but I know Bill Irvine. The book consists of a compilation of his addresses.

As a platform orator, Mr. Irvine is sincere; a fluent speaker, and a brilliant thinker. If you have heard his addresses you will enjoy his book. If you have not heard him, and read his book, you will wish you had heard him. Read his book and pass it on to your neighbour.[10]

The rather odd tone of this introduction suggests that Wood was not entirely happy about the fact that Irvine had become the chief, and certainly the clearest, spokesman for the idea of "group government," and that by claiming not to have read the book he was absolving himself from any responsibility for agreeing or disagreeing with its contents. However, since Irvine's introduction is dated 2 December, and Wood's foreword is dated 16 December, it may be that it was written in haste and at short notice.

Despite its origins in separate public addresses delivered at different times and places, the book is well written and makes a coherent whole. Except for a chapter entitled "The New Economics," in which he gives a succinct account of his views on the necessity for monetary and financial reform, Irvine's opinions do not substantially differ from those in his first book. There is the same concern for establishing truly democratic forms of government but also a new depth to his criticism of parliamentary practices, which arose from nine years of frustrating experiences in the House of Commons.

Co-operative Government got wide distribution in Alberta where there was a special United Farmers' edition, price one dollar, and a few months later, in 1930, it was followed by a pamphlet, *Federal Affairs in Review*, which emphasized the difference between the UFA and the traditional parties. The pamphlet was issued by the UFA members of the House of Commons in the name of the secretary of that group, Henry Spencer. Spencer said later, however, "We all talked it over but Bill wrote it."[11] Its purpose was to set forth clearly for the people in the constituencies exactly what the UFA MPs were doing in Parliament, and to establish the close relation between the policies pursued in the House and those established at the annual conventions of the UFA. One paragraph, perhaps, pointed towards the next stage of political development. In it Irvine wrote:

> The splendid co-operation between the labour, Progressive, Independent and UFA groups, has strengthened our confidence in the possibility of the co-operative principle in governments of the future. The UFA members have not been alone in their advocacy of the record under review. All groups outside of the ranks of the two major parties have worked together in harmony.[12]

NINE

The Founding of the CCF

By 1930 it was apparent to the Ginger Group that the penetration of the parliamentary system through the organization of economic groups was not making headway. After nearly nine years, labour's representation had risen from two to three, and the farmers' representation had dwindled, except for the solid block of UFA members, to a mere handful. Common economic interests, while they were certainly a necessary foundation for political action, apparently were not enough to unite and sustain an attack upon the powerful and wealthy class establishment.

On the other hand, the Ginger Group, chiefly through the writings of Irvine, had formulated a consistent social philosophy, had been able to maintain itself and had brought about co-operation between labour and farmer groups in the House of Commons. The idea gradually began to emerge that this co-operation might be extended beyond Parliament, to build a national social and political movement in which labour and farmer and other groups might work together to bring about fundamental social change.

Perhaps the first turn in this direction occurred in January 1931, at the twenty-third annual UFA convention, when Robert Gardiner, leader of the UFA group at Ottawa, became the president of the UFA, upon the retirement of Henry Wise Wood. A year later, in his presidential address to the twenty-fourth convention, Gardiner told the farmers:

> This is a task which we as farmers' groups cannot accomplish alone, even if our industry be organized effectively

from coast to coast. We must be prepared to co-operate with other social units who suffer today as the result of the breakdown of the economic system.... Co-operation involves continuous consultation and co-ordination of effort. It involves action... on a Dominion-wide scale, for it is only on such a scale that the co-operating groups can make a bid for power to bring about the fundamental changes in the economic system upon the necessity of which they are agreed. In order that the whole people of the Dominion may be able to identify the various groups as part of a great national movement, it is desirable that the nation-wide movement should be known under a single national name.[1]

The same convention also received a report from its educational committee in which the term "co-operative commonwealth" was defined as:

1. A community freed from the domination of irresponsible financial and economic power, in which all social means of production and distribution including land, are socially owned and controlled either by voluntarily organized groups of producers and consumers, or — in the case of the major public services and utilities and such productive and distributive enterprises as can be conducted most efficiently when owned in common — by public corporations responsible to the people's elected representatives.
2. Since in the advanced stages of the present competitive or capitalistic social order, the key to economic power is possessed by those who are in control of the mechanism of finance, the transfer of such control from private interests to bodies responsible solely to the people's representatives is an essential step towards the attainment of the Co-operative Commonwealth.[2]

The 1932 convention followed this up by issuing an open invitation to all interested political groups to meet with them for the purpose of discussing the establishment in Canada of a co-operative commonwealth, the conference to take place that summer. J.S. Woodsworth attended this convention and when back in the

House on 2 March, he moved a resolution, which stated: "... the government should immediately take measures looking to the setting up of a co-operative commonwealth in which all national resources and the socially necessary machinery of production, will be used in the interests of the people and not for the benefit of the few."[3] In elaborating on this theme, Woodsworth referred to the definition of co-operative commonwealth given at the UFA convention, and the support for the idea to be found among western farmers. He got little support in the House, except from his fellow Gingerites, and his resolution was talked out without a vote.

A few months later, on the afternoon of 26 May, a meeting held in Irvine's office was attended by Woodsworth, Irvine, Macphail, Gardiner, Garland, Spencer, Coote, Kennedy and MacInnis. Also present were M.J. Coldwell, president of the Saskatchewan Labour party, and several young lecturers from Toronto and McGill Universities, who had formed a Fabian-type society called the League for Social Reconstruction.* They discussed plans for forming a nationwide organization that they tentatively called the Commonwealth party. Woodsworth was chosen as temporary president and others were allotted areas in which to promote the new organization. Agnes Macphail was given Ontario; M.J. Coldwell, Saskatchewan; Robert Gardiner, Alberta; while Manitoba and British Columbia were to be in the care of the Socialist Party of Canada and the Independent Labour party, both of which had some following, chiefly in Winnipeg and Vancouver.

In Saskatchewan the following July, M.J. Coldwell succeeded, with the assistance of G.H. Williams, in bringing together for political action three organizations, the United Farmers of Canada (Saskatchewan section), the Farmers' Political Association, and the Independent Labour party. They agreed to run joint candi-

---

* The LSR was formed in January 1932. Frank H. Underhill was its first president and Frank Scott its second one. The secretary was Isabel Thomas, the daughter of Rev. E. Thomas, with whom J.S. Woodsworth had been associated in his early social service work under the auspices of the Methodist Church. Woodsworth was made honorary president of the LSR.

dates in the provincial election under the farmer-labour banner and also to participate in the creation of the new organization initiated by the Gingerites and the UFA convention.

For several years there had met each summer a Western Labour Conference, which worked at co-ordinating the political labour parties of the four western provinces. To this conference came representatives of the Socialist party of British Columbia, the Canadian Labour party, the Dominion Labour party of Alberta and the Independent Labour parties of Saskatchewan and Manitoba. In 1931, the Western Labour Conference decided to invite representation from farmers' groups. In 1932, a meeting was planned for Regina but in order to take advantage of the invitation of the Alberta farmers, the conference met in Calgary on 30 July. Two days later, they were joined by the farmers' representatives and the conference to form a Canada-wide socialist political movement was underway.

The delegates were a cross section of the working people of Canada:

> There were fifteen farmers, twenty construction workers, two lawyers, six teachers, one miner, one professor, six housewives, three accountants, six railway workers, three journalists, two steam engineers, one hotel keeper, one retired minister, one motion picture operator, three nurses, two union executives, twelve members of Parliament and the legislature, nineteen unemployed men and women.[4]

W.C. Good, the Gingerite from Manitoba who had retired from Parliament in 1925, remarked of them, expressing a sentiment which would have been appreciated by Henry Wood: "Surely a motley lot!" However, Grace MacInnis more appropriately said: "Together they possessed a practical knowledge of the needs of the working people of this country." From Ontario came A.R. Mosher, representing the Canadian Brotherhood of Railway Employees, and also from the east came representatives of the League for Social Reconstruction. A motion by J.S. Woodsworth was passed, permitting the representatives of the LSR to attend the conference but without voting rights.

The naming of the new organization provoked a good deal of

discussion; the Co-operative Commonwealth Federation was suggested by two delegates — Walter Mentz (Edmonton) and John Fenstein (Regina) — the latter proposing unsuccessfully that the words "Farmer-Labour-Socialist" should also be included. This name was adopted as best expressing the aims, ideals and structure of the new political movement. M.J. Coldwell chaired the resolutions committee, which brought in a draft program of fourteen points. After some discussion, an eight-point provisional program was adopted:

1. Establishment of a planned economy;
2. Social ownership and control of financial institutions, utilities and natural resources;
3. Security of tenure for the farmers;
4. Extension of social security legislation;
5. Equality of opportunity, regardless of sex, nationality or religion;
6. Encouragement of co-operative enterprises as steps to the attainment of the co-operative commonwealth;
7. Socialization of all health services;
8. Suitable work or adequate maintenance to be provided by the federal government for those unemployed.

The officers of the new organization consisted of a president, a secretary, and a national council of seven elected from the delegates present. Woodsworth was unanimously chosen president and Norman F. Priestley (vice-president of the UFA), secretary. The members of the national council were: Angus MacInnis (British Columbia); William Irvine (Alberta); George H. Williams (Saskatchewan); John Queen (Manitoba) and A.R. Mosher (Ontario).

Agnes Macphail was not at the Calgary meeting, since the United Farmers of Ontario were not yet involved, but during the fall of 1932, she and Irvine toured Ontario in order to gain support for the newly formed CCF. Their tour culminated in their participation in two mass meetings in Toronto at the end of November. The first, on the evening of 30 November 1932, was the Toronto debut of the CCF and the gathering in Hygeia Hall overflowed into a second hall, which also rapidly filled, and hundreds of people were turned away. The huge audiences were addressed nonstop for three hours by a battery of speakers. Agnes Macphail, Robert Gardiner, William Irvine, Salem Bland and J.S. Woodsworth spoke to the crowds. It is significant that the only speaker who was not a westerner was Agnes Macphail, the sole Ontario MP to be involved in the new movement. The next night the UFO convention met at the King Edward Hotel, Toronto. The convention was addressed by Robert Gardiner, Agnes Macphail and Irvine. They persuaded the convention to vote overwhelmingly for affiliation with the CCF, although the UFO later withdrew their affiliation, finding it too radical for comfort.

Woodsworth, Irvine, and other members of the Ginger Group soon brought the formation of the CCF to the attention of the House of Commons. On 1 February 1933, Woodsworth resurrected his resolution of almost a year before in which he put forward the co-operative commonwealth as the solution to the country's economic and social problems. He said:

> When I introduced this motion a year ago, there was no large body of organized opinion behind it. Today the situation is altered, for last August there was organized the Co-operative Commonwealth Federation, — a federation of organizations whose purpose is the establishment in Canada of a co-operative commonwealth in which the basic principle regulating production, distribution and exchange, will be the supply of human needs instead of the making of profits.... The object of the federation shall be to promote co-operation between the member organizations and to correlate their political activities. We endorse the general viewpoint and program involved in the socialization of our economic life as these have already been outlined and accepted by the labour, farmer and socialist groups affiliating.[5]

In the subsequent discussion of Woodsworth's resolution, Irvine rose to support it:

> This resolution implies... first, public instead of private ownership, co-operation instead of competition, production for use instead of production for profit. It stands for a

planned control of our national economy instead of the present anarchy. It stands for the priority of human needs over property rights. It stands for international peace to come as a natural consequence of co-operation, instead of international strife inevitable in a condition of competition such as we have at the present time.

We want to nationalize or socialize the resources of the country. Next we propose to socialize the credit system of Canada, which represents 90 percent of all the money distributed in Canada. That money is distributed by the banks of Canada. The banks themselves have no credit; they are simply empowered to administer the credit of the people of Canada.... The next fight in Canada will be between capitalism and socialism.... In the place of private ownership, competition, debts and unemployment, we advance co-operation, social ownership, and the use of commodities instead of holding them for profit.[6]

In the period between the Calgary and the Regina meetings, Irvine was to make up his mind about what kind of organization he wanted the CCF to be. At this time he also tried to reach a wider audience than that provided by the relatively infertile ground of the House of Commons, and to this end he produced a forty-eight-page pamphlet entitled *Co-operation or Catastrophe: An Interpretation of the Co-operative Commonwealth Federation and Its Policy*. The pamphlet, published from Ottawa, is undated, but it is fairly clear from internal evidence that it belongs to the period between the Calgary and Regina conventions. In it he stressed the need for unity between farmers and labour under the CCF banner.

At the conclusion of the Calgary convention, Woodsworth and others decided that a more comprehensive program was needed than the eight points arrived at in Calgary, and so Woodsworth asked the LSR and Frank Underhill its president in particular to prepare a draft for such a program to be presented to the Regina convention.

Most accounts of the founding of the CCF assume that this draft produced by Underhill was in substance what finally emerged as the Regina Manifesto (see Appendix C). Since for a dozen years or more, farmers and radical urban workers had been assimilating and developing political ideas and expressing them with eloquence and power, it might be wondered why the LSR should be given this job, particularly as it was not one of the affiliated bodies and by its own constitution precluded itself from joining a political movement. It is sometimes thought that what these Canadian academics, who had studied at Oxford, Cambridge and the London School of Economics, had to provide was a strong ideological injection of radical socialism. More likely Woodsworth involved the LSR because he wanted some representation from the east, so that the CCF would not look like a purely western movement.

When Underhill and other members of the LSR had finished with the draft of the Manifesto, it was discussed, paragraph by paragraph, by the provisional national council and it was the draft as revised by the council which was read to the convention by Norman Priestley. When he came to the concluding paragraphs, his audience of 131 people rose and cheered, attesting to their enthusiastic agreement:

> Emergency measures, however, are of only temporary value, for the present depression is a sign of the mortal sickness of the whole capitalist system, and this sickness cannot be cured by the application of salves. These leave untouched the cancer which is eating at the heart of our society, namely, the economic system in which our natural resources and our principal means of production and distribution are owned, controlled and operated for the private profit of a small proportion of our population.
>
> No CCF government will rest content until it has eradicated capitalism, and put into operation the full program of socialized planning which will lead to the establishment in Canada of the co-operative commonwealth.[7]

The Regina Manifesto was clearly at one with most of what Irvine had thought and said in the past, and he welcomed it without reservations. Some eleven months later, he produced another pamphlet, *The Forces of Reconstruction: A Review of World Conditions Under Capitalism, and the Forces Working Towards the Co-operative Commonwealth*, in which he stressed the federated nature of the CCF and claimed that its program was not imposed by any single group but grew logically from the common needs of many groups.

As the farmer and labour delegates were meeting in Calgary in the summer of 1932, to bring into being the CCF, two hundred miles north in Edmonton William Aberhart was engaged in an intellectual crisis that would result in his conversion to Social Credit. An Edmonton high school teacher, Charles Scarborough, had for some time been trying to convince his friend Aberhart of the truth of C.H. Douglas's theories without much success, until he finally hit upon the expedient of giving Aberhart a copy of *Unemployment or War* by Maurice Colbourne, in which a popularly written and much simplified version of Douglas's social credit theories was presented. It did the trick, and shortly thereafter Aberhart embarked upon his crusade for social credit.

In the fall of 1932, Aberhart received permission from the board of management of the Calgary Prophetic Bible Institute to introduce economic questions into his Sunday afternoon religious broadcasts, which were sponsored by the Institute. The increasingly economic and social credit content of his broadcasts aroused interest and soon he was engaged in a full-scale campaign to win converts to social credit as he conceived it. In addition to speaking engagements, he distributed a series of pamphlets in which he set forth his version of social credit. The most controversial of these was the "yellow pamphlet" issued in May 1933, in which he reiterated the proposal to pay a $25 "dividend" each month to every adult Albertan.

At this time, Irvine did not consider Aberhart a threat. He was preoccupied with the task of preparing for the Regina convention of the CCF. In 1933, Amelia Turner (later Mrs. Norman Smith) had been the first to run on the CCF ticket in a provincial by-election. Labour and UFA groups had co-operated in supporting her bid for a Calgary seat. She did not win but polled an impressive

12,307 votes. This had encouraged a good deal of activity on behalf of the newborn organization. Irvine was in the thick of it and also, partly in consequence, was at odds with the leaders of the UFA Alberta government.

Herbert Greenfield, who had reluctantly agreed to be the first UFA Premier, resigned towards the end of 1925, and was replaced by Attorney General John E. Brownlee. Brownlee was not a farmer but had formerly been legal counsel for the UFA and the Grain Growers' Association,* and was a friend of Henry Wood, who thought so highly of him that he had wanted him to be Premier when the UFA first came to power in 1921.

The UFA had taken office during a period of depression and had survived because it was a hard-working, efficient, and to some degree, innovative government. In the 1926 election, under Brownlee's leadership, it markedly improved its representation in the legislature from thirty-nine seats to forty-three. At the 1930 election it slipped back to thirty-nine, which was still, of course, a substantial majority.

However, things were not well, since Alberta was in the midst of an even greater depression than that of the Twenties. Farmers were shipping wheat and livestock to markets across the country only to discover that the costs of transportation were greater than the market value of their products. At the 1932 UFA convention, the question of farmer indebtedness loomed large and a resolution calling for a government-declared moratorium on debts was narrowly defeated by a vote of fifty-nine to fifty-five, and then only because Brownlee, who had a basically Conservative outlook, strongly opposed it. Subsequently, the government passed a Debt Adjustment Act, whereby foreclosures and seizures for debt were stopped until the creditor had proved to the Debt Adjustment Director that the debtor actually had the ability to pay.

As in the rest of Canada, the Depression was making a tremendous impact on miners and urban workers. The coal mining area in the southwest of Alberta, particularly in Blairmore, became a

---

* Brownlee also belonged to the legal firm of R.B. Bennett and James Lougheed (grandfather of the present Progressive Conservative Premier of Alberta).

centre for conflict between miners and mine owners, with strikes, lockouts, blacklists and violent clashes between the miners and the RCMP.[8]

Premier Brownlee's first response to this situation was to issue an edict prohibiting miners from parading, and to refuse to meet a delegation of miners who trekked to Edmonton on 18 July. On the following day, 100 miners were arrested in Blairmore for defying the ban on parades. However, by August, the situation was so acute that Brownlee was persuaded to intervene. Brownlee visited the area and spoke to representatives of both the mine owners and the miners and a compromise was worked out between them by Labour Day, 1932.

In December of the same year, over 1,000 unemployed workers and destitute farmers met in Market Square in Edmonton for a hunger march on the legislature. The Premier told a delegation that he would not submit to mob rule and that the march would not be allowed. Meanwhile the numbers in Market Square had swelled to 2,000, who angrily attempted to defy Brownlee's edict. As they marched down Jasper Avenue, they were met by a contingent of city police and mounted RCMP, who made several baton charges on the marchers and finally dispersed them. Some made their ways back to Market Square, where they sang *The Red Flag* and gave three cheers for the Communist Party of Canada. Two were arrested and charged with unlawful assembly.

In a letter that is undated, but which was probably written in December 1932, Irvine described the situation to Norman Smith:

> Brownlee is getting ready to quit. He was very much put out over my speech in Leduc on the 22nd. I spoke after him and gave the same speech which I made in Calgary on the Sunday night previous. At the close he told me that I was more radical than Lakeman and that he would have to call a meeting and have a show down to see whether his view or mine was to be the UFA policy. He has called the meeting for the 28th and 29th, as you will no doubt know. I think that Brownlee is getting ready an excuse for going to the tariff board. If not, we will have to fight hard to retain the CCF revolutionary ideas. Better tell Bob [Gardiner], Brownlee is

liable to make the fight personal on me so that my defence of the CCF would be regarded as a personal one. Garland and Bob will have to fight the thing with me or we will be sunk.[2]

The confrontation foreseen in this letter from Irvine either never took place or was smoothed out without becoming a matter of public debate.

Years later, Irvine said on this matter:

There were no differences between the UFA members of the legislature and those of the federal UFA members, in so far as the rank and file members of the movement were concerned. But every elected member to the federal Parliament under the UFA banner had been a member of the UFA long before it was decided to take direct political action. It is true that after the so-called Ginger Group was formed, the reactionary provincial leadership began to murmur that our radicalism might disturb their reactionary repose. But fortunately for the federal members, the UFA movement was behind us and gave us unqualified support. . . . The Premier once suggested that we should agree to be CCF in the federal field and UFA provincially. This, while it no doubt reflected the difference between the Premier's and the federal members' views, never became an issue in the UFA to the best of my knowledge. The suggestion merely brought into relief the ineptitude of the author and the impracticability of the idea.[9]

Irvine is correct in saying that the federal members had strong support from the UFA rank and file as expressed, for instance, at the annual conventions. However, their attitude towards the provincial MLAs, and more particularly Brownlee and his Cabinet ministers, must have been more equivocal, since the latter were considerably more conservative than the UFA members who attended annual conventions. The UFA conventions indeed initiated and gave strong support to the CCF, and at the same time they were for monetary and credit reform. It has sometimes been supposed that within the UFA there was a conflict between those who were socialists and those who were for monetary reform.[10]

At the Calgary and Regina conventions, the LSR members proclaimed the two to be incompatible, but there was no such conflict in the minds of most of the UFA, as is shown by the statement accepted by the 1932 convention:

> Upon attainment of the Co-operative Commonwealth the forces of production developed under capitalism can be operated to the fullest extent necessary to provide for all essential needs without danger of glut. This becomes possible because through social credit, purchasing power in the hands of consumers is at all times adequate to acquire the goods produced.[11]

This statement was subsequently echoed in the Regina Manifesto. On the other hand, Brownlee and his Cabinet were very cool to both ideas, and it was probably in deference to their views that no steps were taken in rural areas to replace UFA locals with the CCF, and so the efficient organization of the CCF was delayed.

At the UFA convention in January 1934, one resolution urged that the CCF executive give serious consideration to the Douglas proposals when drafting plans for the co-operative commonwealth, and another requested the provincial government to consider the Douglas system and to press for action so that it might be given a fair trial. As a result, the UFA government agreed to hold an enquiry into the Douglas system of social credit before the Agricultural Committee of the legislature. The enquiry was timed to take advantage of the fact that Major Douglas would be returning to the United Kingdom via Canada following a speaking tour of Australia and New Zealand. Meanwhile, Aberhart had not been responsive to the arguments of Irvine and others urging him to rethink his version of social credit. Norman Smith wrote an editorial in the *UFA*:

> Major Douglas's strong individualism would possibly not permit him to agree fully with the program of the UFA and the CCF, but to the writer this appears not to be a matter of major importance. The first task of any government elected to carry out the policies of our movement would be to bring the financial system of Canada under social ownership and

control. Until that is done no government can be master in its own house. For the successful performance of that task there is no instrument more likely to be effective than the Co-operative Commonwealth Federation in which the United Farmers of Alberta are the most influential single unit.[12]

Both on this visit and on a subsequent one, Douglas avoided any outright repudiation of Aberhart and he never unequivocally stated that Alberta did not have the legal power to implement social credit. It is clear that he had no respect for Aberhart's intellectual powers, but on the other hand, he understood that Aberhart was a spellbinder who could possibly win votes and form a government, at which time he thought the task of implementing social credit would be handed over to experts. He seemed to believe that the question of provincial versus Dominion powers in monetary matters was one for others to determine, and that his role as monetary expert did not begin until these other matters were satisfactorily set forth. Douglas's caution did not contrast well with Aberhart's unbounded, although ill-based, confidence that there were no problems in establishing his version of social credit at the provincial level.

Brownlee, in the meantime, had added to the UFA's mounting difficulties by getting himself involved in a sex scandal. On 22 September 1933, suit claiming heavy damages was filed against him because of his alleged seduction of a young woman for whom he had found employment in the legislative offices. The ensuing court case, with its unsavoury allegations against Brownlee, made headlines for weeks, until late in June 1934, the jury found for the plaintiffs and awarded large sums of money to both the young woman and her father.

Brownlee resigned, although he remained in the legislature, and was succeeded by R.G. Reid. It was widely believed in UFA circles that Brownlee was the innocent victim of a Liberal conspiracy. Certainly the Liberals made political use of the case in Brownlee's constituency and elsewhere. Aberhart and his supporters wisely remained silent, leaving the mud-slinging to the Liberals. It remains a moot point as to which was the most damaging to the UFA, Brownlee's political conservatism or his indiscreet behaviour.

By this time, Irvine was acutely aware of the UFA's desperate position. He wrote to Norman Smith on 31 October 1934:

> Have just come from five rallies in Gardiner's riding; 75 percent of the people are for Social Credit.... In my opinion, there is only one hope and that is to accept the Douglas proposals officially. Then get on the air every day that Aberhart is on the air, only follow him and answer his arguments and show him up as the jackass he is. This radio program should be kept going up to the election.[13]

Irvine, by now thoroughly disillusioned with the provincial UFA leadership, still battled on, addressing an incredible number of meetings throughout Alberta and elsewhere.

At the 1935 convention of the UFA, the main subject on the agenda was the proposal, "that a system of social credit, as outlined by Mr. William Aberhart of Calgary, be put as a plank in the UFA provincial platform, to be brought before the electorate at the next provincial election." Aberhart, as an invited guest, spoke for an hour and a half, and followed this up by answering questions for a further two hours.

Gardiner and Priestley made trenchant attacks upon Aberhart's theories and emphasized the considerable difficulties in implementing monetary reform at the provincial level. Irvine also gave an impassioned speech clearly aimed at stealing Aberhart's thunder by advocating a more rational version of social credit. His speech was enthusiastically received, and he succeeded in getting a resolution passed which called upon the UFA government to engage Major Douglas as a consulting economic engineer, to give advice on the possibilities of either Alberta or the federal government applying plans for social credit.

When the Aberhart resolution was finally voted on, it was lost by a large majority. However, the anti-Aberhart victory was a Pyrrhic one, for the UFA had exhausted and divided itself in the contest, and many desertions to the Aberhart camp followed.

As a consequence of the Irvine proposal passed by the convention, Premier Reid, in February 1935, cabled Douglas offering him the post of Chief Reconstruction Adviser to the Government of Alberta. A month later, following the passing of a resolution in the legislature, the government invited Aberhart to prepare and submit a social credit plan for Alberta. The government was prepared to arrange for him to have leave of absence, a clerical and research staff, compensation for lost time and out-of-pocket expenses. Aberhart heeded the counsel of his supporters and refused to make a submission.

It is likely that in making these moves, the UFA was at last responding to some of Irvine's criticisms and adopting his proposed strategies by creating situations in which Aberhart would be forced to expose the confusion and inadequacies of his monetary theory. Reid, Priestley and others had also been using radio to criticize Aberhart, but it was now too late. Aberhart had already captured the imagination and the loyalty of a large section of the Alberta public.

When Douglas came to Alberta for ten days in May and prepared an interim report, he did nothing to change the situation. His report made no mention of Aberhart and suggested that there might be steps Alberta could take in order to create its own credit. He neither publicly condemned the Aberhart proposals, nor put forward definite concrete proposals of his own. During his brief stay in Alberta his relations with Aberhart did not improve. Aberhart feared that Douglas might repudiate his version of social credit, and he was not aware of the extent to which Douglas had decided to let him off the hook.

Irvine too was disappointed by Douglas's attitude. He thought that a man should be prepared to defend the integrity of his own ideas, and he certainly could not agree with Douglas's view that it is better not to explain one's ideas in any depth if one wants to win support for them from the mass of people.

On 23 August 1935, the provincial election was held. Of the sixty-three seats, the Aberhart Social Crediters won fifty-three, leaving five for the Liberals and two for the Conservatives. Not a single UFA or labour candidate was elected.

Some seven weeks later came the federal election, and this time Social Credit took fifteen of the eighteen seats in Alberta. In Wetaskiwin, Irvine ran third, just behind the Liberal candidate, but the Social Credit candidate, Norman Jacques, had an overwhelming majority of 4,800.

Elsewhere, eight CCFers were returned, and Agnes Macphail again represented the United Farmers of Ontario. Woodsworth, Heaps and MacInnis retained their seats. They were joined by M.J. Coldwell and Tommy Douglas, from Saskatchewan. They carried on the tradition of the Ginger Group, but the name now ceased to be appropriate since so many of the original members were gone, and the new group had run for the first time under the banner of the CCF.

In explanation of the final defeat and demise of the UFA as a political force, Irvine said:

> Why did the UFA fail? Why did it pass from the scene when it had so much promise? Here are some of the reasons:
> 1. Incompetent political leadership who loved power rather than achievement. They were not reared in the movement's philosophy; they were chosen from outside to lead a movement they did not understand nor even believe in. They should have chosen their candidates and their leaders from their own ranks. But they had an inferiority complex and thought a lawyer would be better than a farmer.
> 2. The farmers' government was so steeped in Toryism that they lived to serve it without even knowing what they were doing. They killed the UFA, not because they wanted to do so but because of lack of understanding.
> 3. Fear on the part of the leadership to move in any direction other than along that path which was beaten smooth by the feet of reaction led to destruction and destined their efforts to abortion.
> 4. The farmers quit at the first defeat which should have been only a temporary setback.[14]

The causes of the UFA defeat are numerous and complex, but Irvine was correct in placing most of the blame on the leadership of the provincial government. The drive to get the UFA into politics was primarily directed towards the federal government in Ottawa, because it was thought, rightly enough, that it was here that all the most crucial decisions were made. It is not surprising therefore, that the radicals in the UFA sought federal seats. In one case, Donald Kennedy (later a member of the Ginger Group in the House of Commons) gave up his seat in the legislature soon after his election, to make way for Herbert Greenfield, who was chosen to be Premier, although he had not run in the previous provincial election. Kennedy immediately got the federal seat for Edmonton West. More unfortunate was the fact that Robert Gardiner ran in a federal by-election in Medicine Hat and won it overwhelmingly, just before the provincial election took place in 1921. If Gardiner had held off and run for the Alberta legislature, he would undoubtedly have got in and would have been a prime candidate for Premier. In that event he would have given better and more radical leadership than did Greenfield, Brownlee or Reid.

Irvine, as an MLA, would not have had the farming credentials of Robert Gardiner, and so might not at first have been acceptable as Premier, but he would certainly have put some fire and energy into the provincial cabinet. In his case, he deliberately held back and waited for the chance at a federal seat. The crucial mistake of the UFA was to put all its "ginger" into the federal basket.

A significant cause of the decline of the UFA that Irvine surprisingly does not mention is the effect of the Depression. Those who lived through this experience can never forget its mind-destroying effects, which were most keenly felt on the drought-ridden Prairies. In circumstances such as these, it was a constant struggle to maintain membership and activity in the local associations of the UFA. In 1921, the membership of the UFA and its auxiliary organizations reached a peak of 38,000. In 1923, the membership had dropped to 19,468, and by the end of the same year there was a further drop to 11,185. This coincided with the comparatively minor depression of the early Twenties. Irvine and others toured Alberta on membership drives, and between 1924 and 1934 the membership fluctuated between 14,000 and 15,000, but in 1935 it plummeted to 9,838.

This fluctuation in grassroots activity had its effect on the provincial leadership, and they also reacted to Depression conditions. Many progressive plans were curtailed, changed, and even abandoned to make way for projects of family and farm relief, soup kitchens, debt adjustment, and other attempts to help the farmers and workers of Alberta to survive. In such an economic climate, the not so radical leadership became increasingly conservative in its outlook.

Added to this, there was the failure of the labour movement to get something going politically comparable to and in co-operation with the farmers' movement. Labour elected four members to the Legislature in 1921, and six in 1926, and four in 1930. Only two of these, Alex Ross (who lost his seat in 1926) and Fred White, had any real talent for leadership, so that even Henry Wise Wood deplored the fact that labour had not yet asserted itself as an economic group. No doubt labour was suffering from the repressive aftermath of the Winnipeg Strike and also from numerous internal dissensions; but for whatever reason, its failure to adequately represent itself in the Alberta legislature had an adverse effect on the UFA. The *Alberta Labour News,* edited by Elmer Roper, and Norman Smith's *UFA* publication, were mutually supportive of the labour and farmer causes, but their efforts were not sufficient to overcome the lack of a strong labour contingent in the legislature.

Then there was radio. It was sheer accident that William Aberhart had sufficient experience in this new medium to be able to adapt it to political purposes. When, under the pressures of economic depression, other forms of communication and association were breaking down, the radio remained the last lifeline of communication for rural people. The UFA was geared to personal contact at meetings, and they were overwhelmed by this revolutionary means of communication.

The sex scandals were the last straw which broke the UFA's back. In addition to Brownlee's court case, another cabinet minister, Oran L. McPherson, Minister of Public Works, had been involved in a headline-catching divorce suit, which led him to resign at the same time as Brownlee. McPherson had the satisfaction of knocking a scandal-mongering Edmonton *Bulletin* reporter down the steps in front of the legislature, but this did little to improve the image of the UFA government.

So, for many reasons, the UFA political movement passed into oblivion. It left behind an heir, the CCF, born in Alberta, with its origins in the radical farmers' movement. It did not ripen and flower there, but spread and flourished in other Western provinces.

In his last year as MP for Wetaskiwin, Irvine ventured into a new field of endeavour, the theatre, and wrote two plays. The first of these, *The Brains We Trust*, drew capacity audiences at Margaret Eaton Hall, Toronto, for both of its performances 29 and 30 March 1935. It was produced by the Morris Players, a group of CCF members whose purpose was to "accumulate and present plays on social themes." They were directed by Frank E. Hemingway, who was well known in Toronto for his direction of the various pageants held during its centennial celebrations the previous summer.

Although Irvine said that "all the incidents and characters of this play are wholly imaginary," the plot concerned contemporary Canadian political conditions and the audience had no difficulty in identifying the leading characters with those on the actual political scene in Ottawa. The play introduces us to the home of a St. James Street financier, Sir John Horn, who, with two cronies and a rascally lawyer, assumes the right of finance to dictate political policies and acts on that assumption. The scene purports to reveal the cold-blooded attitude of "big business" towards its political puppets; it pays the piper and calls the tune. The tycoons are rather worried by the growing popularity of the "socialist" party, and also by the sudden conversion of the Hon. Hector Dictorson, Prime Minister and leader of the "Loyalist" party, to a reform program. They profess to have no doubt as to the willingness of Mr. Middleton, leader of the "Patriot" party, to obey "his master's voice." Audiences readily identified Dictorson with the then Prime Minister, R.B. Bennett, while Middleton, a character who never appears on stage, is a less easily identifiable Mackenzie King.

When the Prime Minister abruptly leaves the meeting with the financial magnates, after a final outburst of oratorical defiance, one of them remarks quietly, "That settles it. Our money goes on Middleton." But the political paymasters see that their real problem is to offset the menace of the Socialist party, led by Robert McGregor. As the plot develops, it appears that their legal cat-spaw has induced a young woman to take employment in the office of the party, and that a conspiracy has been hatched whereby the Socialist leader is to be charged with seduction.

Irvine skilfully works in a scene in which Socialist party workers discuss the question of principles versus "practical polit-ics." Both sides of the argument are presented but McGregor's principled stand clearly dominates:

> There is confusion of thought about what is meant by win-ning an election. An election is only a means of measuring real progress in political thought. Any device which might show progress to be greater than it really is would be like a merchant tampering with the weights and measures. . . . If by a change in phraseology or through some spurious promise we increased our vote by 300,000, that vote would not really be for socialism. . . . We want to win socialism. The election is incidental. It is true that we cannot win socialism without first winning the election. But it is just as true that we might win the election in such a way as to lose Socialism. . . . I can-not permit any modification of policy with a view to getting votes. To do so would be to yield the principle for which the votes are sought. . . . It is better to have a following which is positively committed to the building of a new social order, than to be overwhelmed by a mob which is running in panic from the crashing structures of the old.[15]

All seems to be going well with the Socialist party when the young woman in the office disappears, and just prior to the elec-tion much publicity is given to the utterly unfounded charge of seduction. This is sufficient to turn the tide in favour of the Patriot party. The play ends with the shouts of the victorious and jubi-lant Patriots in the background, while the following dialogue takes place:

> *McGregor*: The people are weak and foolish, but Horn and his ilk can't keep them in blindness for ever. They're easily frightened, easily swayed, bullied, cajoled, exploited, until the hour strikes.

Miss Wilson: The hour?

McGregor: The hour of desperation, when men's burdens are so heavy that they would rather risk death than carry them a moment longer. It struck in France in 1789; in Russia. . . .

West: Canadians won't tackle anything unconstitutional!

McGregor: Have you ever seen a panic at a fire, or a shipwreck? There are codes, but there's a time when people forget them. There's a law, but people can be driven beyond it. Then we have not reform but revolution.

Miss Wilson: But I thought you wanted revolution.

McGregor: Not that kind. I wanted to build up, not tear down— build a newer and better social order. Well, I've failed. Someone else will succeed. Even if it comes through bloodshed, it's coming. It's bound to come.[16]

It is clear that Robert McGregor was a stand-in for J.S. Woodsworth, and this final speech echoes some of the remarks made by Woodsworth when speaking in the House of Commons in 1933.[17]

The play got a good press with general agreement that it was clever, witty and entertaining. A few critics thought that dramatic interest was drowned by political discussion, and on the other hand, a few complained about the ending: they presumably wanted virtue to be triumphant. Still others thought the theme of the play to be an exaggeration of certain features of political life. In fact, Irvine's play struck rather close to reality. Although transferred to Ottawa, much of it was derived from the Alberta scene, and some from Irvine's own experience. The political use of the seduction scandal was clearly inspired by the Brownlee case, and the attempt to bribe the Socialist leader was drawn from an actual attempt to bribe Irvine:

In 1921, when I ran in East Calgary, a Liberal heeler came to me a day or so before official nomination, [and said] if I would be a little late for nomination so that I wouldn't be running in East Calgary, he would pay me $10,000, he would give me a home — a good house on the North Hill of Calgary — and he would use his influence with the Liberal party to get me a job in the Immigration Department. Now my answer to him was this, exactly as I said it: "If you offered to make me God Almighty I would not be late for nomination tomorrow" and I left him. ... That is just an incident to show you the type of things that are done by political parties.[18]

Despite its Toronto success, Irvine did not have the play performed in Alberta until after the provincial election. It was presented in Edmonton on 26 and 27 September 1935, shortly before the federal election, by the CCF youth movement of Edmonton under the direction of Sam Bancroft. The *Alberta Labour News* reported:

Added interest was given to the presentation on Friday night when William Irvine spoke briefly at the conclusion of the last act. It was decidedly an Irvine night, for in addition to the personal appearance of the author himself, Ronald Irvine, the playwright's son, carried off the part of Mr. Lomer Hogg* the dynamo of St. James Street, with great artistry, while Harry Irvine's baritone solo was also a pleasing feature of the program.[19]

Encouraged by the reception of his first excursion into drama, Irvine proceeded to write another play, this time with a "national credit" theme. *You Can't Do That*, written in collaboration with Edmonton playwright Elsie Park Gowan,[20] was a comedy whose plot revolved around Linda Strome, the Prime Minister's spirited and intelligent niece, who becomes thoroughly disgusted with a dilatory, chicken-hearted group of Cabinet ministers who never do anything but offer excuses for their deficiencies. So Linda, while she calmly passes tea and angel cake to her uncle's guests, conjures up in her head a scheme to kidnap her pompous uncle and four of his ministers. Then, with the cabinet safely out of the way, marooned on an island in the Gulf of St. Lawrence, she passes on faked instructions from the Cabinet over her uncle's forged signature to the Deputy Prime Minister in Ottawa. In this

---

* Ronald Irvine played the same part in the Toronto production.

way, the Dominion government proceeds to take over the "national credit" and make purchasing power available, to get the economy moving and to eliminate unemployment. An incipient rebellion by the bankers is quelled by threatening to cancel their charters. When the Prime Minister and his Cabinet return to Ottawa, they find that the economy is working so smoothly and the majority of people are so satisfied that the process is irreversible, and they are forced to maintain it and to take credit for it.

Clearly Irvine's intent is not as serious in this play as in the previous one. He did not think that changes could happen in this manner, nor that they would meet with so little resistance but, nevertheless, the point is made — if only men and women of intelligence and goodwill had the power and the opportunity, they could accomplish social changes which are now declared impracticable.

You Can't Do That was performed in Edmonton on 13 and 14 March 1936. Again the players were members of the CCYM, this time directed by Elsie Park Gowan, and it was judged a success. The play had a similar reception at Wetaskiwin and several other townships outside of Edmonton. It is to be noted that the monetary and credit reform thesis of the play was quite acceptable to leading members of the CCF in Edmonton and elsewhere in Alberta, who collaborated in putting on the play and in publicizing it.

Mrs. Gowan describes these efforts to give a political education by means of dramatic performances:

> In the depths of the Depression, the Edmonton CCYM made efforts to use drama to spread the word. In Edmonton they produced Irvine's two full-length plays, *The Brains We Trust* and *You Can't Do That*. The latter comedy we also took to a rural community (Smithfield) forty miles west of Edmonton.
>
> The production was an adventure. The community hall (now a general store) had a small raised platform but no curtain. A wire was strung across, and a curtain improvised with a few flannelette blankets hung on safety pins.
>
> The show was well received, but D.L. Shortliffe, who accompanied our party, got into hot arguments afterwards.

The Aberhart gospel of social credit had local converts who debated the "national credit" of the play's thesis.

Bill Irvine accompanied the CCYM Players when they went to the country with a Depression one-act play, *Glorious and Free*. This had originally been written by Jim F.C. Wright, of Saskatoon, rewritten with Gowan dialogue. It was a melodramatic picture of a farm family, in desperate straits. The young son eventually held up the local bank, and was killed attempting to jump a freight. The plot was hokum, but the picture of the family rang true. . . .

We took this short play to points like Camrose and Ft. Saskatchewan, with Irvine as the second half of the act. That is, the play gave Bill an emotional jumping off place for a fiery and indeed eloquent speech on the need for change. I remember Chester Ronning saying to us in Camrose, "You could sweep through Alberta with this like Joan of Arc through France."[21]

After this second play, Irvine did not pursue this line of endeavour, but instead returned to the more usual types of political persuasion. Almost certainly with practice he would have improved his technical skills and his expressive powers as a playwright and perhaps he would have developed the genre of the political play with some distinction. However, this was not to be and he returned to the very necessary but more humdrum task of political journalist and propagandist.

TEN

Building the CCF

At the close of 1935 Irvine, having lost his seat in Parliament, found himself without a source of income, so he naturally turned to journalism. He had already been a frequent contributor to the *Alberta Labour News* and he had known the editor and owner, Elmer Roper, since his early days in Calgary when Roper was president of the Calgary Trades and Labour Council. In 1936 the *Alberta Labour News* became the *People's Weekly*, which although not an official organ of the CCF strongly supported the new political movement.*

Early in January 1936, Irvine made an attempt to get back into the House of Commons. Prime Minister Mackenzie King had appointed J.G. Gardiner, former Premier of Saskatchewan, to his Cabinet as Minister of Agriculture, and consequently Gardiner was seeking to gain a seat in Parliament. The Assiniboia riding was made vacant and Irvine and Gardiner contested it in a federal by-election. In the circumstances it was a forlorn hope, but although defeated by a large majority, Irvine managed to save his

---

* With Roper in control of editorial policy and Irvine assisting and supporting him as associate editor, there was little if any criticism of the paper by CCF members. There was, however, a growing feeling that the CCF should have its own official organ, so in 1944 Roper offered to turn the paper over to the Alberta CCF. The offer was accepted and from 6 January 1945, the paper was owned and officially controlled by the Alberta CCF. Roper retained the position of editor, and Irvine continued his association with the paper.

deposit. It was the first time that he sought election under the CCF banner.

Shortly afterwards he settled down to his job as associate editor of the *People's Weekly*. The first issue appeared on 26 January 1936, and it contained the first of a series of open letters from William Irvine to Premier Aberhart. There were sixteen letters in all, appearing almost every week for four months. They constituted a devastating attack upon the performance of the Aberhart government in its first nine months of office. At the conclusion of the series, the letters were reprinted in pamphlet form with a foreword by Irvine. Irvine criticized the Social Credit government for increasing taxes, reducing social services and not implementing the basic tenets of social credit as propounded in election promises. He eventually accused Aberhart of fascist tendencies because he implemented legislation that allowed him to govern by Order-in-Council over Parliament:

> In your amendment to the Social Credit Bill you take to yourself that power and authority which properly belongs to the legislature and thereby have robbed the people of a liberty for which other generations fought and paid dearly in the past.
>
> You may argue that any policy within the jurisdiction of the province which the government might bring before the legislature, your majority would vote for it in any case. That is probably true, but still there would be open discussion on it and the people would know something of what was being proposed and would have a chance to register either protest or agreement before the thing is undertaken. In other words, the people do not desire to transfer the power of the legislature to any government or any dictator.
>
> It is true that a government may by Order-in-Council carry through details of a principle which has received the endorsation of Parliament, and when Parliament is not in session. But for a government to take to itself the power to deal with all the principles which might be involved in the implementing of a Social Credit policy and without referring each phase of it in the form of a bill to be passed by the

legislature, is a departure from democratic principles which is unwarranted and dangerous....

Finally, Irvine proposed to Aberhart constitutional measures by which he might try to relieve the farmer of his burden of debt and provide him with security of land tenure:

> I suggest that you begin by taking the first step, which is to make it a policy of your government that from now henceforth all the lands held by the province shall continue to be held by it. That neither homesteads nor leases on the old basis will be given and that not an acre shall be sold to any one.
>
> The second step is to tax large landholding companies, including mortgage companies, so high that they will be forced either to put their land to productive uses or get rid of it. If this were done much of the best of Alberta's lands would be returned and would become the property of the commonwealth.
>
> The third step, and the one which is essential to be taken in the interests of debt-ridden farmers, is that when a farmer has been ejected by a mortgage company you should at once grant him a perpetual lease of land belonging to the province.

In only one case was Irvine's criticism wide of the mark. He had characterized the Recall Act of 1936, by which an MLA could be unseated by petition, as ineffective; however, in 1937, the necessary 4,400 signatures required for Aberhart's recall were collected in his riding of High River-Okotoks. In order to save Aberhart, the provincial cabinet had to sponsor and push through the legislature a motion to repeal the Recall Act.

Irvine's trenchant attack may have played a part, combined with general disenchantment, in reducing Aberhart's support, so that at the end of the Social Credit government's first term in office in 1940, it suffered not a defeat but a serious setback in the provincial election. With 43 percent of the vote, Social Credit won thirty-six seats, while a motley crew of former Liberals, Conservatives and some former UFAers, comprising the Independent party, received 46 percent of the vote and twenty seats. The CCF, with 10 percent of the vote, won no seats. It had previously scored its first success in the Alberta political field when Chester Ronning, principal of Camrose Lutheran College, ran as a CCF candidate and won the Camrose constituency in a 1933 provincial by-election. Ronning supported the UFA government in the legislature and was admitted to the UFA caucus. He suffered defeat along with all the UFA members in 1935.

The development of the CCF was hampered by the subsequent political hesitation and uncertainty of the UFA, which, at its convention in 1936, was unable to reach any decision regarding its political future. Soon after, the Alberta CCF called its first provincial convention and elected an Alberta CCF council consisting of William Irvine as president, Robert Gardiner as vice-president and Fred White as secretary, each officer representing respectively the general membership, the UFA, and the Canadian Labour party (Alberta section).

From its beginnings in Alberta, the CCF had been a true federation. Through mutual decision and co-operation, it became a movement composed of labour and farmer organizations, further augmented by local groups operating through a provincial constitution and charter as economic reconstruction association clubs. These clubs were formed to provide an appropriate place in the new movement for those men and women of progressive thought who were not eligible to belong to either farm or labour organizations. The constitutions of these three groups were arranged to allow for joint participation in nominating conventions and other matters concerning direct political action.

In the early years, the UFA, both as the dominant farm group in an agricultural province, and as the government of Alberta, was the strongest single part of the federation, and in deference to its political position no steps were taken in rural areas to replace UFA locals with the CCF. However, even before the first Alberta CCF convention in 1936, a CCF council had been set up consisting of the presidents of the three main groups participating in the federation. In 1935, a further step forward had been taken when it was agreed that in several federal constituencies the groups would hold joint nominating conventions and the nominees from these conventions would contest the election as CCF candidates.

In 1937, the UFA decided to vacate the provincial political field but to remain in the federation in federal affairs. This decision literally forced the CCF into a position of separate political action and in that year, at its second provincial convention, the CCF launched a program of direct active organization in both rural and urban areas of the province. Irvine was appointed as provincial organizer on a full-time basis with the necessary financial support coming through regular monthly contributions of individual members, "dime" funds, and other money-raising schemes.[1] The "dime" funds were a revealing indication of the depression conditions that prevailed in Alberta throughout the Thirties. CCF membership was only fifty cents per year but it was not feasible to increase this so as to provide more revenue for the party. As an alternative, the CCF office distributed to members and sympathizers sheets of paper on each of which there were spaces, rendered suitably adhesive, for ten dimes. The recipient was expected to stick on a dime whenever one became available. When all the spaces were filled, the sheet was folded over and mailed in. Mary Crawford, the party's treasurer for many years, had the unenviable task of gouging out and depositing in the bank hundreds of sticky dimes.

Meanwhile, the CCF had been growing on a national scale and was now recognized as a potentially powerful political force. Other provinces, with a clear field before them, had outstripped Alberta in terms of organization and activity. In 1938, the Alberta CCF was honoured with the decision to hold the national convention in Edmonton, but in the same year the UFA continued to maintain its indecisive position in regard to political action. This led to the calling of a special CCF provincial convention to be held in July in Calgary. The delegates decided to commit the CCF to full-scale political activity within the province and to proceed at once to the setting up of local club organizations throughout Alberta. They also agreed that as soon as club membership reached 1,000, another convention would be called for the purpose of preparing a provincial program and constitution for the Alberta CCF.

At its thirty-first annual convention held in Calgary in January

1939, the UFA finally withdrew from politics after twenty years. It was a hard blow to the CCF to lose its chief progenitor and the most important constituent of its federation, but it was softened by the fact that at last several years of indecision and uncertainty were resolved. Also, the UFA that came to this decision was a shadow of its former self. In its heyday UFA conventions had drawn as many as 1,000 delegates and there had been as many as 1,200 local associations. At the 1939 convention, there were only 272 delegates and active locals had dwindled to perhaps 300.

At the end of July 1939, the general membership section of the CCF held a provincial convention at the Masonic Temple in Edmonton to discuss the situation. Irvine, who was president of this section, acted as chairman. There was an immediate need for the provincial CCF to form constituency organizations to fill the gap left by the withdrawal of the UFA, and Irvine was appointed provincial organizer, having declined the presidency. Irvine also chaired the first joint convention of the two remaining affiliated units of the Alberta CCF on 2 August 1939, immediately following the general membership convention.

One important item of business was the election of someone to the new post of leader of the provincial party. Chester Ronning, Fred White and Irvine were nominated. Irvine declined, stating that his experience had been in the federal field and since he was accepting a federal nomination in the 1940 election, it would be impossible for him to effectively act as provincial leader. Fred White also refused the nomination, so that Ronning was elected leader by acclamation.[2]

For the next few months until the federal election on 26 March 1940, Irvine campaigned in the Cariboo riding just across the border from west-central Alberta. He had chosen to run in B.C. because of the lack of CCF constituency organization in Alberta. Working from an office in Prince George, he campaigned throughout the riding, which was difficult for someone of limited financial resources. Later Irvine succinctly described what happened:

> My best vote was among labour in the hard-rock gold mines. There happened to be a strike on during the election.

Men were demanding not only better pay but better protection from silicosis. Two days before the election, seventy-five policemen came to the camp. It turned out that the workers were living in houses which belonged to the company. Presumably they could not pay the rents while on a prolonged strike and the policemen herded them off to Vancouver. I stood there watching while my supporters in the election were driven out of their homes and every one of them thereby disfranchised. So again I lost the election.[3]

Nevertheless, Irvine made a good showing with 5,000 votes to the Liberal's 6,000, while a third candidate trailed with 2,300.

During the early Forties, the organizational structure of the CCF gradually changed. More and more local clubs were organized, provincial and federal constituency associations were formed, and direct membership became larger until it exerted a major influence upon the policies and activities of the movement. At the same time, the Canadian Labour party (Alberta section), despite strenuous efforts on the part of its leadership, failed to grow significantly.

At a special convention called in early 1942 to reorganize the Alberta CCF, the Alberta Labour party amalgamated with the CCF clubs. The Alberta CCF thereby lost its federated nature and became a direct membership body operating a provincial organization from an Edmonton office with Irvine as field organizer and a small office staff, though constitutionally it remained theoretically possible for trade union and farm organizations to affiliate with the Alberta CCF.

Irvine set about writing a brief but lucid pamphlet which set forth CCF policy as it applied to Alberta. The pamphlet reproduced the CCF provincial platform and this was followed by Irvine's explanation of the ideas behind the CCF proposals. A central feature of the CCF program was the prominence given to the concept of public ownership, and in a few pages Irvine gave an explanation and justification of this philosophy. He argued that institutions and resources used by all people should be publicly owned so that a few were not allowed to capitalize on the needs of many. He made it clear that this did not mean the abolition of all private property. He also pointed out that although nationalization could obviously not take place without the support of the federal government, it was nevertheless up to the Alberta government to socialize those means of production which fell under its jurisdiction. He suggested that the Alberta oil industry was the place to start in a program of provincial nationalization.

The former UFA provincial government had succeeded after protracted negotiations with the federal government, in gaining jurisdiction over the province's natural resources. All these, and the revenues derived from them, were handed over to the province of Alberta to administer as it thought fit. In view of the subsequent exploitation of Alberta's natural resources, a resolution passed at the CCF provincial convention in November 1942 is of particular interest. It read in part:

> ... The CCF is also concerned about the development of the McMurray oil sands which are said to contain an almost unlimited supply of oil. The public should be informed about the arrangement by which the sands are now being worked. Not only is it felt that not sufficient progress is being made in bringing the potential oil resources of the McMurray field into use, but there is public uneasiness lest private interests instead of the people through their governments should gain and keep control of what may turn out to be one of the greatest sources of oil and oil products in the world.[4]

Earlier in the year, Elmer Roper won an Edmonton seat in the legislature at a by-election, and at the 1943 CCF convention he became the leader of the party. At the same time, Irvine added to his duties of organizer those of party secretary; he held these two posts, along with his associate editorship of the *People's Weekly*, until 1945. At the 1943 convention, he reported that membership had grown from 2,000 in the previous year to 6,000. Despite this impressive rate of growth, the Alberta CCF was unable to make a major breakthrough in either the provincial or the federal field.

These were hard years for Irvine. Not only did he perform a threefold task but he did so on a minimal income, and in 1940 he faced a major financial crisis. He had embarked upon the project of building a home for his family in Wetaskiwin, and when the lumber he had ordered arrived he found himself without the means to pay for it. In desperation he wrote to the national secretary of the CCF in Ottawa, David Lewis, asking the party to lend him $500, the cost of the building materials, to be repaid with interest. In his letter to Lewis, Irvine mentioned another possible source of income: during his years in Ottawa he had frequently functioned as preacher and pastor for the Unitarian church there, and in 1940 the pulpit was vacant and had been offered to him. Although Irvine's role throughout his connection with the Unitarian church had been to raise social issues rather than religious ones, he was reluctant to return to the ministry and preferred to stay in Alberta working for the CCF, provided he could sustain his family. He wrote:

> As to the Unitarian proposal, you may be sure that I will stay in Alberta if that is possible, and what you are doing to help me will go far to make it possible. Once I have got a place to live in I can hold out a long time on very little. My heart is not in the church as you know, but in the CCF. To have to go to the church for a living would be unfair and most difficult for me.[5]

Lewis apparently replied that there was no way in which the CCF would be able to lend Irvine money to meet his pressing needs. He was urged to continue supplementing his income, as he sometimes did, by writing anonymous articles for the labour press at the rate of $8 for 12,000 words. In this way he might earn as much as $25 to $40 per month. Lewis also promised to seek assistance from individual supporters of the CCF. It appears that Irvine received some remuneration from these sources and the remainder from CCF friends in Alberta and thus was able to complete the construction of his house in Wetaskiwin.

Nevertheless, he continued to be in financial straits, and around 1944, the following incident occurred, as described by Elmer Roper:

> Bill had gone to Ottawa to attend a meeting of the national council of the CCF. When he did not return after the meeting

and we did not hear from him, we were somewhat mystified as the days and then weeks went by. I received a note from him indicating that he was living at the Windsor Hotel, but he gave no hint of why or how he happened to be holed up in what was then Montreal's most luxurious hotel. The mystery was solved only after he arrived home unexpectedly one day and he told me the story.

While in Ottawa he met an old acquaintance who admired Bill's speaking and writing style. He was an executive in one of the major advertising agencies. The job he offered Bill was that of writing what are in the trade called "readers." In this case the "readers" were to be items of interest or little stories that would in a subtle way say or infer something favourable about one of the agency's clients, a kind of innocent-looking bit of brainwashing. These "readers" are distributed to newspapers and they provide useful fillers, especially for country weeklies; and since the weeklies depend heavily on business from the advertising agencies, use of the "readers" is so general that they provide easy employment for clever writers employed by the agencies.

That was the job Bill took, with a fat payment for his work and a room at the Windsor. I have no doubt that he could have continued to haul down the big paycheck for as long as he wished. But he came back to his meagre little pittance as CCF organizer. He couldn't (as he put it) prostitute his talent by polishing the image of some interests whom he regarded as enemies of his fellow Canadians.[6]

In addition to his financial hardships in the Forties, Irvine suffered a grievous loss (as did the CCF) with the death of J.S. Woodsworth, in March 1942. When Canada declared herself at war in September 1939, Woodsworth was the sole person to rise in the House of Commons and oppose Canada's participation in the conflict. Although they respected his views and agreed that he should speak his mind, none of his CCF colleagues was prepared to support his position. Irvine's own attitude to the war was reflected in a resolution later passed at the Alberta CCF convention in 1943, which stated:

We reiterate the stand of our national organization regarding the full utilization of all our resources for an effective prosecution of the war. We commend the activities of our CCF members in Parliament in this respect. While recognizing the magnificent response of the Canadian people to every call which the nation has made upon them, and recognizing also that Canada has made a very great contribution to the war effort of the United Nations, we deplore the inadequacy of the manpower policy of the present government and its failure to take the farmers and industrial workers into full partnership in the war economy, while at the same time it has been submissive to the influence of the financial and industrial interests.[7]

Woodsworth's health rapidly declined during 1940 and having suffered a severe stroke he was unable to attend the national convention in Winnipeg that year; instead, he sent a letter to the convention resigning as national president and suggesting that the CCF members should also choose a new House leader to replace him.

The convention unanimously, by standing vote, supported Irvine's resolution that the resignation of the president be not accepted, and that the question of House leader be referred to the parliamentary group for decision. The convention sent Irvine and S.J. Farmer, a labour man closely associated with Woodsworth during the Winnipeg Strike, as delegates to speak with Woodsworth. The next day Irvine reported to the convention that Woodsworth stood firmly by his decision to resign. However, Irvine suggested that Woodsworth would be prepared to accept an honorary position. Whereupon the convention proceeded to abolish the office of president and replace it with that of honorary president, to which post Woodsworth was duly elected by acclamation. He was never again to play an active political role and within less than two years he was dead. M.J. Coldwell had already assumed some of Woodsworth's responsibilities under the title of national chairman, and shortly thereafter he became House leader.

Irvine was called upon to give the main address at a memorial service held in Vancouver. He paid eloquent and moving tribute to Woodsworth before a large gathering, calling him a true prophet and a man of courage:

> He not only had courage of a physical kind, the courage to face a hostile crowd, to become a longshoreman, to go to prison. But he had that courage expressed in lines which he himself quoted, the courage "to go on forever and fail, and go on again" — the courage which enabled him to rest "with the half of a broken hope for a pillow at night."[8]

Irvine had been closely associated with his friend for thirty-five years, and with Woodsworth's passing an era came to an end.

From the time of his electoral defeat in 1935 to his re-election in June 1945, Irvine produced a constant output of week by week political journalism in the *People's Weekly* and elsewhere. In addition Irvine was heavily involved in politics, not only as organizer for the CCF in Alberta, but also as a candidate for the federal riding of Cariboo.

Irvine's second son, Harry, was also a CCF candidate, for the Jasper-Edson constituency in Alberta. An RCAF officer, Harry was thirty when in January of 1944 he was sent overseas. Subsequently he was promoted to the rank of flying officer. His wife and two children helped to make Harry an ideal candidate, but on 15 January 1945, Harry was reported missing in action. Although the loss of his son was a bitter blow to Irvine, he continued his work almost unabated. Only one issue of the *People's Weekly* failed to carry his regular contributions and he cancelled a few speaking engagements.

Irvine was forced to fight the 1945 election on the issue of the essentially democratic nature of socialism. The CCF had been under attack as a Nazi-like organization, particularly by right-wing pamphleteer B.A. Trestrail, who characterized socialism as "social suicide." Trestrail had some success in gaining big business support against the CCF. In 1945 Irvine published a booklet entitled *Is Socialism the Answer?: The Intelligent Man's Guide to Democracy*, which was intended to counteract anti-socialist propaganda and reassert the democratic basis of socialism. Unfortunately it was not off the press until two days before the election, so that it had little influence on the campaign even though it was subsequently widely distributed.

At the polls on 11 June, Irvine defeated the incumbent Liberal and also the Progressive Conservative and Social Credit contenders for the Cariboo seat. His victory was warmly greeted by CCF supporters in general and by the Albertan contingent in particular. The party had hoped to make great gains, and although they raised their membership in the House of Commons from ten to twenty-eight (by-elections subsequently raised the number to thirty-two), this figure did not meet their expectations. There was particular disappointment that no CCF members were from Alberta.

At the age of sixty, after a lapse of ten years, Irvine re-entered the House of Commons. Only one of the other CCFers, Angus MacInnis, had previously served with him. Despite his years and long absence from the parliamentary scene, he entered into debate with all his former zest and in the course of the four-year life of the twentieth Parliament spoke some 225 times, often at considerable length.

In June 1946, there was a seamen's strike on the Great Lakes and a lumber strike in B.C., both related to the hours of work. Irvine spoke up in the House, defending the eight-hour day for all categories of workers and pointing out that during the period of the war these groups had, in the national interest, refrained from pushing their claims for an eight-hour working day. Irvine called for government intervention to ensure that all workers operated an eight-hour day:

> According to the information which I have, there are some 5,800 seamen affected by the seamen's strike. I am informed that there are as many as 37,000 affected by the woodworkers' strike in British Columbia. To imply that we should be careless about taking active part in settling a strike because it is alleged that some communist is in the leadership is to ignore the actual conditions which govern the lives of 37,000 men in British Columbia and 5,800 seamen. The Ca-

nadian Great Lakes seamen work twelve hours a day, seven days a week.... Can the shipowners afford to pay for an eight-hour day? I am not going to enter into the profits they made during the war, although that might very well be done. But I would say that morally this nation cannot afford to allow the continuation of a twelve-hour day, seven days a week. Any industry which cannot afford to employ its men on an eight-hour day should either cease operation or be subsidized by the public, so that one class of worker may not have to bear more than its share of the national burden.[9]

The following year, during a debate on the question of rescinding emergency powers adopted by the government during the war, there was considerable opposition to allowing Canadians of Japanese origin to return to the area of the Pacific coast from which many of them had been deported. Irvine vigorously defended the rights of these people and in response to a member who had questioned their loyalty, Irvine replied:

Let me suppose that the hon. member for New Westminster had been an immigrant to Japan. Suppose they had taken all his goods out of his home and sent him with his bagpipes under guard to the top of a high mountain! Suppose they told him to stay there, told him how much he was to get for his daily work, how many hours he had to work, and all the rest of it. Then suppose a year or two later they came along and said: "Now, Mr. Reid, will you tell us to whom you owe your greatest loyalty? Is it to Canada or is it to Japan?"
... The whole question, it seems to me, is this: Shall we have one law for citizens of Japanese origin and another law for the rest of us? That is the real issue before Parliament.... There can be no ifs, ands or buts when applied to the principles of freedom extended under Canadian citizenship. Every citizen must be treated equally.[10]

In the same year, Paul Martin, Minister of National Health and Welfare, introduced a bill to amend the Old Age Pensions Act. It provided for the federal government to assume the full responsibility for paying pensions at the rate of $30 a month to all persons in Canada seventy years and over who passed a means test. Also the federal government undertook to pay, on a fifty-fifty basis with the provinces, the cost of pensions to the aged between the ages of sixty-five and seventy and to the blind from the age of twenty-one. Previously the pension had been $25 per month at age seventy, or at age forty for the blind. Some provinces paid supplemental amounts.

The inadequacy of the proposal raised a storm of protest in the House, which was in part expressed by Irvine, who recalled:

> I had the honour of being on the first committee appointed to consider old age pensions. From the evidence given before us at that time [1924], I came to the conclusion that a pension of $50 a month should be paid to the people of Canada who had reached the age of sixty or sixty-five and that this should be a federal responsibility. I was alone in the committee in that regard, but I have not seen any good reason to change my mind on the matter up to this time.…
>
> I want to emphasize the point of view that my group has constantly put forward, that there should be an overall social security program for Canada, which would have to be carried out through federal legislation, whether by co-operation with the provinces or whether by an amendment to the constitution which gives the federal government the complete right to pass such legislation.… I want to press the Minister when he closes the debate, to indicate that he is willing to allow this bill to go to the appropriate committee for more careful consideration. I venture to say that if it had not been that an amendment to the motion for second reading, to send the bill to a committee, might have had the effect of killing the bill, such an amendment would have been moved long since. No one wants to kill the thing, though it is only a matter of $5 a month or $60 a year for every old man and every old lady of seventy.… But none of us is satisfied with it.[11]

Despite a long and vigorous debate and much criticism, the government pushed the bill through almost unchanged. As late as 1962, the federal old age pension was only $40 a month at age seventy for those who had lived in Canada for twenty consecutive years.

In April and May 1948, the House of Commons had a major debate on the direction of Canada's foreign policy. The Cold War had already begun and Irvine was practically alone in urging what was later called co-existence, and which more recently has been called détente between the major world powers:

> The Russian people think they gained by their revolution something which they would rather die than give up. Some of us, all of us I think, feel that during the centuries, in our struggle for liberty, we have gained something which we would rather die than give up; and as things are presented to us now, it appears that Russia must either die or give up some of the things she believes in, or we must either die or give up some of the things we hold so dear. I believe that history will prove that neither the Russians nor the western democracies need either die or give up the things they hold dear.
>
> On the other hand, there are features of our way of life which we ourselves do not want and which we are struggling day by day to eliminate; and no doubt there are in the Russian way of life features which we certainly do not want and which even the Russians themselves may not want, and which they may be struggling to get rid of and ultimately will get rid of just as they got rid of the Czar.
>
> A world war, however, to determine which of these two ideologies shall dominate in the world, would, in my view, be the greatest of all great tragedies of all time; for in such a war, whichever of the two was victorious, it would mean that there would be foisted on the world a system which the peoples of the world do not want — because there are elements in our system which we do not want, while there are elements in the Russian system which we do not want and which perhaps they do not want.
>
> Perhaps there is not enough knowledge and goodwill among men today for us to discover that desirable synthesis

between these two extreme ideologies without our fighting it out on the battlefield, as has been the custom in the past. I hope we shall be able to struggle through to that synthesis without a third world war.... It is said that even the beasts of the forest which ordinarily prey on each other herd together when they are overtaken by a forest fire. Surely it is not too much to hope that nations of human beings will be able to find some basis of co-operation before we are herded together in what would be much worse than a forest fire — an atomic war.[12]

In September 1948, Irvine had the opportunity of observing the situation in Europe at first hand. The British Parliamentary Association was holding a conference consisting of delegates drawn from the Parliament of the U.K. and the parliaments and legislatures of the other member nations of the Commonwealth. Three CCFers were invited: M.J. Coldwell, House Leader and National Chairman, Tommy Douglas, Premier of Saskatchewan, and Irvine. The purpose of the conference was to enable legislators from all parts of the Commonwealth to meet and exchange views and become acquainted with each other and the problems of Commonwealth countries.

The trip, which lasted five weeks, also gave Irvine the chance to visit some of the countries in Europe and to pay his second return visit to Shetland. The trip occurred during the Berlin blockade, which lasted from 24 July 1948 to 12 May 1949.

Irvine, with his companions, visited the blockaded city, and as a result he wrote two articles on the situation for the *People's Weekly*. Essentially, Irvine looked upon the Berlin crisis as a dangerous power play between the two great superpowers, the U.S.A. and the U.S.S.R. He deplored the Russians' use of the blockade and thought that their policy in this regard was mistaken and endangered peace. Nevertheless he continued to hope that war would be avoided and that the two powers would eventually learn to settle their differences in more rational ways.

On his return to Canada, Irvine was immediately involved in preparing for the federal election of 27 June 1949. Unfortunately, the CCF suffered another setback, their numbers in the House of

Commons being reduced from thirty-two to thirteen. Irvine was one of the casualties. Again his Cariboo riding had been gerrymandered. Some fifty square miles had been cut out of it, removing his support from miners. Even then, with a reduced electorate, Irvine received about 100 more votes than in the previous election. However, the Progressive Conservatives and Social Credit refrained from running candidates, leaving the Liberal candidate to fight for capitalist free enterprise unhampered. Thus Irvine went down to defeat, bringing to an end a long and honourable parliamentary career.

ELEVEN

The Cold War

After his electoral defeat, Irvine returned to his former roles as associate editor of the *People's Weekly* and organizer for the Alberta CCF. There were now two other organizers in the field, Nellie Peterson[1] and J.P. Griffin. Irvine became the director of CCF organization, and for the next twelve years or so his activities centred around Woodsworth House, where his office was established.

Woodsworth House had been acquired earlier in the year, in circumstances described in the *People's Weekly*:

> Barely a month ago an appeal went out for $10,000 to make the down payment on a property costing $18,000. By last Thursday the whole $18,000 had come in and on Friday April 1st, the Alberta Woodsworth House Association obtained a clear title to the property with not a dollar owing to anyone outside the CCF.
>
> Alberta Woodsworth House Association is an incorporated society composed of the persons who subscribed the funds to buy Woodsworth House. The Association owns Woodsworth House...
>
> ...Suites on the second and third floors and in the basement are rented. There is a large fireproof garage to be rented.
>
> Revenue from the property will be enough to pay interest on the investment with a surplus to go toward retirement of debentures held by members of the Alberta Woodsworth

House Association. All surpluses and all donations will be
used to build up the equity of the CCF in the property, with
complete ownership by the CCF the ultimate goal.[2]

This aim was never achieved. The CCF did come to own a few of
the debentures, but because of its insecure financial position, it
was desirable that the Woodsworth House Association should retain ownership, otherwise there was a great risk of losing a potentially valuable property.

The ground floor of Woodsworth House was put to multiple
use. The front office was occupied by whoever was doing secre-
tarial duties, usually Nellie Peterson, while the rear office was
given over to Irvine. Adjacent to Irvine's office there was a bath-
room and kitchen, so that he could use it as living quarters on the
occasions when it was not convenient for him to drive the forty-
five miles to his home in Wetaskiwin. The larger board room and
reception room were also available for meetings of up to fifty
people. The control and maintenance of Woodsworth House was
mainly carried on by Nellie Peterson and Floyd Johnson,* who
collected the rents, paid the bills and supervised the carrying out
of necessary repairs. The house became a well-known centre for
CCFers. For many years there was a large notice in the front of
the house proclaiming that "The CCF Puts Humanity First." Perhaps because of this, the house became a regular port of call for
transients and others down on their luck. Irvine was a generous
and indiscriminate giver, often disposing of all his ready cash and
on one occasion, in the depths of winter, making a gift of his
overcoat.

Irvine made three more attempts to get back into Parliament, in
1953, 1955 and 1958, in Cariboo, Battle River and Wetaskiwin
respectively. In Cariboo, he made a respectable showing, but in
the latter two attempts he trailed his opponents badly. This was
due partly to the fact that the Social Credit government was
firmly established on the basis of its exploitation of the oil re-

---

* Floyd Johnson (1908-1974), an Edmonton building contractor, was
  a tireless worker for the CCF. He was annually elected leader of the
  Alberta CCF from 1958-1961.

sources of the provinces, and partly due to the Cold War atmosphere, which developed in the late Forties and reached its height in the Fifties.

The Cold War not only affected the electoral performance of the CCF but it also penetrated its ideology and particularly its approach to international affairs, which became almost identical with that of the Liberal government: support for the UN, for NATO and for foreign aid and, generally, support for the rearmament that was necessary to meet the NATO commitment. In defence of the CCF's policy of NATO support, David Lewis wrote:

> Socialists could not ignore the Soviet threat. They abhorred capitalism, particularly the arrogant variety governing the United States, but they could live and work under it. Under Soviet communism they knew they could not remain socialists and live.... Therefore, socialists everywhere and the CCF in Canada support NATO. But we cannot ever lose sight of the fact that our most powerful partner is a country whose capitalist leaders are concerned not only with protecting the west against Soviet aggression but also with protecting American profits and the capitalist system....
>
> We support NATO but not all its policies. We are in favour of western collective security, but not of unbalanced rearmament at the expense of European recovery. We are prepared to work with the United States but not on its terms alone. We will fight communism with all our vigour, but we will not permit capitalism to turn the clock back. NATO must become an agency of economic and social advance and not merely an armed camp.[3]

It is odd that this defence of CCF support for NATO makes no reference to the much hotter issue of the Korean war. Here actual warfare was taking place, men were being killed, including Canadians, and there was imminent danger of the war becoming a worldwide conflict. The national leadership of the CCF was able to get endorsation of its support for what was essentially U.S. policy in Korea at both national and provincial conventions, but not without a good deal of uneasiness and rumblings of discontent among the rank and file of the membership. The possible consequences of this policy became so ominous that even M.J. Coldwell began to have second thoughts.

On 1 February 1951, his reply to the Speech from the Throne dealt almost entirely with Canada's stand on the Chinese-Korean issue. Coldwell expressed his fear that the UN resolution branding China an aggressor would be "followed by an intensified bitterness and demands for the institution of sanctions which, if approved, I fear will push China more and more into the orbit of the Soviet Union."[4]

Coldwell placed on the record the resolution passed by the national executive on 28 January, which said: "The CCF does not doubt that the invasion of Korea by the Chinese armies was unjustifiable and contrary to UN policy. But at this moment every effort must be made to prevent a general war. We must not give way to resentment or hysteria, or assume that war is inevitable."[5]

Less than a week later, Premier Douglas voiced a stronger statement in the Saskatchewan provincial legislature in which he said that he was convinced that the people of Saskatchewan were willing to fight to protect freedom, but were not willing to go to war merely to "bolster up discredited regimes," and he offered "to test the opinion of the people on that important matter." Irvine promptly sent a wire congratulating Douglas on his stand.

However, the war within the CCF continued unabated and it was reflected in the pages of the *People's Weekly*. Letter writers and columnists began to express dissent and discontent with the party's foreign policy and this led to counterattacks from other letter writers and indeed at times from the paper's own editorial columns. Editor Elmer Roper was personally convinced of the rightness of CCF policy on the Korean war and he exercised his power to edit and reject articles, and to a lesser extent letters, which seemed in conflict with that policy.

The chief offender was Walter Mentz, who wrote a regular column under the pseudonym "De Bunker," although a recognizable photograph of Mentz appeared at the head of the column. Mentz's comments emphasized that side of the dilemma (which the CCF had created for itself) criticizing the capitalist aims and motivations of the United States. Mentz was vigorously abused by several letter writers who accused him of being a "Moscow-

Communist." Anyone who reads Mentz's columns carefully cannot imagine how he could be regarded as a proponent of anything but democratic socialism; nevertheless, the situation led to a crisis in the *People's Weekly* and the Alberta CCF over whether the *People's Weekly*, as an official organ of the CCF, should publish articles critical of party policy. Roper was emphatically against allowing such criticism to be printed.

Irvine himself was in a difficult position, with a conflict between his convictions and the policy of the CCF as established at national and provincial conventions, and with the added complication of sharing editorial duties and reponsibilities with Elmer Roper. Irvine refrained at this time from writing in the *People's Weekly* on the controversial topic of international affairs, but he was in close contact and sympathy with those who wished to publish controversial material in the paper and he tried to seek solutions to the problem.

The Alberta CCF board met in Woodsworth House on 9 April 1951 to discuss the issue. Following Roper's presentation, a number of board members including Irvine, Walter Mentz, Nellie Peterson and Sig Lefsrud, contended that although the *People's Weekly* was a party organ, articles critical of party policies could appear, as long as editorials adhered to the party line. After a lengthy discussion by board members of most aspects of the situation, measures were taken intended to have the effect of opening the paper to constructive discussion or criticism of CCF policies provided that use of the letter column space was not abused. This motion was defeated by ten to eight.

J.E. Cook then moved that the board express complete confidence in the editor, but that it should also provide a would-be contributor with the right of appeal against editorial decisions. In speaking to his motion, Cook argued that, in view of the national council's resolution in favour of freedom of discussion within the party, as reported by Irvine earlier in the meeting, there was no longer any conflict. He declared that to prohibit free discussion in the *People's Weekly* would be a violation of CCF policy as formulated by the national council. His motion was carried. Roper, who was absent from the latter part of the meeting, subsequently wrote to the national secretary Lorne Ingle, asking if

Cook was indeed correct in assuming that the national council intended to rule against restriction on discussion in CCF papers. Ingle replied that Cook's interpretation was not correct and that the national council's resolution only intended to reaffirm that there was already plenty of room for debate and discussion inside the existing framework of the CCF.

Roper sent Ingle's reply to the provincial board but by this time he had already summed up and concluded the whole matter in the pages of the *People's Weekly*. On 14 April 1951, he wrote of the special board meeting:

> In all good faith, and with what may have been completely justified anger if their conception of the situation had been correct, some correspondents have written letters about somebody in the CCF conducting a "purge" of certain of the paper's contributors. There was of course, nothing of the kind, although the temporary absence of De Bunker's column from recent issues may have given that impression, due to a misunderstanding that has been fully resolved. The situation still remains that regular contributors to the paper are asked to use their talents positively to promote public support of CCF policies. The letter columns are open to anyone to say anything they wish, within the usual bounds of good taste and observance of the laws respecting slander and libel. In all cases the editors have the responsibility of deciding what is to be printed, subject to appeal to the provincial executive or provincial board in any case where a contributor may wish to challenge the editors' decisions. Most important is the fact that there is now no remaining dispute and little likelihood of any new one developing. In these circumstances, none of the letters now in hand dealing with the matter will be published.

Actually, nothing much had changed. Contentious letters continued to appear in the paper and De Bunker's column reappeared. It is clear that during these years there was a strong minority that found CCF policies on the Cold War unpalatable.

This dissatisfaction spread to other matters. At the provincial convention in November 1950, a resolution in favour of accepting only advertising that did not conflict with CCF policies was moved and seconded. The motion was lost, and one can only suppose that the convention was swayed by the argument that the paper needed the money. Certainly the *People's Weekly* was in trouble, and on 20 December 1952, it brought out its last issue before it was absorbed into the *Commonwealth*, the official organ of the Saskatchewan CCF. No doubt the paper lost readership and support for a complex variety of reasons, but at least one significant factor was discontent with the established CCF policies it reflected. Irvine soon became a regular and popular contributor to the *Commonwealth*, writing a number of different columns: one was called "Ginger", and for another he wrote under the unusual pseudonym "Iplin Berrier", after two of the islands offshore from his birthplace in Shetland. However, Irvine was having increasing difficulty in containing himself within the confines laid down by the necessities of of the Cold War. Even the *Commonwealth* was careful about just what it would publish and Irvine's articles were often edited to conform to editorial policy.

About this time two British Columbia MLAs were causing a stir among the CCF leadership. The Canadian Peace Congress, a section of the World Peace Congress, was circulating a petition calling for the settlement of international differences by peaceful negotiations at a summit meeting. The World Peace Congress, not unnaturally, included members from the communist countries of Europe and Asia, and received support from communist parties throughout the world. It also included many supporters who were not communists. It would seem to be a prerequisite of a viable world peace movement that it should have wide support from communists and non-communists alike. However, the CCF executive ruled that CCF members should not belong to the Canadian Peace Congress and should not sign the peace petition. Ernest Winch and Arthur Turner signed the petition in defiance of the ban. Irvine wrote two letters to the national council in Ottawa, urging that disciplinary action should not be taken against them. He received a reply from the national secretary, Lorne Ingle, pointing out that the CCF national convention of July 1950 had passed a unanimous resolution rejecting the peace petition and the peace congress organization. Winch and Turner, however, were not moved by pressure to repudiate their signing of the petition.

Irvine continued to be preoccupied with the problems of international conflict, and on 22 December 1952, he again wrote to Premier Douglas, this time suggesting that the most critical issue in the forthcoming election was foreign policy. Irvine proposed that Canada should ease itself out of NATO by means of a worldwide economic co-operative commonwealth composed of voluntary nations that would share a common currency and enjoy a free trade situation. Irvine thought such a union would free Canada and other nations from U.S. domination and break the deadlock of the Cold War, which threatened to lead to another global crisis.

In the postwar years the CCF had made increasing efforts to get its voice heard on radio. M.J. Coldwell, as a national party leader at Ottawa, got some broadcasting time; and in Alberta, Roper, Liesemer and Irvine and others had been able to get a limited amount of radio time, but it was a major breakthrough when Irvine was invited to participate in the CBC's public affairs debate program, *Citizens' Forum*. The topic was "Can Canadian Capital Develop Our National Resources?" The chairman was Donald Cameron, director of extension at the University of Alberta, and in addition to Irvine, the speakers were Andrew Stewart, president of the University of Alberta, who presented the viewpoint of an economist; and a businessman. The CBC encountered some difficulty in finding a businessman who would agree to participate (the fee was only $50) but finally they persuaded Carl C. Nickle, editor of the *Daily Oil Bulletin*, to fill the third position. The program was aired on prime time across Canada on 25 January 1951. No record remains of Irvine's talk, nor of his response to debate and questions, but he received much fan mail from CCFers across the country. There is no doubt that he spoke in favour of Canada's developing her own resources, rather than letting them pass into the possession of foreign investors and multinational corporations.

A year later, on 7 February 1952, Irvine again participated in the *Citizens' Forum*. The subject was "Canada's Foreign Policy," and we have a fairly accurate summary of what he said on that occasion from the two pages of notes he made:

> This subject crystallizes a definite popular feeling that Canada has been too ready to agree to policies with the made-in-America label. There is nothing reprehensible in Canada agreeing in many things with a neighbour nation so geographically near and so similar in cultural background and ideals. But it is one thing to agree, another to echo.
>
> There have been times when our representatives have spoken in Canada's real voice, as when our Minister of External Affairs spoke strongly against declaring the Chinese to be aggressors in Korea. But when it came to voting, the real voice was smothered and the world heard nothing from Canada but the echo of the Pentagon.
>
> Canada has never had a foreign policy of her own making. We were docile followers of Britain until recent years.... Between the wars, Canada's leaders switched from British leadership to pursue the isolationist policy of America. After World War II we continued to be "Ready, Aye Ready" to dance when America fiddled.
>
> Canada cannot be excused for failure in her foreign policy on the grounds of her youth as a nation....
>
> There are those who say that America is in the position of such power, economic and otherwise, that Canada can't do other than acquiesce in the American will. Canadians will hardly accept that craven defeatist position. The logic of that would be that Canada is joining with America to protect the freedom of the world because we have no freedom from America to do otherwise.
>
> Canada is committed to democratic objectives and methods. Accordingly we should have disagreed sharply with America on some matters to which we have agreed in recent years. We are now helping to fight a war in Korea, in the name of the United Nations, which was declared by President Truman before consulting that body. Under American influence the UN forces crossed the 38th parallel despite warnings by China. Apparently because of American views,

Canada still recognizes Chiang Kai Shek as the representative of the people of China, refuses to recognize the People's Republic, or to lend its weight to the admission of China to the United Nations. And under that influence Canada signed the Japanese treaty which was certainly open to question on some important points.

In Europe we are agreeing with the rearmament of Germany, thus breaking faith with our sons who died to disarm her a few short years ago.

There is nothing to contemplate but world war as long as force is the cornerstone of our peace policy. Official America refused to entertain a Russian proposal to negotiate on the ground that they would talk with Russia when they were sure that their military strength was greater than that of Russia.

Moreover, as a nation that really does want peace, Canada should spend at least as much in building an economic foundation for the world's hope of peace as she spends in preparation for war.

In October of 1955, National Secretary Lorne Ingle wrote to Irvine urging him to write a pamphlet stressing the benefits of international co-operation and the relationship of this policy to the CCF philosophy in general. Irvine lost no time in complying, and by the end of the year he had written a 20,000-word pamphlet entitled *Challenge to the "Free Enterprise" Capitalist Way of Life*. In it Irvine made an uncompromising attack upon capitalism and unravelled the misconceptions and illusions fostered by the phrase "free enterprise." His pamphlet was written in the radical tone and spirit of the Regina Manifesto, and it is not surprising that the national leadership, who were moving towards the replacement of that document by a less radical one, were not impressed. Irvine's manuscript was not even returned to him but languished in the national office files until they were handed over to the Public Archives of Canada, where this unpublished work now rests.

No doubt the leadership were unappreciative of Irvine's criticisms of CCF international policy, specifically: "the refusal to recognize China at the moment when we should have demanded it; failure to make an issue out of the U.S. policies in respect to the Korean war and to Chiang Kai Shek in Formosa; the adoption of the negotiation-from-strength policy of capitalism as the basis for settling international differences; backing of NATO and failure to lead the fight against the rearmament of Germany."[6] Irvine saw the continued Canadian support of U.S. foreign policy as a betrayal of the ideals of "social democracy" on which the party was founded.

The CCF leadership, however, was set on the opposite course; instead of accommodating their international policies to domestic ones, they were busy deradicalizing their domestic policies to bring them into line with their international policies. This process culminated in the adoption of the Winnipeg Declaration, which was presented to the fourteenth national convention in Winnipeg in August 1956. It specifically superceded "all other statements of philosophy and principle adopted at previous conventions." This document was presented to the convention by the national chairman, David Lewis, who claimed then and later that the new statement did not differ in principle from the Regina Manifesto, but merely cleared up misunderstandings that might have been created by the language of that document. He managed to persuade the majority of delegates to the convention, who overwhelmingly voted for the new statement of principles.

However, the account given in the *Commonwealth* indicates a real, not merely a verbal, shift in fundamental attitudes towards social change:

> The Regina Manifesto proclaimed by the party in 1933, a year after its foundation, called upon CCF governments to ensure that capitalism is "eradicated." This phrase has frequently been used in the past by opponents of the CCF to suggest that the party is opposed to private enterprise in any shape or form. The corner store grocer and the owner of a single share in a large corporation have been warned of the dire consequences to their investments that would attend the electoral success of the CCF.
>
> CCF leaders, on the other hand, have stated repeatedly

that only monopolistic and oppressive concentrations of power and wealth would be eradicated. The Regina Manifesto specified that — in the light of conditions and circumstances of the early 1930s — it was felt that banking, insurance, transportation, mining, pulp and paper and other services essential for social planning would be brought under public control.

In dealing with the question of the part which the CCF feels that public, co-operative and private ownership must play in the national economy, Premier T.C. Douglas of Saskatchewan stressed that "there must always be an element of choice." Public ownership is a means to an end, but in no way the only means to that end. He was applauded loudly by delegates when he stated that complete public ownership is "not desirable" and that thousands and thousands of middle class Canadians, including the small businessman and the farmer, had an important role to play in the economy. With complete state ownership, Premier Douglas suggested, "You would destroy parliamentary democracy."[7]

In place of the Regina Manifesto's assertion that capitalism must be "eradicated" and that reformist measures will "leave untouched the cancer eating at the heart of our society," the Winnipeg Declaration contented itself with saying that there was a useful place for "private enterprise" in the Canadian economy, although private profit and corporate power must be "subordinated" to social planning.

Irvine's unpublished pamphlet was contrary to both the letter and the spirit of the Winnipeg Declaration. Although unpublished as a whole, he nevertheless presented a good deal of it in a succession of articles in the *Commonwealth*. These included the substance of his attack upon capitalism and free enterprise but omitted his direct strictures on the CCF and its international policy. As we have already seen, he was subject to editorial censorship.

Even before the Winnipeg Convention, Irvine was already embroiled in a new heresy. Some years before he had been invited to form part of a delegation to the U.S.S.R. He received an invitation in July 1953 from Dyson Carter, a Canadian scientist with a long-standing interest in the Soviet Union who had been instrumental in forming the Canadian-Soviet Friendship Society, to accompany the Society on a trip to the U.S.S.R. Although he was not able to accept, for health and financial reasons, apparently a seed had been planted in Irvine's mind, and a little over a year later, in October 1954, he wrote to David Lewis in Ottawa proposing a CCF-sponsored official group visit to Russia. The party endorsation Irvine requested was not forthcoming, and so in 1956 he began to organize a private tour. His travelling companions were Harold Bronson, first vice-president and organizer of the Alberta CCF, Floyd Johnson, president of the Edmonton CCF, and two members of the party from southern Alberta, Otto Wobick and Byron Tanner. They planned to make a six-week tour of Europe, twenty-one days of which would be spent in the U.S.S.R. and the remainder in Holland, Czechoslovakia, Scandinavia and Britain. Irvine applied to the Soviet Embassy in Ottawa for the necessary visas and subsequently received a reply from the ambassador of the U.S.S.R. in Canada welcoming the group. Later Irvine explained the reasons for his visit to the Soviet Union:

> Why did we go? Well, all of us had travelled to many parts of the world but none of us had ever before pierced the iron curtain, so-called. That in itself was a challenge. A healthy curiosity also played a part. To what extent did the Soviet Union resemble the picture drawn for us by the capitalist press during the years of anti-Soviet propaganda? Then there were the two great nations of the world facing each other, each backed by its satellites, menacing the entire world with a total war which, with atomic weapons, threatens the human race with annihilation. We knew that the ordinary people of the United States were kindly, generous folk who would much prefer peace to war. We wanted to know what the ordinary people of the Soviet Union were like; was their economy geared to war, like Hitler's, as had been alleged by its critics, or was it such as could flourish best in time of peace? We wanted to find out if the common people of the U.S.S.R. had been taught to regard war between them and the Western world as being inevitable, or

whether they believe that they can build their way of life without interference either from or with us.[8]

The group left for Europe in early July and travelled from Amsterdam to Prague to the Soviet Union, where they visited Moscow, Leningrad, Kiev and other places of interest such as the Dneiper Dam. Shortly after arriving in Moscow the group wrote a letter to Soviet Premier Khrushchev requesting an interview, which was granted.

Irvine writes:

> We spent the most interesting hour of our entire visit in Mr. Khrushchev's office. . . . We discussed the Near East situation and the hope for avoiding a third world war. We were convinced, not only by the passionate hatred of war and the avowal of peaceful intentions toward all nations which he evinced, but by the overwhelming sentiment of the people of the U.S.S.R. that they want peace and that they will go any honourable distance to gain it.
>
> We found this busy and very hard working man, a brilliant conversationalist, with a keen sense of humour which bubbled out naturally at the proper time and place. He appeared intellectually keen, a shrewd man, competent and determined to make a success of agriculture to keep the U.S.S.R. out of war and to build a new and better way of life for his people. In reiterating the view he expressed at the Party Congress a few months before, he proved that he was no tight-laced doctrinaire. He frankly expressed the view that other countries might not gain socialism by following in the footsteps of the U.S.S.R.; that different traditions and conditions would determine to some extent the particular course to be taken.[9]

When they returned to Canada the travellers were met with a barrage of criticism, both from the press and from a number of their CCF colleagues at both the national and the provincial level. Through translations of Tass Agency reports and the *Soviet News Bulletin* issued by the Soviet Embassy in Ottawa, Irvine was reported as saying that the Soviet Union was more democratic than

Canada and was a new Mecca for socialists from other countries. The impression was also given that Irvine made these remarks on behalf of the "Social Democratic Party of Canada," (i.e., the CCF). M.J. Coldwell, who embarked for Europe prior to Irvine's return, was widely reported in the press as saying that the president of the Alberta CCF would be questioned on his return to Canada and that if there was any suggestion at all that he had expressed approval of a political system based on a one-party dictatorship, it would be immediately and completely repudiated by the CCF. Irvine asserted that his remarks had been distorted when Reuters News Agency mistranslated a Tass report. His comment that the Soviet Union was a "new Mecca" was a casual remark made in response to the fact that there were numerous delegations from many countries in Moscow at the time of his visit.

In Alberta, two CCF provincial board members, Bert Ryan of Calgary and Jack Leavens of Edmonton, were calling for an executive meeting to discuss Irvine's statements in the Soviet Union. About a month later, Irvine reported in a letter to a friend:

> As you truly say, there does not appear to be any valid reason why anyone should have taken objection to our visiting Russia. Indeed, we should have been sent as a CCF delegation. But it seems as if our leaders, in particular, have soaked up American propaganda like sponges and when one impinges on their prejudice they ooze poison like a Dulles.
>
> You may be interested to know that we are all on trial before the provincial board which meets on November 10th. This was inspired by Mr. Roper, who I have reason to believe is acting under the urgings of Coldwell and Lorne Ingle. So we are prepared for western-style liquidation.[10]

The minutes of the board meeting referred to above are not now available, but from some of those present we know that Irvine did not attend the meeting and that Elmer Roper called for Irvine's removal from the presidency on the grounds that his actions were damaging to the CCF. The provincial board, presumably after some heated discussion, decided not to take any action.

The national office also decided not to take any action and the matter was considered closed.

Previously, a small group of Alberta CCFers (not including Elmer Roper) had written to the national office asking if they could withdraw from Alberta membership of the CCF and retain membership as national members only. Clearly this was unconstitutional and could not be implemented, but as a result, Carl Hamilton came to Edmonton to sound out the situation. Before meeting with the elected officers of the Alberta CCF in Woodsworth House, he met with the half a dozen or so dissidents in a downtown hotel. After meeting with them, and later with Irvine and other CCF members, he reported back to the National Office that there was no way in which the majority of Alberta party members would consent to remove Irvine as president.

Meanwhile, Irvine set about writing a short book on his thoughts and experiences arising out of his trip to the Soviet Union. He described his intentions in a letter to Norman Smith:

> Here is the first installment of my "opus." Please be as critical as you would with your own work. I do not wish to become the champion of communist theory. On the other hand, I want to show, among other things, that revolution was the only open door from the regime of the Tsar; that democracy or any part of it was unknown to the Russian people; that they do not miss it even now; that the Soviet Union has done one thing for which it must be given credit, something of fundamental importance to human life and basic if ever a democracy is to be built anywhere, and that is that the resources of a nation and the industries built thereon, must belong to the people and be devoted to the needs of people, rather than to the profits of a few. Also I want to show that despite political dictatorship, the health service, the educational system, the welfare of the working people, reveal a real desire to promote the principle of humanity first, which no capitalist country has shown so far that it possessed.
>
> Then I want to show that the Soviet Union wants peace, the very survival of its system depends on it; that this fact

explains the armament race begun by the West; that it is the basic economic reform introduced in the U.S.S.R. that capitalism fears and that its beneficiaries are willing to risk the survival of the race in a battle to retain the private enterprise system.

Finally, I want to show that it is unlikely that either communism or capitalism has reached the end of all improvement; that neither system is faultless; that the best way to find what is best is for both to exist side by side.... [11]

Irvine's book was published early in 1958 with the title *Live or Die with Russia*. When it first appeared, the CCF was involved in the campaign of the 1958 general elections and Irvine in particular was fighting his last electoral battle in Wetaskiwin. Irvine chose not to publicize his book at that time, fearing it might hinder his and the party's success with the voters. The appearance of Irvine's book, however, was certainly overshadowed by the Conservative victory in the federal election and the reduction of the CCF contingent in the House of Commons from twenty-five to eight, with leading members such as M.J. Coldwell and Stanley Knowles losing their seats.

Unsuccessful himself in winning a seat in Parliament, Irvine had by now decided to put almost all his remaining energy into the struggle for peace. If he could do this and remain in the ranks of the CCF so much the better, but he was no longer going to be deterred from this necessary task by the possibility of expulsion for political heresy. He enthusiastically joined with a group of people in Edmonton who had decided to support the Stockholm World Peace Congress on Disarmament and International Co-operation, and he and Harold Bronson were chosen as delegates. The Congress was supported by over 2,000 delegates from eighty countries, including many moral and religious groups, representatives from co-operative and trade union movements, and members of writers', artists' and scientific organizations from all parts of the world. Peace movements in general, and this one in particular, were still on the proscribed list but many people ignored the ban.

Irvine and Bronson attended the congress, with Irvine later

making a three-day visit to "the old rock," as he affectionately called Shetland. On their return they were both engaged in a series of meetings. The CCF leadership was apparently too busy licking its wounds and preparing for the formation of a "new party" to take any disciplinary action. If Irvine had lived another eighteen years, he would have been pleased to hear that there was a Second Stockholm Appeal (1975) calling for an end to the arms race and for convening a United Nations disarmament conference which was widely supported by trade union organizations and endorsed by Ed Broadbent, leader of the NDP.[12] He would also have had an ironic appreciation of the report that in 1975 a group of NDP leaders visited the U.S.S.R. and exchanged views with members of the Communist Party political bureau on Canadian-Soviet relations and the need to promote world peace and security.[13]

TWELVE

The Last Years

In the latter half of the 1950s, when he was already past seventy, Irvine was still tremendously active. He fought two gruelling and unsuccessful election campaigns; travelled abroad; wrote two lengthy political pamphlets, as well as a weekly stint of column writing for the *Commonwealth*; and carried on the day-to-day activities of organizer for the CCF. Apparently in vigorous physical health, he suddenly discovered in 1959 that he had cancer of the prostate. The circumstances of the early stages of his illness are laconically revealed in a letter he wrote to Norman Smith: "The laboratory test in the University Hospital revealed that I have cancer of the prostate. But I do not intend to die right away." Three weeks later, in response no doubt to anxious enquiries, he replied:

> It is painless and it is slow to develop. I have had it for five years now and would not be surprised if I should be around for several years yet. I really feel as well as I ever did, eat well, sleep well and do a lot of physical work in the garden and on the farm.[1]

He had an operation a few weeks later and further surgery in 1959 and in 1961. In 1960 he had brought to his attention a substance, Krebiozen, which was an alleged cure for cancer. Although Krebiozen was not endorsed by medical authorities, Irvine tried it anyway. He reported that it improved his condition and indeed his regular doctors are said to have been surprised by evidence of such improvement. But this effect, if genuine, was only temporary and in the circumstances Irvine's case provided no clear evidence either way concerning the efficacy of the drug.

Apart from the hope of curing his illness, Irvine was interested in Krebiozen because of the alleged persecution by the American Medical Association of the doctors who promoted it. In his column "Ginger," Irvine wrote a lengthy account of the case in two successive issues of the *Commonwealth*:

> American doctors, like their counterparts in Canada, are no doubt anxious to protect ignorant people from being exploited by quacks. It is of course, a very easy matter for a person dying of a hopelessly incurable disease, to be persuaded to try almost anything, regardless of the cost. It is therefore right and proper for a medical association to prevent profiteering exploiters of the sick from mulcting unfortunates by selling them useless and even dangerous drugs at extortionate prices to enrich quacks.
>
> It is indeed commendable for the medical profession to protect the public from quackery. But there were no quacks involved in this matter. Dr. Durovic is a fully qualified physician and Dr. Ivy, as is well known, was and is an outstanding medical scientist. Perhaps those who continue to administer drugs to patients for a disease for which no cure is yet known might be nearer to quackery than Drs. Durovic and Ivy.
>
> It is unscientific and unworthy of the medical profession to deliberately stand in the way of careful scientific experimentation of any alleged remedy for any disease, even if it were advanced by so-called quacks. Men who might be called quacks have made some remarkable contributions to medical science.[2]

Irvine had been president of the Alberta CCF for six consecutive years when, some weeks prior to the 1960 provincial convention, he announced his intention of retiring for health reasons and in order to lessen his responsibilities. Since 1955, he had been receiving the niggardly $40-per-month old age pension he and others had fought so hard to get for the elderly of Canada, but in 1952, Parliament instituted a pension for ex-MPs who had served at least three terms. To qualify for a full pension, a member had not only to be elected three times, but he must also have served for at least seventeen sessions. Irvine had all these qualifications but he was ineligible because he was no longer a sitting member. To have made the legislation applicable to qualified members no longer sitting in 1952 would have extended the pension to a mere handful of old-timers such as Irvine, A.A. Heaps, and Agnes Macphail, but the MPs concerned with drafting the legislation were apparently unmoved by representations made on behalf of this group.

In these circumstances, Irvine's many friends in the CCF took up a private collection to be presented to him on his retirement, and approximately $2,500 was collected for this purpose. This was presented to him along with a carved wooden bust of himself made by the leader of the Alberta CCF, Floyd Johnson, which now stands in Irvine House, the NDP provincial office in Edmonton. There were a number of spoken tributes to Irvine, one from Elmer Roper who was then Mayor of Edmonton, and numerous messages came from across the country. Irvine was touched and somewhat overwhelmed by the appreciation. Some of these messages came from political non-sympathizers, but Irvine had the rare capacity of being able to relate to people with whom he had deep intellectual and political disagreements and to elicit a similar response in return.

Irvine did not allow his appreciation of the tributes he had received from some of his foremost critics in the CCF to alter or modify his opinions. During the 1960 convention, Irvine had given his valedictory address as president, in which he took the opportunity of making a firm stand on the need to replace capitalism by democratic socialism and made a trenchant attack upon the attempt by the CCF and other socialist groups to depart from this position:

In recent years and due largely to the false prosperity of a hot and Cold War economy and assisted by constant insidious propaganda, even some socialists have begun to doubt the need for socialism.

It was said, four years ago, that capitalism had reformed, that there would never again be unemployment or depression. It will be recalled that even the CCF reeled on the brink and drew back a little from its original manifesto.

This reactionary effort has been expressed in a strong tendency to minimize the basic differences between capitalism and socialism; in trying to rub out by rhetoric the basic and irreconcilable antagonisms which still exist between a system which has private profit for an aim and another which seeks to devote all the national production to meeting the needs of all the people. To do this is to sell the socialist principle ... down the river. ...

Make no mistake. In a mixed economy the bank accounts of the wealthy will not be mixed with the bank accounts of the wage earners. The incomes of the monopolist profiteers will not be mixed with that of the semi-bankrupt farmers nor with the pittance which might be allowed to the unemployed. We may rest assured that as long as capitalism dominates the economy any mixture will be like the famous hamburger made from one horse and one rabbit.

The provincial CCF convention, held in Union Hall, Edmonton, on 24 and 25 June 1960, was attended by well over 100 delegates from urban and rural areas, as well as by visitors and a considerable contingent from the CCF youth groups. Following the election of a new president, Robert Carlyle, to replace Irvine, a resolution was passed unanimously, to the effect that, in recognition of Irvine's devoted service to the party, the convention appoint him as honorary president for one year and to a lifetime honorary membership of the provincial executive. The convention also went on record as extending best wishes to Irvine for his impending tour of Asia (including the People's Republic of China) and requesting him to bring back firsthand information.

Further support of Irvine's viewpoint was expressed by the convention when it proceeded to pass resolutions in favour of

Canada's aligning herself with other neutral countries and dissociating herself from military blocs such as NATO and NORAD; and in favour of the position that public ownership is a desirable and necessary means of achieving our economic goals in a just, moral and democratic society.

At the World Peace Congress in Stockholm in 1958, Irvine had met delegates from the People's Republic of China and this, in addition to the fact that he had already travelled to the Soviet Union and published a book about it, led to an invitation to visit China. The trip was delayed by Irvine's illness in 1959, but in the following year he again organized a party of six. His companions were Harold Bronson and Byron Tanner, who had also been with him on the Soviet trip; Nellie Peterson and her husband, Roy, and Wilbert Stevens, Irvine's son-in-law. They left on 6 July for Japan and proceeded after a few days to Hong Kong and thence to the Chinese mainland, where they spent three weeks visiting Canton, Peking and Shanghai. On occasions the party split up to pursue different interests and four of them made a trip to the industrialized northeast (formerly known as Manchuria). They met with Chen Yi, vice-chairman of the Chinese People's Republic and with leading members of the Chinese Peace Council.

Irvine's health was not good during his stay in China, and instead of taking the trip to the north, he had to spend some days in hospital. Nellie Peterson also stayed in Peking so that he would not be left alone. She wrote in letters home:

> Bill has had to spend three days in hospital. He was taken to one, near the hotel, which was built by the Rockefeller Foundation years ago. It's a beautiful building, but being older, not so bright or modern as the one we visited. His doctor, an outstanding specialist, spoke English, as did his nurse. His treatment was the same as that given at home and appears successful. Our hosts were kindness itself – there seemed nothing they would not do, including driving me to visit him twice a day, bringing him a bouquet of gorgeous lotus blooms and roses, and keeping his room pleasantly cool with fans at strategic points. When Bill was leaving he, of

course, offered to pay for his care. The doctor smiled and said "Medical care is not sold, it is given."[4]

The purpose of the visit to China was similar to that of Irvine's previous trip to the Soviet Union, and the conclusions of the group too were similar. With a vastly different history and set of circumstances from those of Canada, China was doing its utmost to build a new society, and although not without reason they felt threatened by the outside world, the Chinese leaders and people were well acquainted with the horrors of war and had no wish to experience them again if they could avoid it.

Two of the party, Bronson and Tanner, returned to Canada from Peking by air via Moscow, while the others returned to Hong Kong. From there they flew to India to visit Irvine's old friend Chester Ronning, now Canada's High Commissioner to India. After making comparisons between the two most populous nations of Asia, they continued on to Moscow and thence to Britain and Canada. Irvine, despite continued ill health, took the opportunity to pay a three-day visit to his birthplace. It was to be his last.

This time there was no publicity surrounding Irvine's trip on his return to Canada, and he quietly settled down to produce a book. The travellers agreed that it should be a symposium with each traveller making his or her own contribution. Irvine's chapters, including the foreword, amounted to seventy-five pages, while his companions contributed the other ninety-five. The book appeared in June 1961 and was fittingly titled *The Twain Shall Meet*. It was printed at the expense of the authors and of friends and supporters in the CCF. As a result of a review in the *Commonwealth* the first 1,000 copies sold fairly easily. A second printing of another 1,000 was never completely sold since there were no easily available channels for publicity; however, sufficient revenue came from sales to pay everyone who contributed towards the printing of the book at least two-thirds of his or her original outlay.

Throughout 1959 and 1960, the CCF gradually turned to the left, away from the established Cold War policies and toward a stronger socialist position. This was expressed in the resolutions

passed at the Alberta provincial convention in 1960 and reinforced by the Saskatchewan provincial convention held soon
after. When the CCF met for its sixteenth national convention
(which was to be its last), at Regina on 9 August 1960, the change
soon became apparent. With 420 people present at the opening, it
was the largest convention ever held by the party. Three things of
importance occurred. The first was the agreement, strongly endorsed by the party leadership, to go ahead with the formation of
a new party in association with organized labour. The other two
events were a grassroots expression of opposition to the leadership. M.J. Coldwell, after losing his federal seat in 1958, had expressed his desire to retire after many years of service as leader. In
the meantime, the remaining eight CCF MPs in the Commons
unanimously chose one of their number, Hazen Argue, to be parliamentary leader, and were strongly in favour of his election as
national leader on Coldwell's retirement.

Argue, at thirty-nine, was the CCF Member of Parliament for
Assiniboia (Sask.). When first elected in 1945, he was the young-
est MP in Canada and he had held the seat continuously since
then, being one of the survivors of the debacle of 1958. During the
two years he had already served as parliamentary leader, he had
given sympathy and strong support to the left wing of the party,
and by the time of the Regina Convention he was immensely
popular with his parliamentary colleagues and, more impor-
tantly, with many of the rank and file of the party, but he was by
no means popular with the leadership. They feared that the
official position of party leader would give him an edge in the
contest for the leadership of the new party and they were determined to draft Tommy Douglas for this role, even though up to
this point (and for some time later) Douglas refused to seek the
post. In defiance of the National Executive, an overwhelming
majority of convention delegates elected Argue as national
leader.

The third important issue to come before the convention was
the question of Canada's membership in NATO. The CCF national council had recently decided that it was necessary for Canada to withdraw from NORAD, on the grounds that it provided
no effective defence for Canada, and only hampered her from

pursuing a more independent policy, but the council still stood fast in support of Canada's role in NATO. The ensuing debate on the resolution to advocate withdrawal from NATO was lengthy and heated, and the vote in favour of withdrawal was a close one, but again, the convention voted against the stand taken by the leadership.

Irvine was absent from the convention because it conflicted with his China trip, but he was of course, immensely pleased with the results. His satisfaction however was tempered by growing doubts about the proposed new party. From one point of view it represented the fulfillment of what he had long struggled for: the active participation of labour in a socialist political movement. On the other, he feared the compromise of socialist ideals in the interest of forming a broadly based party. Irvine, like many other CCF socialists, was particularly disturbed by the manner in which new party clubs were being created, drawn from the ranks of the "liberally minded," with an invitation to them to share in the process of making party policy before and at the founding convention of the new party. The Alberta executive committee was so incensed at this development that it circulated a letter of protest to a number of prominent CCF leaders. Irvine was also disturbed by the treatment meted out to Hazen Argue by some of those who resented his bid for the leadership of the new party and he wrote to Argue offering encouragement and advice.

On 23 and 24 January 1961, at Edmonton, the Alberta CCF held its last annual convention. The shadow of the new party hung heavy over the convention and its formation dominated the discussion. Guest speakers were Hazen Argue, now national leader, and William Mahoney, Canadian director of the United Steelworkers of America. Argue's address was geared to the left wing of the CCF, now strong in the Alberta sector of the party, and he received a standing ovation. When Mahoney spoke he assured delegates that labour was not coming into the new party in order to take it over but in order to work side by side with other participants. He said that labour would bring to the new party the "organizational know-how." Organization, he said, was the main point. He maintained that "doctrinaire socialism" was no more an answer than Diefenbaker's "doctrinaire conservatism." His remarks, understandably, were politely but not warmly received.

A resolution was proposed by the Alberta CCF that their members would convene to discuss the new party program prior to the national founding convention. It was obvious that the Alberta CCF had not yet irrevocably committed itself to the new party.

Irvine was of two minds about whether or not to attend the founding convention of the new party, but finally decided to do so. The convention was on a grand scale; there were 2,083 registrations, and the American-style political ballyhoo, which Irvine despised, was much in evidence, particularly in the leadership contest.

In the event, Douglas defeated Argue by a vote of 1,391 to 380. The most dramatic event of the convention was the debate over the NDP's attitude to NATO. Numerous resolutions had come in from CCF constituencies in favour of continuing the anti-NATO stand of the last convention. When the matter came up for discussion, long lines of delegates, anxious to speak on the question, appeared at all the microphones on the floor of the convention. It looked as if a heated and protracted verbal struggle was about to ensue. After a hurried consultation with other leading members, the chairman announced that this was such an important issue that it should be debated from the platform and pro- and anti-NATO forces were requested each to pick a panel of four to speak briefly on the question. On the pro-NATO team were David Lewis and Tommy Douglas. Immediately after the debate from the platform, without further participation from the floor, the vote was taken and support for NATO continued as part of NDP policy.

There was no doubt that the founding convention of the New Democratic Party was a major setback for socialists in the movement. Disappointment, disillusionment, and in some cases confirmation of their worst fears produced different reactions in different people. Hazen Argue, who had staked his future position in the party on the resurgence of the socialist left, now clearly despaired of the continued viability of any left-wing movement, either inside or outside the NDP, and having incurred the displeasure of the party leadership now saw no future role for himself in the movement. Six months later he defected to the Liberal

party. Irvine, however, saw that there was no acceptable democratic socialist alternative to the New Democratic Party. Although
old and sick, he decided to stay with the NDP and continue to
fight for socialism within that framework, unpropitious though it
seemed.

On 25 November 1961, the Alberta CCF held its special (and
last) convention to make its final decision on the manner in
which it would participate in the provincial section of the New
Democratic Party. The provincial board had already discussed the
question and it presented the convention with three alternatives:

(1) The CCF dissolves as a separate political entity upon the
    founding of the Alberta section of the NDP;

or

(2) The CCF applies for affiliation with the NDP and retains
    CCF identity as an association of like-minded people within
    the framework of the NDP;

or

(3) The CCF, before dissolving as a political party and merging
    with the NDP, will make provision for the setting up of a
    democratic socialist association for the purpose of education
    and study, and further, that it be recommended to the New
    Democratic Party that this association be granted the same
    privilege as the New Democratic Party national executive
    now grants to the Canadian Labour Congress, namely that
    of appointing a small advising committee from the associa-
    tion to the provincial executive committee of the New
    Democratic Party.

It might be noted that of these proposals only (1) and (2) were,
strictly speaking, alternatives. The third was certainly compatible
with (1) and not incompatible with (2), although in certain circumstances the adoption of (2) would have made (3) redundant.
In any case, all three propositions were discussed fully.

Elmer Roper urged acceptance of proposal (2) on the grounds
that a CCF section, affiliated with the NDP, would vastly
strengthen the party by providing an organized, participating
group to which farmers would more readily belong and through

which the vital contributions of CCF thought could be expressed to the NDP. Roper said that such an affiliation should not in anyway be considered anti-labour. He pointed out that he himself was a strong supporter of labour unions and that he had grown up in the labour movement. Finally he said that he did not consider that the implementation of this proposal would raise either financial or organizational difficulties.

Irvine supported Roper and made a strong plea for proposal (2) by pointing out that the CCF had originally been a federated organization and that therefore affiliation did not present any insurmountable difficulties. He said that he had no fear of labour and indeed welcomed it into full participation in politics, but he thought that the CCF had a great deal to offer the NDP in philosophy and principles. Socialism versus capitalism was basically the issue upon which the Canadian people must decide. The NDP was refusing to face up to this issue and was substituting planning within the framework of capitalism for planning toward the achievement of socialism. The CCF's democratic socialist philosophy could be maintained within the NDP only if it were an affiliate organization speaking with a definable voice.

The Roper-Irvine position in favour of preserving the identity of the CCF, while affiliating with the NDP, was defeated by those who continued to claim that this involved major organizational difficulties. The second part of proposal (3) was also rejected. The resolution finally adopted said:

> That the CCF participate in the NDP by dissolving as a separate political party upon the founding of the Alberta section of the NDP, and that the CCF make provision for the setting up of a democratic socialist association for the purpose of education and study.[5]

It is interesting to note that the CCF's "participation" in the NDP was limited to that of bringing about its own dissolution; since both affiliation and an organizational link with the proposed socialist education association were rejected, and although there must have been an underlying assumption in the minds of many of those present that the ex-CCFers would join the NDP, there was no explicit statement of this assumption, nor was there any urging of members to do so.

The net effect was that the Alberta CCF proceeded to wind up and conclude its affairs, and then went out of existence, leaving its former members without formal guidance, advice or recommendations concerning the NDP. This situation probably arose because the major disagreement at the Convention was between those who wanted to make an entirely new start with the NDP and those who wished to salvage as much as possible of what they considered to be important in the CCF. However, this state of affairs was modified by the fact that earlier in the year, before the national founding convention, a provincial committee for the new party had been formed and it in turn had set up program and constitution committees on which CCF members were numerous and prominent.

The provincial board of the CCF had also set up committees to draft recommendations in respect to the constitution and program of the proposed new party. These recommendations were considered at the final Alberta CCF convention, and those that were approved or amended were sent to the founding convention of the Alberta New Democratic Party. In fact, a considerable amount of time at the final CCF convention was devoted to a consideration of the constitution and program of the new party. The board in its report to the convention also made recommendations concerning the disposal of the CCF's assets. These assets were chiefly debentures in Woodsworth House transferred out of the earnings of Alberta Woodsworth House Association to the CCF and placed under the care of CCF trustees appointed for that purpose.

In recognition of Irvine's long years of devoted service to the CCF at a minimal salary, the board unanimously approved a motion to transfer to Irvine $1,000 in AWHA debentures held by the trustees, and to transfer ownership of the 1957 Chevrolet car (used by Irvine in CCF organization work) to him. Similar transfers of party assets were made to two other longtime CCF workers.[6]

Irvine continued to write for the *Commonwealth* and he spoke at a number of meetings for the NDP, but in the last year of his life the group he worked most actively with was the Woodsworth-Irvine Socialist Fellowship. This group came into being as the result of the resolution of the last CCF convention in 1961, which said, in part, that the CCF would make provision for the setting up of a democratic socialist association for the purpose of socialist education and study. In January 1962, therefore, at the final meeting of the Edmonton CCF co-ordinating committee, its members accepted the responsibility and steps were taken to establish such a group in Edmonton. A letter was sent to all members and friends of the CCF or the NDP who might be interested in participating in such a project.

At the first meeting it was decided, over the strong protestation of Irvine, to call the group the Woodsworth-Irvine Socialist Fellowship. Its basic purpose, in line with the last directive of the CCF, was to encourage discussion and promote the ideas and ideals of democratic socialism. Its first activity was the initiation of regular monthly meetings at which invited speakers introduced topics and led discussion on matters of interest to socialists. Membership was open to all those who subscribed to the ideals of democratic socialism; they could belong to any political party or none. The annual fee was initially $1.50. A great number of the membership, which soon exceeded 100, were also members of the NDP, but this was never a requirement. However, in 1963, the then provincial secretary of the New Democratic Party, Grant Notley, entirely unsolicited by the fellowship, but acting on instruction from the party's provincial executive, invited the fellowship to apply for affiliation to the New Democratic Party, and to send delegates to the 1963 provincial convention. After much discussion and considerable concern lest political affiliation should restrict the scope and function of the fellowship, a majority decided in favour of accepting this invitation, and delegates from the fellowship participated in the NDP provincial convention and submitted resolutions.

Subsequently, the national executive of the NDP refused to ratify the fellowship's affiliation as recommended by the provincial body, on the grounds that, unlike labour unions and farm organizations (of which none were actually affiliated), the fellowship was not eligible for affiliation. The fellowship accepted this decision and was content to pursue its original and basic aims of education and research. In the ensuing years, the fellowship, in addition to its monthly gatherings, sponsored a number of public meetings and for ten successive years arranged summer seminars on topics of current social and political interest. For a number of years, the fellowship also published in various forms a paper of socialist comment, which it named after Irvine's first paper, the *Nutcracker*; it now takes the form of a page, sometimes two, in the Alberta NDP monthly paper, the *Alberta Democrat*.

In 1972, the fellowship again received an unsolicited invitation to affiliate with the NDP. This time the proposal was first cleared with the national council and since then the fellowship, while retaining its uncommitted membership (as do trade unions), has been affiliated to the NDP.

In the last years of his life, fully aware that his time was limited, Irvine set to work to write his final statement. It is significant that he again returned to a topic which had preoccupied him throughout his life, namely, democracy. In spite of his appreciation of the achievements of the Soviet Union and China, and although he thought the political process in Canada, while claiming to be democratic, actually fell far short of that ideal, Irvine never wavered in his conviction that the road to socialism in Canada was a democratic one. Hence his last work reiterated and developed his critique of democracy in Canada and tried to suggest ways of bringing it a good deal closer to the ideal.

His manuscript ran to 72,000 words and was entitled *Democracy — Fact or Fiction?* His central theme was the power of the wealthy to subvert democracy by buying politicians and political parties in a variety of ways and he argued that at least a partial solution to this problem was to pay all legitimate election expenses out of public funds. Irvine also described an early temptation to which the CCF did not succumb:

> Mr. J.S. Woodsworth and I had addressed a well-attended meeting in Massey Hall, Toronto. A few days later, Mr. Woodsworth came to my office and displayed a cheque for $5,000 toward our campaign. He was worried. We both knew that the man who sent that cheque was sincere, and that he was not seeking any favours. . . . It was, therefore, not easy to risk

insulting such a man by refusing to accept his sincerely offered financial assistance.

Nevertheless, Mr. Woodsworth could not conscientiously accept that cheque, and I agreed with him.... We saw the danger that, if we once opened the door to this method of financing the party, there would be no excuse for refusing cheques even for much larger sums from people with ulterior motives, if it happened that the CCF ever came near enough to power to make it worthwhile for anyone to try to buy our party to serve their private interest aims.[7]

By the time Irvine had completed his manuscript, his health had deteriorated considerably and the cancer had now reached his lungs, but he was still mentally and physically active.

On Friday, 26 October 1962, the world seemed on the brink of nuclear war, with Kennedy and Khrushchev in deadly confrontation over the missile bases in Cuba. In the evening, the Woodsworth-Irvine Socialist Fellowship held its usual monthly meeting at Woodsworth House. It was well attended and the chief topic of discussion was the Cuban missile crisis. Irvine was an active participant and one of a small committee chosen to draft telegrams urging sanity upon the world leaders concerned. The meeting adjourned about 11 p.m., but a few of Irvine's friends stayed behind to talk and sip wine in Irvine's office, which he still retained. After an hour or so of friendly conversation, they left him cheerfully preparing to go to bed.

Sometime in the early hours of 27 October 1962, Irvine died, apparently suddenly and quietly, since he was found sitting up in bed with a book in his hands. In the centre of his desk nearby was an old calendar pad which he had used for jotting down notes. The latest page recorded in Irvine's handwriting two quotations which presumably he had recently culled from his readings:

"How shall we ever learn toleration? The last lesson a man ever learns is that liberty of thought and speech is the right for all mankind, that the man who denies every article of our creed is to be allowed to preach just as often and just as loud as we ourselves."

Wendell Phillips

"May you live all the days of your life."
>> Jonathan Swift

To these we may add a third quotation from the verse of Ralph Chaplin as an appropriate epitaph for William Irvine:

> Mourn not the dead that in the cool earth lie —
>> Dust unto dust —
> The calm sweet earth that mothers all who die
>> As all men must.

> But rather mourn the apathetic throng —
>> The cowed and meek —
> Who see the world's great anguish and its wrong
>> And dare not speak!

EPILOGUE

The story of Irvine's political life is essentially the story of the vicissitudes of the democratic socialist movement in Canada from 1907 to 1962.

It is a history of struggle on two fronts. On the one hand, there is the struggle to build a radical movement with sufficient strength and support to enable it to bring about basic changes in Canada's economic and social structure; and on the other hand, there is the internal struggle, common to all such movements, between those who are willing to accept reforms within the status quo and those who are determined to maintain the original driving force behind the movement — the desire for fundamental and far-reaching social changes. It is appropriate to attach the label "social democracy" to the former attitude and to name the latter "democratic socialism."

When Canadian historians and political scientists lament (as some do) the demise of the Progressive farmers' movement in the federal Parliament in the Twenties, and their failure to establish a viable political party, they are in effect deploring the failure of the farmers to establish a "social democratic" type party, which would have become a normal and permanent part of the Canadian political scene. This "failure" they attribute in part to the intransigence of the radical Ginger Group within the Progressives and its opposition to the party system.

Most of the time, what goes on in the political scene might properly be called "normal" politics. Its actual function is the preservation of the status quo while a political game of shadowboxing goes on between political parties that are as interchangeable as Tweedledum and Tweedledee. In this context, the success and failure of a political group is measured by its ability to play the "game."

The Ginger Group (of which Irvine was a leading member) was not interested in playing this game. Its members wanted to practise what might be called "significant" politics, in contrast to "normal" politics. They wanted to use the political process as a means of bringing about social and economic changes that would abolish the inefficiencies, the injustices and the exploitation which prevail in capitalist society. Significant politics comes into existence when in times of stress political groups bent upon radical change break into the political scene.

In part, and especially in its early career, the United Farmers of Alberta was such a group and, unlike the Progressives in Ottawa it succeeded in establishing a strong political organization and won political power in the province. During its fourteen-year rule in Alberta, the radical proclivities of the UFA gradually suffered the process of normalization, and in consequence it failed to make an adequate response to the economic depression of the Thirties and was swept from office. However, the roots of western radicalism remained and from them sprang a new democratic socialist movement — the CCF. This too became subject to conflict between those who were social democrats and those who were democratic socialists.

Left-wing critics of the UFA and the CCF have tended to explain the drift away from radical positions in these movements in class terms. It is claimed that since the bulk of the support for these movements came from the farmers they were understandably less militant than movements firmly based upon the urban working class. This view depends upon an *a priori* conception of the political and social roles played by different classes and there is little evidence to support it. In the advanced capitalist countries of the world, such as Britain, Australia, New Zealand, Scandinavia, and other western European nations, working class and organized labour support has produced typically "social democratic" type parties in which the interests of the working class are pursued almost entirely within the limits of the capitalist economic order. In times of affluence, "social democratic" parties are able to force through legislation and measures of social welfare that benefit the majority of the people, while in times of economic depression these gains are under attack and subject to retrenchment. Often social democratic governments are the instruments used to bring this about in the hope that this will encourage "free enterprise" to get the economy going again.

One might plausibly argue that the "social democratic" governments which have been in power for lengthy periods in the provinces of western Canada as a result of UFA, CCF and NDP political actions compare favourably in their level of achievements with "social democratic" governments in other countries, which rely much more heavily and exclusively on labour support. It is a feature of this Canadian movement that it has throughout preserved a radical democratic socialist core which, although often suppressed, and sometimes even expelled (as happened to the Ontario Waffle group in 1972), continues to function as the socialist yeast that leavens the movement.

The changeover from the CCF to the NDP, although its proclaimed, and no doubt genuine, objectives were eminently reasonable, namely, to get more support from organized labour and from Canada's central and eastern provinces, nevertheless sought to achieve these aims by emphasizing the social democratic nature of the movement at the expense of its democratic socialist element. The NDP achieved only limited success in attaining its objectives, since "social democracy" does not draw the widespread support from the working class in Canada that it does in some other countries; neither, of course, does any other party of the left. The NDP, except for the connection with organized labour, is therefore now pretty well where the CCF was — capable of electing provincial governments in the west and drawing support from 15 to 20 percent of the electorate across Canada.

In general, parties of the "social democratic" type need their socialist component. Since such parties have no coherent philosophy of their own the socialists wihin the movement provide at least a vicarious one, and thus help to maintain the dividing line from the other parties, from which they might otherwise be indistinguishable. As the case of the NDP illustrates, attempts to eliminate the socialist element from "social democratic" parties are usually unsuccessful since, as with the salamander's tail, amputation stimulates new growth.

Democratic socialists, becoming weary of the struggle within the social democratic context, have often considered (and sometimes acted upon) the possibility of creating a new and separate socialist party, untarnished by compromise and accommodation to the capitalist system. This is not a viable option in those countries where the social democratic party is the strongest and largest movement on the left, for this is where the primary audience for socialism is to be found. If one cannot first convince NDPers that capitalism must be replaced by socialism, it is unlikely that others will be more easily convinced. Also in such a context a new socialist party, as it begins to gain in numbers and in electoral success, will develop the same symptoms of degeneration as the party it has abandoned: the conflict between democratic socialist attitudes and social democratic ones will begin all over again. This is a struggle which cannot be avoided, but which must be faced and fought. It might therefore just as well be fought on the original battleground within the "social democratic" type party. In such circumstances, the first task of socialists is to change social democratic parties into democratic socialist ones.

Some socialists have proposed that as an alternative to working within social democratic parties, socialists should seek to establish roots in the working class, but this can only be done through the organized labour movement, and this is subject to the same compromising process as social democracy itself. The organized labour movement, which struggles for the interests of wage earners entirely within the framework of capitalism and does not envisage changing that system in a radical way, is itself a part of the "social democratic" syndrome. It is necessary for socialists to work within the institutions of organized labour, but this is essentially a task of the same nature as that of changing the social democratic party.

The struggle to build a genuine socialist movement is often associated with adherence to a Marxist outlook, and the question may be raised: to what degree was Irvine a Marxist? This is not easy to answer, since in recent times the nature of Marxism has become problematic and there are widely differing opinions about what constitutes the essential elements of Marx's thought. It is unlikely that Irvine ever asked himself this question. In building up his socialist philosophy, he drew upon a variety of sources and traditions (including Marxism), and tried to weld them into a workable and consistent position. He would have claimed that the truth is more likely to be found by gleaning it from many places rather than by looking for it in one source.

Nevertheless, it is worthy of note that he shared Marx's conviction that whatever one's day-to-day tactics, it is necessary to adhere to the objective of replacing a capitalist economic system with a socialist one and, like Marx, he believed that sooner or later this social transition would take place. Irvine also believed, like Marx, that the fundamental division within capitalist society was between the few who exploited others and the many whose productive powers were exploited. He thought that the urban worker would play an essential and necessary role in bringing about social change, but perhaps unlike Marx, he thought that other groups, particularly the farmers, had at least an equal role to play. Irvine was firmly convinced that in the circumstances of Canadian life, the road to socialism would be a democratic one, involving the electoral and parliamentary process, although he conceived the process of social change to be broader than this and at times laid a great deal of stress upon the interests of particular economic groups and the development of organizations to pursue these interests. At one stage he thought that an understanding of the social structure and the will to change it arose almost inevitably from one's social circumstances. Experience with both farmer and labour groups taught him that this was not necessarily so, and that upon the economic foundation one must still build a socialist understanding.

Irvine is perhaps best understood when conceived as a democratic socialist engaged on the one hand in a critique of capitalism, and on the other hand in fighting in a more subtle and complex way the compromises of "social democracy." Throughout most of his life, therefore, Irvine devoted himself to the twin tasks of organizing people for political action and then educating them to a proper perception of the task of bringing about radical social change. Where no people's movement existed, Irvine was in the forefront of creating one. When progressive mass movements developed, he joined and worked in them. The struggle that Irvine engaged in is still with us. We can learn from his story the nature of our own problems, for although he may not have always found the right answers, he posed the right questions.

UFA Principles of Political Action, 1925

This declaration was published in the *UFA*, 2 February 1925:

1. That each elected member who has been nominated by the UFA organization in any constituency, shall be known only as a UFA representative and shall be expected to attach himself to no other legislative group or party, and further, that each UFA member is responsible directly to his own UFA constituency organization and that organization is responsible to the UFA as a whole.
2. That each candidate so elected shall be expected to co-operate as an individual with all other UFA members, thereby forming and organizing a parliamentary group unity; and that this UFA group unit should be expected to co-operate as such, with other parliamentary parties, groups or individual members, when practicable to do so in the interests of desirable legislation.
3. That each constituency shall have the fullest autonomy in nominating and electing a candidate, as outlined in the two above clauses, but this Convention specifically declares that no constituency shall have the right to use the UFA organization in that constituency for the purpose of nominating and electing a candidate on any other understanding than that outlined above, in clauses one and two of this Resolution. And be it further:
4. Resolved, that nothing in the above resolutions shall be so construed as to prevent the UFA parliamentary group from

acting with, and inviting into their group councils, individual parliamentary members, especially those elected by other farmers' organizations, similar to the UFA, when a majority of the said UFA group decide that it is expedient and advisable to do so. And be it further:

5. Resolved, that when a bona fide farm organization such as the UFA from another Province elects a group of legislative members and these members organize themselves into a legislative group unit representative of that organization, it is the desire of this Convention that our UFA legislative group should co-operate with such a legislative group or groups in the organization of a larger agricultural group containing all such provincial groups, or as many as will so organize. And be it further:

6. Resolved, that the principles and policies, as declared from time to time by UFA Convention, broadly interpreted, shall be the general guiding influence of the UFA members and the UFA legislative group, and that with these principles in mind, they are expected to use their best judgment in dealing, in a practical way, with all matters of legislation, in the interests of industry as a whole and further that the UFA members and the UFA legislative group shall not be considered as in any way bound by any declaration of principles, or any platform coming from any other source.

7. Be it further resolved, that when a special service is required that calls for special training in order to render that service efficiently, the nominations for a constituency need not necessarily be limited to UFA members, nor even to farmers. The object should be to select a candidate who will be loyal to the UFA and capable of giving efficient service.

C.B. Macpherson's Account of UFA Social Theory

C.B. Macpherson wrote the first and what is still the closest analysis of the social theory of the UFA as expressed by Wood and Irvine, and all subsequent students of the matter are heavily indebted to him. Macpherson argues that the social theory of the UFA and its merits and deficiencies must be understood in class terms. The fundamental fact about western farmers was that they were independent commodity producers, owners of the means of their own labour. The great majority of them, together with their families, worked the land they owned. This clearly distinguished them from industrial workers, who depend upon wages paid by those who own the means of production and the product.

Macpherson recognizes that Irvine cuts across this distinction in his writings, which reflect a consciousness of the goals of organized labour which Wood lacked.[1] Macpherson goes on to argue that because of their class position the farmers, insofar as their ideas were accurately expressed by Wood or Irvine, did not understand the exploitative nature of capitalism, particularly the command of capital over labour. Instead, they looked at the economic process as a matter of trade between producers in the marketplace, and what they protested against was the unfair competitive strength of the non-productive classes. For this reason also, Macpherson alleges, farmers did not understand the nature of classes and the class struggle and tended to identify classes with occupational groups. Since such occupational divisions can be expected to persist in any society, the farmers' solution was to replace conflict between them by co-operation, and so they believed that class struggle could be transcended.

Prices, tariffs, credit and banking regulations, and the problems of marketing and transportation affect the farmers more directly than industrial wage-earners, for the farmers are direct producers for the market and carry through the whole productive process. On the other hand, the wage-earner has a more direct and immediate knowledge of wages, hours and conditions of work, than he has of the position of his industry's product in the market. Macpherson contends, therefore, that the farmers' viewpoint is a limited one which fails to give an adequate overall view of what is going on in the economic system.

He further argues that the UFA had two conflicting concepts of democracy: firstly, a non-exploitative social order to be striven for and attained in the future, and secondly, a scheme for the popular control of elected representatives. The two are alleged to be incompatible because to attain the first "nothing less than party organization will serve," so that all the apparatus of the party system, parliamentary procedure, and cabinet domination, as they now exist, must be accepted by a group wishing to gain power, even though this is incompatible with the democratic control of representatives.

Macpherson recognizes in part the truth of the farmers' contention that the exigencies of party politics defeat the purpose for which radical parties are formed, but he claims that this is not true in all circumstances:

> Now it is apparent that in countries where there is one economic class large enough to sustain singly a party able to take office, there is no necessary tendency for a party to become unprincipled. In such a country a labour party, for instance, does not need to appeal much beyond its own class and hence need not lose that singleness of aim and that stable basis in identity of class interest which Wood rightly saw must be kept by any democratic reforming organization.[2]

Macpherson's arguments, although superficially persuasive, are fundamentally wrong-headed, and one can imagine the response the UFA in general, and Irvine in particular, might have made to them. Certainly it is true that western farmers were independent commodity producers and therefore looked at the economy from that standpoint. However, there are other important characteristics of this group to be taken into account. First, they had not lived on the land in one place for generations. Many came from eastern Canada and the United States, and a sizable contingent came from Great Britain and Europe. They also came from a great variety of backgrounds and previous occupations, and their outlook was not bounded by their occupation.

If it is true, as Macpherson says, that the farmer cannot appreciate the problems of the wage-earner because he is not a wage-earner, then it must be equally true that the wage-earner does not understand the problems of the farmer. It would follow, then, that since both are necessary to the economy, the wage-earner and farmer need to appreciate and respect each other's role in society. Irvine recognized that these two groups had much in common, that both were producers, were exploited by the same class, and were badly represented in government. Irvine and others forcefully put the case for co-operation between farmer and labour organizations, and it was no part of the theory of group government that farmers should legislate for industrial workers.

The problem of distinguishing between class and occupation was in effect solved by Irvine. What he and Wood called the "plutocratic classes," who exploit others but do not themselves produce, were to be distinguished from the productive classes. There was no place for the plutocratic classes in a co-operative commonwealth. But even when these parasitic classes were abolished by one means or another, distinctions would remain between occupational groups. These cannot be eliminated, since doctors, teachers, shop assistants, coal miners and farmers have differing needs concerning remuneration and conditions of work. To assert in this sense that classes still exist and that they should settle their respective claims through co-operation rather than competitively is in no way to ignore or deny the importance of the class struggle in the primary sense of a distinction between exploiting and exploited groups.

It is therefore inaccurate to say, as Macpherson does, that the UFA political movement had an inadequate knowledge and understanding of the class struggle. They had this knowledge practically forced upon them by their semi-colonial relationship with eastern Canada, which looked to the west to provide cheap food for the domestic market and for export, raw materials and golden opportunities for profit-making on the part of the railway companies and land speculators. And above all, there were the banks with their stranglehold on the economy. In fact, both labour and farmers from Winnipeg and points west were more militant than their eastern counterparts. The OBU had its strength in the west and almost every other manifestation of radicalism was stronger and more militant in the west.

As already shown above, the difficulties, problems and choices open to farmers' movements were strikingly similar to those of the labour movement, and this was why Irvine throughout his career could maintain a role in both movements, frequently acting as a liaison between them. Not only did farmers and industrial workers have common economic interests against those who exploited them, they were also exposed to the same set of ideas. The OBU, for instance, distributed cheap editions of works by Darwin, Huxley, Kropotkin, Marx, Engels, Owen, Herbert Spencer, H.G. Wells and other writers considered to be radical.[3] Many of the works of these authors were reviewed by Irvine in the *Nutcracker* and its successors and the works of Herbert Spencer were as widely known among farmers as they were among industrial workers.

There is of course a difficulty about attributing any ideology to a large group of people, as its members will understand and adhere to its ideas in varying degrees. No doubt there were many members of the UFA who were only superficially and peripherally influenced by its ideology, so that in certain circumstances they were prepared to attach their allegiance to other movements. But the same situation exists in the labour movement; by no means do all industrial workers recognize the nature of exploitation under capitalism. All too many accept the status quo and think that the wage-earner's problem consists entirely of attaining a good bargaining position inside the system.

In the 1920s in Canada, farmers looked to be a better instrument than industrial workers for achieving social change. They were more numerous, at least in western Canada, if not possibly throughout Canada. They were better organized and more unified than urban workers and could draw support from a greater number of people in their own economic group. Then and now some critics would say they should have formed a political party. But this is to ignore the cogency of their argument against the efficacy of party politics.

Macpherson accepts the argument but claims an exception in the case of a party overwhelmingly composed of one economic group or class, which in numbers dominated both the party and the electorate at large. He does not believe that the farmers across Canada at that time occupied this position but, on the other hand, he does not suppose that labour in Canada has ever held this position either. In fact his set of conditions for making party politics work in a radical direction have never prevailed anywhere. No doubt, in countries like Great Britain, the industrial workers compose a majority of the population but since large numbers of them are neither politically active nor politically conscious, the Labour party has had to swell its ranks beyond the working class and, even more to the point, to get sufficient votes at the polls, it has had to appeal to large sections of the middle class. Certainly, like many other ostensibly radical parties, to win votes it has abandoned its far-reaching aims and proposals for radical social change and has consequently been condemned to remain within the orbit of the capitalist system.

It might be asked of Macpherson: what course of action would he have recommended to someone like William Irvine in the 1920s?

I suppose his advice would have been: sit, preach and wait until the industrial workers outnumber other sections of the population and are sufficiently politically conscious and organized to sustain a principled and radical socialist party, immune from the corrupting effects of the party system. But even fifty years later we have not arrived at that happy set of circumstances.

The UFA in particular and the farmers' movement in general did not fulfil the hopes of Irvine and others that it would bring about a new and better social order in Canada. Nevertheless the UFA laid important foundations during the fourteen years in which it was in office in Alberta, and during which it also had a group of MPs who acted as a social conscience in the House of Commons. It established, despite mistakes and shortcomings, a radical tradition that lives on in Canada.

The League for Social Reconstruction

By January 1932, the LSR had already produced its own manifesto. Its strongest statement was:

> We are convinced that these evils are inherent in any system in which private profit is the main stimulus to economic effort. We therefore look to the establishment in Canada of a new social order which will substitute a planned and socialized economy for the existing chaotic individualism, and which, by achieving an approximate economic equality among all men in place of the present glaring inequalities, will eliminate the domination of one class by another.[1]

This was followed by a nine-point program:

1. Public ownership and operation of the public utilities connected with transportation, communications, and electric power, and of such other industries as are already approaching conditions of monopolistic control;
2. Nationalization of banks and other financial institutions with a view to the regulation of all credit and investment operations;
3. The further development of agricultural co-operative institutions for the production and merchandising of agricultural products;
4. Social legislation to secure to the worker adequate income and leisure, freedom of association, insurance against illness, accident, old age and unemployment, and an effective voice

in the management of his industry;

5. Publicly organized health, hospital and medical services;
6. A taxation policy emphasizing steeply graduated income and inheritance taxes;
7. The creation of a National Planning Commission;
8. The vesting in Canada of the power to amend and interpret the Canadian constitution so as to give the federal government power to control the national economic development;
9. A foreign policy designed to secure international co-operation in regulating trade, industry and finance, and to promote disarmament and world peace.

There is nothing here which goes beyond or adds to the position arrived at by farmers and other western radicals years before, with the possible exception of point 8, with its implied reference to the BNA Act. Most of the proposals can be found in the programs of the Labour Representation League and the Alberta Non-Partisan League, which Irvine played a large part in formulating in 1917. In fact, western radicalism had more to teach the LSR than vice versa, and it is likely that the LSR did learn something transmitted through their association with J.S. Woodsworth.

With such western Canadian influences seeping through to them, in addition to the excitement of being in on the founding of a new socialist organization, the LSR may have had a brief flowering of radicalism, but the history of the development of some of its leading members suggests that if this was so it was uncharacteristic.

In his own account of his intellectual and political development, Frank Underhill tells of the years he spent at Oxford (1911-14):

My chief tutor in Greats was A.D. Lindsay who was a notorious socialist and whose wife went out addressing women's suffrage demonstrations. I joined the Fabian Society, though only as an associate member, since I wasn't quite sure that I believed in the full socialization of the means of production, distribution and exchange. I was also a member of the Russell and Palmerston Club, it being possible in those days to be both a liberal and a socialist. I was swept off my feet by the iconoclastic wit and high spirits of Bernard Shaw's plays, I read H.G. Wells and the Webbs, and became a member of a Balliol Fabian group in which the leading spirit was G.D.H. Cole.[2]

After a period of war service Underhill came to the University of Saskatchewan in 1919 and witnessed the development of the Progressive movement among the farmers:

> I experienced for the first time what a democracy is really like when it is thoroughly alive. It thrilled me to attend conferences of the Saskatchewan wheat growers and to watch the executive on the platform keeping a precarious hold over the earnest, excited, opinionated, anti-authoritarian delegates in the body of the hall.... Bliss was it in those days on the prairie to be alive, but to be young was very heaven. I exulted in the refusal of the prairie farmers to be fitted into the old two-party system of eastern Canada, or into the orthodox denomination of Ontario — the United Church was born on the prairie — or into the dominant banking or financial system of Montreal and Toronto. (page 10)

Underhill acknowledges the influence of the friendship of two men — J.W. Dafoe, liberal editor of the *Winnipeg Free Press* and J.S. Woodsworth. This posed a conflict after which he followed Woodsworth to the left. He describes his relation to the Regina Manifesto:

> I made the first draft of this; and my version, as revised by a small group of LSR friends in Toronto, was sent to Woodsworth just before the Regina meeting.... That first draft...was a better piece of writing than the document which emerged from the Regina discussion. I recall that, none of us having had any farm experience, we were very clear as to what should be done about the Canadian agricultural crisis. And I don't think that our document had in it that final declaration that a CCF government would not rest until it had eradicated capitalism from Canada. But I cannot

find a copy of the original draft anywhere, and my friends cannot supply me with one.

I was one of the first in the CCF who began to have doubts about the far-reaching socialism of the Regina Manifesto. I wrote articles and delivered speeches about the need for a new political party in Canada until I was wearied with my own arguments. This was good for me because I discovered thereby that I was not cut out to be a practical politician, since the more I repeated my arguments for my party the more I began to doubt them or to feel that the cause needed revision. I never doubted that socialism must be liberal (with a small l). By the 1940s I was annoying my political friends by writing revisionist articles and book reviews in the *Canadian Forum*; and I welcomed the revised Winnipeg Declaration of 1956. By the 1950s I had become considerably less interested in the fortunes of political parties as such and more concerned with the climate of opinion in our time which determines to a great extent what parties accomplish or try to accomplish. (page 11)

It is clear that Underhill's own political philosophy was never firmly established but vacillated between socialism and liberalism, with a strong bias towards the latter. His liberalism finally won; he left the CCF and joined the Liberal fold.

Most of the other leading figures in the LSR revealed by their subsequent actions and comments that they were never happy with the radical socialism expressed in the Manifesto. They all welcomed the more moderate Winnipeg Declaration in 1956 and approved of the passage in it which read:

The CCF will, therefore, extend public ownership wherever it is necessary for the achievement of these objectives. At the same time, the CCF also recognizes that in many fields there will be need for private enterprise which can make a useful contribution to the development of our economy. The Cooperative Commonwealth will, therefore, provide appropriate opportunities for private business as well as publicly owned industry.

But the LSR group had already arrived at this position around the time of the Regina meeting. Shortly thereafter they set to work to produce a volume called *Social Planning for Canada*. It appeared in the fall of 1935. Over 500 pages in length, in dark brown covers, and weighing over two pounds, it was a formidable volume.

This work was reprinted in 1975 with a new introduction by six of the seven LSR authors which says in part:

> A re-reading of these chapters today indicates that the general approach was more pragmatic — not to say reformist — and less socialist than we might have admitted at the time. On economic questions, for example, the conclusions were not always doctrinaire. They can be better described as a mixture of Fabian socialism, Keynesianism (a new thing in 1933-35) and the Welfare State (still unchristened as such). In short, while the book emphasized the need for public ownership of those large industries and financial institutions which occupy the commanding heights of the economy, it gave equal emphasis to such ideas as the stimulation of the economy by new fiscal and monetary measures, and to the ways in which greater equality could be brought about by tax reforms and an enlarged social assistance program. (pp. xvii-xix)

In the light of this examination of the views of the LSR, it becomes evident that no matter who penned the first draft of the Regina Manifesto, the ideas and sentiments it expresses in its final form did not spring from the LSR but from the radicalism of the prairies and the west coast.

William Irvine's Electoral Record

Alberta Provincial General Election, 7 June 1917
CALGARY SOUTH

Blow (Conservative)	3275
Irvine (Labour)	2248
McNeil (Independent)	1296

Federal General Election, 17 December 1917
CALGARY EAST

	Civilian Vote	Soldiers Vote	Total
Redman (Union)	6208	2155	8363
Irvine (Labour)	3805	106	3911

Federal General Election, 6 December 1921
CALGARY EAST

Irvine (Labour)	6135	*Elected*
Smith (Conservative)	4237	
Marshall (Liberal)	3684	

Federal General Election, 29 October 1925
CALGARY EAST

Davis (Conservative)	5560
Irvine (Labour)	3710
Davidson (Liberal)	2519

Federal General Election, 14 September 1926
WETASKIWIN (ALBERTA)

Irvine (UFA)	3897	*Elected*
Tobin (Liberal)	3150	
Russell (Conservative)	2243	

Federal General Election, 28 July 1930
WETASKIWIN (ALBERTA)

Irvine (UFA)	4750	*Elected*
Russell (Conservative)	4326	
Hayhurst (Liberal)	2809	

Federal General Election, 14 October 1935
WETASKIWIN (ALBERTA)

Jacques (Social Credit)	7601	
Campbell (Liberal)	2801	
Irvine (CCF)	2772	

Federal By-election, 6 January 1936
ASSINIBOIA (SASKATCHEWAN)

Gardiner (Liberal)	7350
Irvine (CCF)	3719

Federal General Election, 26 March 1940
CARIBOO (BRITISH COLUMBIA)

Turgeon (Liberal)	6063
Irvine (CCF)	5070
Stephens (Nat. Gov.)	2354

Federal General Election, 11 June 1945
CARIBOO (BRITISH COLUMBIA)

Irvine (CCF)	5773	*Elected*
Turgeon (Liberal)	4841	
Jameson (Prog. Cons.)	2490	
Phillips (Social Credit)	1080	

Federal General Election, 27 June 1949
CARIBOO (BRITISH COLUMBIA)

Murray (Liberal)	7330
Irvine (CCF)	5870

Federal General Election, 10 August 1953
CARIBOO (BRITISH COLUMBIA)

Leboe (Social Credit)	5562
Murray (Liberal)	5160
Irvine (CCF)	4314

Federal By-election, 20 June 1955
BATTLE RIVER-CAMROSE (ALBERTA)

Smith (Social Credit)	8455
Smith (Liberal)	8067
Irvine (CCF)	3753

Federal General Election, 31 March 1958
WETASKIWIN (ALBERTA)

Speakman (Prog. Cons.)	10557
Thomas (Social Credit)	4314
Larson (Liberal)	1704
Irvine (CCF)	1591

William Irvine was an MP in the following Parliaments:
Fourteenth Parliament, Independent Labour Member for Calgary
    East, 6 December 1921-29 October 1925
Sixteenth and Seventeenth Parliaments, UFA Member for
    Wetaskiwin, Alberta, 14 September 1926-14 October 1935
Twentieth Parliament, CCF Member for Cariboo, British
    Columbia, 11 June 1945-27 June 1949

Irvine spent a total of 17 years as a federal MP.

William Irvine's Writings

PUBLISHED WORKS

The Farmers in Politics. Toronto: McClelland & Stewart, 1920;
re-issued in 1976 with an introduction by Reginald Whitaker.
Capitalism, Communism and Credit, pamph. No. 1 in series
Purchasing Power and The World Problem. Ottawa: Mutual Press
Ltd., 1924.
Social Control of Credit, pamph. No. 2 in series *Purchasing Power
and The World Problem*. Ottawa: Mutual Press Ltd., 1924.
Co-operative Government. Ottawa, Mutual Press Ltd., 1929.
*Political Servants of Capitalism: Answering Lawson and Mackenzie
King*. Ottawa: Labour Publishing Co., 1933.
Co-operation or Catastrophe. Ottawa: Mutual Press Ltd., 1933.
The Forces of Reconstruction. Ottawa: Labour Publishing Co., 1934.
Can a Christian Vote for Capitalism? Ottawa: Labour Publishing
Co., 1935.
The Brains We Trust: A Play in Three Acts. Toronto: Thomas
Nelson & Sons Ltd., 1935.
You Can't Do That: A Play in Three Acts. Toronto: Thomas Nelson
& Sons Ltd., 1936.
Open Letters to Premier Aberhart. Edmonton: Reproduced from *The
People's Weekly*, 1936.
C.C.F. Provincial Policy: What the C.C.F. will do for Alberta.
Edmonton: Commercial Printers Ltd., 1938.
The Trail of a Truth Twister. Edmonton: Commercial Printers Ltd.,
1939.

Let Us Reason Together: An Appeal to Social Crediters and C.C.F.'ers. Edmonton: Commercial Printers Ltd., 1939.

Can Capitalism Survive the War? Edmonton: Commercial Printers Ltd., 1943.

Tribute to Mr. J.S. Woodsworth. (No publisher cited), 1942.

The People Must Choose. Winnipeg: Contemporary Publishers, 1944.

Is Socialism the Answer? The Intelligent Man's Guide to Basic Democracy. Winnipeg: Contemporary Publishers, 1945.

Live or Die with Russia. Edmonton: printed privately, 1958.

The Twain Shall Meet. Edmonton: printed privately, 1961. Other contributors Roy and Nellie Peterson, Bryon C. Tanner, W.A. Stevens and Harold Bronson.

UNPUBLISHED MANUSCRIPTS

Challenge to the "Free Enterprise" Capitalist Way of Life. Written in 1955. Mss. with the CCF Papers, PAC, Ottawa.

Democracy: Fact or Fiction? Written in 1962. Mss. part of the Irvine Papers at present in the possession of A.M. Mardiros.

NOTES

Introduction
1. Professor of Ethics and Social Philosophy, Victoria College, University of Toronto; author of *The Social Credit Movement in Alberta*; in a letter to A.M. Mardiros following Irvine's death.
2. From a tape of speeches delivered at the Memorial meeting held for William Irvine in Edmonton, 7 December 1962.
3. From a tape made at the Sedalia NDP meeting, June 1962.

Chapter One
1. William Irvine, autobiographical notes in manuscript.
2. A.T. Cluness, ed., *The Shetland Book* (The Shetland Times Ltd., 1967), p. 51.
3. This was the name of the international youth organization of the Methodist church until 1941. It was formed in Cleveland, Ohio in 1889 and took the name Epworth League in honour of John Wesley, founder of Methodism, born at Epworth, England.
4. Irvine ms.

Chapter Two
1. Irvine autobiographical notes in manuscript. This is the source of all biographical information in this chapter.
2. *Nation*, 1 May 1920, p. 583.
3. William Irvine, *The Farmers in Politics* (Toronto: McClelland and Stewart, 1920), p. 53.
4. William Irvine, *Is Socialism the Answer?* (Winnipeg: Contemporary Publishers, 1945), p. 89.

5. William Irvine, *Democracy: Fact or Fiction,* unpublished manuscript.

Chapter Three
1. *Morning Albertan,* 31 January 1916, p. 3.
2. *Morning Albertan,* 22 March 1916, p. 50.
3. *Morning Albertan,* 20 August 1917.
4. It was first published biweekly. When it became the *Western Independent,* 1 October 1919, it became a weekly.
5. *Nutcracker,* vol. 1, no. 16.
6. This pamphlet, likely Irvine's first, has been lost.
7. *Nutcracker,* vol. 1, no. 12.
8. *Morning Albertan,* 27 October 1916, p. 3.
9. *Nutcracker,* vol. 1, no. 13, p. 8.
10. *Ibid.,* vol. 1, no. 14, p. 7.
11. *Ibid.,* p. 6.
12. *Ibid.,* vol. 1, no. 6, p. 3.
13. *Ibid.,* vol. 1, no. 22, p. 10.
14. *Eye Opener,* vol. 18, no. 24.
15. *Nutcracker,* vol. 1, no. 7, p. 9.
16. *Western Independent,* vol. 1, no. 26.

Chapter Four
1. *Nutcracker,* vol. 1, no. 3, p. 3.
2. *Alberta Non-Partisan,* vol. 2, no. 9, p. 7.
3. *Ibid.,* vol. 3, no. 12, p. 9.
4. *Morning Albertan,* 6 March 1917.
5. *Ibid.,* 8 June 1917.
6. *Ibid.,* 15 June 1917.
7. *Alberta Non-Partisan,* vol. 2, no. 9.
8. *Ibid.,* vol. 1, no. 25.
9. *Ibid.,* vol. 1, no. 26.
10. *Morning Albertan,* 10 April 1918.
11. Reissued in paperback in 1972 by James Lorimer & Company with a new introduction by Stanley B. Ryerson. It still raises the hackles of big business.
12. *Morning Albertan,* 27 January 1919.

13. *Alberta Non-Partisan*, vol. 3, no. 12, p. 3.
14. *Western Independent*, vol. 1, no. 6, p. 4.
15. *Alberta Non-Partisan*, vol. 3, no. 12, p. 5.
16. *Ibid.*, vol. 3, no. 11, p. 5.
17. *Western Independent*, vol. 1, no. 6, p. 5.
18. *Morning Albertan*, 2 July 1919.
19. *Calgary Herald*, 31 December 1919.
20. Leo Heaps, *Rebel in the House* (London: Niccolo Publishing Co., 1970), p. 53.
21. *Morning Albertan*, 5 April 1920.
22. William Irvine, letter to E. Wolf, 8 February 1961.
23. *Morning Albertan*, 28 August 1919.
24. *Ibid.*, 23 September 1919.
25. *Western Independent*, vol. 1, no. 6. The successful candidate was Alex Moore.
26. *Morning Albertan*, 20 July 1920.
27. *Ibid.*, 5 November 1920.
28. *Loc. cit.*
29. Irvine papers.
30. *Morning Albertan*, 18 March 1921.
31. *Ibid.*, 21 May 1921.
32. *Ibid.*, 30 May 1921.

Chapter Five

1. "The Significance of Democratic Group Organizations," in the first four issues of *UFA*, March and April 1922.
2. *Morning Albertan*, 6 November 1916.
3. W.H. Rolph, *Henry Wise Wood of Alberta* (Toronto: University of Toronto Press, 1950), pp. 14-15.
4. James H. Gray, *The Roar of the Twenties* (Toronto: Macmillan, 1975), p. 124.
5. Rolph, p. 12.
6. *Alberta Non-Partisan*, 18 January 1918, p. 5.
7. *Ibid.*, 15 January 1919, p. 5.
8. *Ibid.*, 30 January 1919, p. 5.
9. *Ibid.*, 22 May 1919, p. 5.
10. *Ibid.*, p. 5.

11. *Western Independent,* 1 October 1919, p. 5.
12. *Alberta Non-Partisan,* 4 December 1918.
13. *Ibid.,* 23 January 1920.
14. William Irvine, taped interview with Floyd Johnson.
15. William Irvine, *The Farmers in Politics* (Toronto: McClelland and Stewart, 1920), p. 11.
16. *Ibid.,* p. 37.
17. All his life Irvine stuck with this choice and tried in one way or another to deal with its difficulties and ambiguities. In his last year he devoted much of his time to the writing of a 240-page manuscript in which he tried to sum up the possibilities of democratic political action as a means of achieving socialism.
18. William Irvine, *The Farmers in Politics,* p. 56.
19. *Ibid.,* p. 156.
20. *Ibid.,* p. 125.
21. *Ibid.,* p. 186.
22. Paul F. Sharp, *The Agrarian Revolt in Western Canada* (Minneapolis: University of Minnesota Press, 1948), p. 147.
23. Norah Story, ed., *The Oxford Companion to Canadian History and Literature* (Toronto: Oxford University Press, 1975), p. 385.
24. William Irvine, *The Farmers in Politics,* p. 236.

Chapter Six
1. *Western Farmer and Weekly Albertan,* 21 May 1921.
2. *Morning Albertan,* 31 May 1921.
3. *Western Farmer and Weekly Albertan,* 15 June 1921.
4. *Morning Albertan,* 8 July 1921.
5. *Ibid.,* 25 October 1921.
6. Edward Garland, on tape, recorded by Floyd Johnson and J.E. Cook.
7. *Ibid.*
8. W.L. Morton, *The Progressive Party in Canada* (Toronto: University of Toronto Press, 1953), p. 162.
9. Henry Spencer on tape, recorded by Floyd Johnson and J.E. Cook.

10. William Irvine, in an interview with Una Maclean, 1960, now at Glenbow Alberta Institute, Calgary.
11. Garland tape.
12. Grace MacInnis, *J.S. Woodsworth, A Man to Remember* (Toronto: Macmillan, 1953), p. 162.
13. Spencer, *op. cit.,* and manuscript, "Bill Irvine Recollections."
14. *House of Commons Debates* 1922, vol. I, p. 214.
15. *Ibid.,* p. 221.
16. Garland tape.
17. *HCD* 1922, vol. I, p. 539.
18. *Ibid.* 1923, vol. II, p. 704.
19. *Ibid.,* vol. IV, p. 3547.
20. *Ibid.,* p. 3557.
21. *Ibid.* 1909, vol. I, p. 1267.
22. *Ibid.,* 1924, vol. V, p. 4578.
23. *Ibid.,* 1924, vol. IV, p. 3860.
24. William Irvine, autobiographical notes in manuscript.
25. *HCD* 1925, vol. V, p. 4425.
26. *Ibid.* 1924, vol. II, p. 1267.
27. *Ibid.* 1923, vol. I, p. 208.
28. *UFA,* 15 July 1922.
29. His subsequent career is of interest. He took little part in the business of the House after his resignation as leader, but continued to sit as a private member until the elections of 1925. He then withdrew from politics and returned full time to his position as manager of the United Grain Growers. In 1929, however, he returned to the House as a Liberal and accepted the railway portfolio under Mackenzie King, along with three other portfolios which he amalgamated into a new Department of Mines and Resources in 1936. He remained in the King government until 1945 and was then appointed to the Senate where he spoke against old age pensions. He died in 1975 at the age of ninety-eight.
30. *UFA,* 1 December 1922.
31. *HCD* 1924, vol. II, p. 1460.
32. Norman F. Priestley and Edward B. Swindlehurst, *Furrows, Faith and Fellowship* (Edmonton: Co-op Press, 1967), p. 92.

33. *Financial Post*, 18 and 25 July 1924.
34. P.D. Smith, *The United Farmers of Alberta and the Ginger Group: Independent Political Action, 1919-1939*, unpublished M.A. thesis (University of Alberta, 1973). An earlier source for this view is W.L. Morton, *op. cit.*, chap. 6.
35. *UFA*, 2 February 1925, p. 12.
36. *UFA*, 22 February 1925.
37. Smith tries to make the point that the UFA federal members were now subject to "group discipline," and not merely to their local constituency associations, but this was never really an issue, for the Ginger Group's appeal to constituency association autonomy was directed against Progressive policies and domination by a Progressive caucus rather than against the authority of the UFA convention. No doubt this latter issue needed clarification, but it was not originally raised by the Gingerites.
38. Kenneth McNaught, *A Prophet in Politics* (Toronto: University of Toronto Press, 1959), p. 213.

Chapter Seven
1. William Irvine, taped interview with Una Maclean, 1960.
2. *House of Commons Debates* 1922, vol. 1, p. 222.
3. W.C. Good, *Farmer Citizen* (Toronto: Ryerson Press, 1958), p. 215.
4. C.H. Douglas, *The Alberta Experiment* (London: Eyre and Spottiswoode, 1937), p. 21.
5. E.C. Manning, *Political Realignment* (Toronto: McClelland and Stewart, 1967), p. 76.
6. C.B. Macpherson in *Democracy in Alberta* (Toronto: University of Toronto Press, 1953) claims that Douglas' social and political theories are important aspects of his thought, at least as important as his monetary theory. He also claims that if we bear this in mind then we can see that the disturbing features of his final position grow quite logically from his earlier beliefs. But the logic is the logic of paranoia not common sense. That is why in his latter phase Douglas lost not only whatever popular support he may have had, but also that of the intellectuals.

7. *HCD* 1922, vol. I, p. 224.

8. *Alberta Labour News*, 6 October 1935.

9. *People's Weekly*, 6 January 1945.

10. *HCD* 1935, vol. III, p. 2324.

11. John A. Irving, *The Social Credit Movement in Alberta* (Toronto: University of Toronto Press, 1959), p. 86.

12. *Alberta Labour News*, 24 August 1935.

13. The pamphlet is undated but it refers to the UFA leaving the political field, an event which took place at the annual convention in January 1939, and makes no reference to World War II, so it probably appeared between January and September 1939.

14. *Edmonton Journal*, 22 March 1938.

15. Letter to Irvine, 9 November 1934. Norman Smith Papers, Glenbow Alberta Institute, Calgary.

16. John Strachey, *Social Credit: An Economic Analysis* (London: Victor Gollancz jointly with the Workers' Bookshop, 1936). A copy of this paper was in Irvine's library.

17. *Alberta Labour News*, 30 December 1933.

18. *HCD* 1922, vol. II, p. 1289.

19. *Ibid.* 1923, vol. I, p. 629.

20. Henry Spencer, on tape, recorded by Floyd Johnson and J.E. Cook.

21. Journal of House of Commons, Committee on Banking and Commerce, 1923.

22. *HCD* 1923, vol. V, p. 4017.

23. *HCD* 1924, vol. I, p. 730.

24. *Ibid.* p. 734.

25. *Ibid.* 1925, vol. V, p. 4330.

26. *Ibid.* 1924, vol. IV, p. 3917.

27. *UFA*, 1 February 1924.

Chapter Eight

1. William Irvine, autobiographical notes in manuscript.

2. *Western Farmer and Weekly Albertan*, 1 January 1925.

3. *Morning Albertan*, 22 September 1925.

4. Henry Spencer, on tape, recorded by Floyd Johnson and J.E. Cook.

5. *Morning Albertan*, 1 October 1925.
6. The great majority of divorce bills came from Ontario. For religious reasons few came from Quebec. Prince Edward Island had the legislative power to set up a divorce court but had not used it and no divorce bills came from P.E.I. to Ottawa.
7. William Irvine, taped interview with Nellie Peterson and Floyd Johnson.
8. The account of the incident given above is based upon the verbal testimony of two members of the constituency board at that time, namely J.E. Cook of Edmonton, and Henry Young of Millet, Alberta. These accounts differ on points of detail but they agree that the offer was made: the officers of the constituency association returned the decision to Irvine, who promptly rejected the offer.
9. Spencer tape.
10. William Irvine, *Co-operative Government* (Ottawa: Mutual Press, 1929), v.
11. Henry Spencer, letter to Nellie Peterson, 27 November 1962.
12. *Federal Affairs in Review*, Ottawa, 1930.

Chapter Nine
1. Margaret Stewart and Doris French, *Ask No Quarter* (Toronto: Longman, Green & Co, 1959), p. 266.
2. Priestley and Swindlehurst, p. 108.
3. *House of Commons Debates* 1932, vol. I, p. 726.
4. Grace MacInnis, *J.S. Woodsworth: A Man to Remember* (Toronto: Macmillan, 1953), p. 266.
5. *HCD* 1933, vol. II, p. 1687.
6. *Ibid.*, p. 1738.
7. Unpublished pamphlet in Irvine papers.
8. For a detailed account of these struggles see Allen Seager, "The Pass Strike of 1932," in *Alberta History*, Winter 1977, vol. 25, no. 1.
9. Irvine interview with Peterson and Johnson.
10. See J.A. Irving, *Social Credit Movement in Alberta*, p. 148.
11. Priestley and Swindlehurst, p. 109.
12. *UFA*, 2 April 1934.

13. Norman Smith Papers, Glenbow Alberta Institute, Calgary.
14. Irvine interview with Peterson and Johnson.
15. William Irvine, *The Brains We Trust*, Act II, Scene 1, pp. 31-3.
16. *Ibid.*, II, 2, p. 47.
17. *HCD* 1933, vol. II, p. 1687.
18. Irvine interview with Peterson and Johnson.
19. *Alberta Labour News*, 4 October 1935.
20. William Irvine and Elsie Park Gowan are named as co-authors, but when the play was published only Irvine's name appeared on it. Mrs. Gowan says that this was entirely due to an oversight on the part of the publishers, Thomas Nelson & Sons, Ltd., Toronto, who had also published Irvine's first play.
21. Elsie Park Gowan, in a letter to A.M. Mardiros.

Chapter Ten
1. Nevertheless he continued as associate editor of the *People's Weekly* and remained president of the CCF. His salary as organizer for many years was approximately $100 a month plus travel expenses, although payment was sometimes irregular.
2. He served in this capacity until 1942 when he enlisted in the RCAF. He entered the Canadian Foreign Service in 1945 and his first assignment was to Chungking, the wartime capital of China. He later served as head of the American and Far Eastern Division in the Department of External Affairs; as Ambassador to Norway; as High Commissioner to India; as Acting Head of Delegation to the Geneva Conference on Korea (1954) and Laos (1961-62) and as a Special Representative to Hanoi and Saigon in 1966.
3. William Irvine, autobiographical notes in manuscript.
4. Minutes of the Alberta CCF convention, 28 and 29 November 1942.
5. William Irvine, letter to David Lewis, 4 October 1940, CCF Papers, Public Archives of Canada, Ottawa.
6. Elmer Roper, letter to A.M. Mardiros, 12 September 1977.
7. Minutes of the Alberta CCF convention, 22 and 23 November 1943.

8. William Irvine, Tribute to J.S. Woodsworth, 29 March 1942.

9. *House of Commons Debates* 1946, vol. III, p. 2562.

10. *Ibid.* 1947, vol. III, pp. 2342-3.

11. *Ibid.* 1947, vol. V, pp. 4411-5.

12. *Ibid.* 1948, vol. IV, p. 3578.

Chapter Eleven

1. In 1949, Peterson also became the president of the Alberta CCF. J.E. Cook, a former president, replaced her as organizer, but by 1951 she had been appointed to the less eminent but more essential role of party secretary, which duties she carried out until the dissolution of the CCF in 1961.

2. *People's Weekly*, 9 April 1949.

3. David Lewis, from an article entitled "Socialists Support NATO," in *Comment*, February 1952, a monthly publication of the national CCF in Ottawa. The whole issue was devoted to defence of CCF policy on NATO.

4. *People's Weekly*, 19 February 1951.

5. *Ibid.*

6. William Irvine, *Challenge to the "Free Enterprise" Capitalist Way of Life*, unpublished manuscript (1955), in the CCF Papers, Public Archives of Canada.

7. *Commonwealth*, 15 August 1956.

8. William Irvine, *Live or Die with Russia* (Edmonton, 1958), p. 5.

9. *Ibid.*, pp. 22-23.

10. William Irvine, letter to Norman P. Finnimore, 24 October 1956.

11. William Irvine, letter to Norman Smith, undated. Norman Smith Papers, Glenbow Alberta Institute, Calgary.

12. *Canadian Tribune*, 19 July 1976.

13. *Ibid.*, 30 April 1975.

Chapter Twelve

1. William Irvine, letter to Norman Smith, 5 August 1967. Norman Smith Papers, Glenbow Alberta Institute, Calgary.

2. *Commonwealth*, 8 June 1960.

3. William Irvine, presidential address to the Alberta CCF convention, 25 June 1960.

4. William Irvine, with N.R. Peterson, H. Bronson, W.A. Stevens, and B.C. Tanner, *The Twain Shall Meet* (Edmonton, 1961), p. 42.
5. Minutes of the Alberta CCF (special) convention, Edmonton, 25 November 1961.
6. It was also moved, seconded and carried unanimously, that when and if the Alberta CCF decided to dissolve or merge with the New Democratic Party, or in any way otherwise surrender its identity, the Alberta CCF, in recognition of past help rendered by the Alberta Woodsworth House Association (approximately thirteen years of rent-free office space), would instruct its trustees holding AWHA debentures to notify the association that the CCF wished the debentures remaining in their trusteeship, after all CCF debts were met (debentures to the value of $4,500 were transferred back to the Alberta Woodsworth House Association), to be deemed forgiven, surrendered, satisfied and paid in full, and that the trustees were released by the party from any further obligation as trustees for the CCF. In effect, this returned the debentures to the ownership of the Alberta Woodsworth House Association, which had previously given them to the CCF. This part of the board's report dealing with the disposal of the CCF's assets was approved unanimously by the convention. The AWHA retained possession of Woodsworth House, using it for purposes related to socialist study and education until 1973, when the area in which it was situated succumbed to the encroachment of developers. The house was sold on 11 September 1973, and was shortly afterwards demolished. In 1976, when the New Democratic Party in Alberta moved to new quarters, which it named Irvine House, the AWHA played a substantial role in financing the purchase of the property.
7. William Irvine, *Democracy — Fact or Fiction*, unpublished manuscript, pp. 13-15.

Appendix B
1. C.B. Macpherson, *Democracy in Alberta*, p. 36. It is possible to name a great number of active Non-Partisans and UFA mem-

bers but none as productive of ideas and as influential as Irvine. In this respect Wood and Irvine dominated the scene. As is shown above, the relation between them and between their social theories is a complex one. In his account of UFA ideology Macpherson has essentially only two sources to draw upon — Wood and Irvine. It is equally misleading to say, as Macpherson does, that Irvine "reached essentially the same conclusions" as Wood. One can get a fairly coherent account of UFA philosophy from Irvine, but the same cannot be said of Wood.

2. *Ibid.*, p. 59.
3. Gray, *op. cit.*, p. 236.

Appendix C
1. League for Social Reconstruction Research Committee, *Social Planning for Canada* (Toronto: University of Toronto Press, 1975), p. 1690. This is a reprint of the 1935 edition with a new introduction.
2. F.H. Underhill, *In Search of Canadian Liberalism* (Toronto: Macmillan, 1960), p. 10.

INDEX